The Official Microsoft® HTML Help™ Authoring Kit

Understanding, Creating, and Migrating to Microsoft HTML Help

For the Microsoft Windows 95 and Windows NT 4.0 Operating Systems

Steve Wexler
WexTech Systems, Inc.

PUBLISHED BY
Microsoft Press
A Division of Microsoft Corporation
One Microsoft Way
Redmond, Washington 98052-6399

Library of Congress Cataloging-in-Publication Data
Official Microsoft HTML Help Authoring Kit / Steve Wexler, WexTech Systems, Inc., and Brett Foster
    p.   cm.
  Includes index.
  ISBN 1-57231-603-9
  1. HTML (Document markup language) I. Steve Wexler, WexTech Systems, Inc. II. Brett Foster
QA76.76.H94034 1997
005.1'5--dc21   97-29233
                                         CIP

Printed and bound in the United States of America.

1 2 3 4 5 6 7 8 9 WCWC 3 2 1 0 9 8

Distributed to the book trade in Canada by Macmillan of Canada, a division of Canada Publishing
Corporation.

A CIP catalogue record for this book is available from the British Library.

Microsoft Press books are available through booksellers and distributors worldwide. For further
information about international editions, contact your local Microsoft Corporation office. Or contact
Microsoft Press International directly at fax (425) 936-7329. Visit our Web site at mspress.microsoft.com.

Encarta, Microsoft, Microsoft Press, Visual Basic, Visual C++, Windows, and Windows NT are
registered trademarks and the Microsoft Internet Explorer logo is a trademark of Microsoft Corporation.

Other product and company names mentioned herein may be the trademarks of their respective owners.

Acquisitions Editor: David Clark
Project Editor: Saul Candib

Acknowledgments

Although I started writing this book over a year ago, most of it has been written over the last six weeks as new features of HTML Help become available (and stable). This much writing in such a short time would not have been possible without the exceptional contributions and support of WexTech Systems' staff, brilliant outside consultants, my friends, and my family.

While my name is on the cover of the book, my friend and colleague, Brett Foster, contributed the chapters on context-sensitive HTML Help, the HTML Help API, and HTML Help on other platforms. I had set extremely high expectations for these chapters and, as with every project Brett tackles, he exceeded these expectations.

The high volume of content over such a short period of time put a lot of pressure on Bill Ash, who handled the production of the book, and Deborah Finn, who handled the copy editing. While I write well under pressure, I don't write *this* well under pressure, and I owe a lot to Bill and Debbie for improving the content and appearance.

Speaking of production, I will give a nice fat plug for WexTech's documentation and Help authoring tool, Doc-To-Help. The entire book was written and produced using Doc-To-Help and it made what would have been a very time-consuming job much, much easier.

While Brett and I produced some of the illustrations in the book, Andre Liu, WexTech's in-house graphic artist, created the really good ones. Andre continues to do a great job of illustrating very difficult concepts and of interpreting my nebulous artistic musings (for example, "can you make that illustration frothier?"). Andre also created all the movies on the CD.

The Microsoft HTML Help team gave me a lot of support and help. In particular, Ralph Walden, the lead programmer for HTML Help, and Kate Harper, the Program Manager, were very generous with their time and were willing to answer any and all questions.

I'd also like to thank Peter Plamondon and Will Greg of Microsoft Corporation for their evangelism of HTML Help and their help bringing this book into fruition. Also Dave Clark, Stuart Stuple, and Saul Candib of Microsoft Press for having the good sense to publish this book and for finding the perfect balance of help and pressure in getting the book published under a tight deadline.

Thanks also to Claudette Moore of Moore Literary Agency for taking such good care of her authors.

And thanks especially to my wife, Laura, and my children, Janine and Diana, for all their love and support.

About the Author

Steve Wexler, an internationally-renowned expert in Help authoring and Help technology, is founder and president of WexTech Systems, Inc., a software company that specializes in online documentation and web software. Steve is a frequent speaker at Help authoring, documentation, training, and Windows programming conferences worldwide. The author of several books, he is a recognized expert in improving corporate use of online information and web technology. His unique blending of technical acumen and an understanding of how to create Help systems that really work has made him an invaluable resource to many Fortune 500 companies.

The Official Microsoft HTML Help Authoring Kit is Steve's latest book. He has also co-authored two other books: *Using WordBasic,* a primer on Word's programming language, which is distributed by Microsoft; and *Microsoft Excel Macros Step by Step,* distributed by Microsoft Press. Steve was also the chief designer and architect for *Microsoft Windows 95 Starts Here,* the official interactive CD-ROM-based training companion for Windows 95 distributed by Microsoft Press Interactive. To date, *Microsoft Windows 95 Starts Here* has been translated into eight languages and has sold several million copies.

Steve has a bachelor's degree from Princeton University and a master's degree from the University of Miami. He lives in Westchester, New York, with his wife, Laura, and two daughters, Janine and Diana.

WexTech Systems, Inc.

WexTech Systems, Inc. is a New York-based software company specializing in Windows-based tools for publishing hypertext and web-based information. WexTech's products include *Doc-To-Help,* the award winning documentation and Help authoring tool; and *AnswerWorks,* the new development tool allowing Help authors to add a natural-language interface to Windows online Help.

Doc-To-Help is the authoring tool that easily integrates with Microsoft Word for Windows and allows users to create powerful Windows Help systems, as well as commercial-quality printed documentation, from a single source. Used by over 300 of the Fortune 500, Doc-To-Help has won 17 major industry awards including Visual Basic Programmer's Journal Readers' Choice Award three years in a row, Windows Magazine Top 100, Windows World Open Winner's Choice Award six years running, and recent similar honors from industry magazines internationally from France to Norway. Doc-To-Help 3, the latest version, also allows users to create HTML and HTML Help.

AnswerWorks, WexTech's newest product, makes getting Help faster and easier. With AnswerWorks, users can ask a question in plain English and get to the information they need. AnswerWorks is the first tool ever that doesn't require programming to add natural language technology to online Help. A free trial copy of this new standard in online Help can be downloaded from WexTech's web site.

In addition to commercial products, WexTech maintains a thriving consulting practice, helping Fortune 500 companies see bottom line results from implementing better help systems. WexTech also maintains a very close relationship with Microsoft Corporation and has developed many tools, templates, and training courses that have been included in Microsoft products, including Word and Excel. *The Official Microsoft HTML Help Authoring Kit* is the latest contribution to that relationship.

WexTech's principals are featured as regular speakers at Tech Ed, Interactive, Computer Training and Support, STC and ASTD conferences and regularly make presentations to user groups throughout the United States. WexTech can be reached at (914) 741-9700 and on the web at http://www.wextech.com.

About the CD

What's on this CD?

This CD contains the following items:

- the HTML Help Workshop
- Microsoft Internet Explorer 4.01
- sample files for examples and procedures
- movies (.AVI files) explaining some of the concepts behind ActiveX

How to Use the CD

Some of the items on the CD need to be installed onto your computer's hard drive before they can be used; others can be run directly off the CD. Following are the specific instructions for each component.

The HTML Help Workshop

If your computer doesn't already have the HTML Help Workshop installed, you will need to install it.

To Install the HTML Help Workshop

1   Click the **Start** button and select **Run**.

    The Run dialog box opens.

2   Type **d:\htmlhelp** (where d: is your CD-ROM drive) and click **OK**.

    An Explorer window opens, displaying the contents of the HTMLHELP folder on the CD.

3   Double-click **SETUP.EXE** and follow the prompts to complete the HTML Help Workshop installation.

Microsoft Internet Explorer 4.01

If you want to follow along with the examples in this book, you will need to have Microsoft Internet Explorer 3.x or later installed on your computer. Version 4.01 of Internet Explorer can be installed from the CD.

To Install Microsoft Internet Explorer 4.01

1 Click the **Start** button and select **Run**.

   The Run dialog box opens.

2 Type **d:\ie4** (where d: is your CD-ROM drive) and click **OK**.

   An Explorer window opens, displaying the contents of the IE4 folder on the CD.

3 Double-click **IE4SETUP.EXE** and follow the prompts to complete the Microsoft Internet Explorer installation.

Sample Files for Examples and Procedures

If you want to work through the examples in the book, you will need to install these files to your hard drive.

To Install the Sample Files

1 Click the **Start** button and select **Run**.

   The Run dialog box opens.

2 Type **d:\hhkit** (where d: is your CD-ROM drive) and click **OK**.

   An Explorer window opens, displaying the contents of the HHKIT folder on the CD.

3 Double-click **SETUP.EXE** and follow the prompts to complete installation of the sample files. By default, a folder named HHKIT will be created on your hard drive to hold the sample files.

Movies

The movie files can be run directly off the CD; they do not need to be copied to your hard drive. Your computer must be capable of playing sound and .AVI files in order to view the movies.

To View the Movies

1 Click the **Start** button and select **Run**.

   The Run dialog box opens.

2 Type **d:\movies** (where d: is your CD-ROM drive) and click **OK**.

   An Explorer window opens, displaying the contents of the MOVIES folder on the CD.

3 Double-click the movie file you wish to view.

Support Information

Troubleshooting

If you experience difficulties installing or working with files from this CD, here are some things to check.

- **System requirements.** In order to run the HTML Help Workshop, your computer must be running Windows 95 or later or Windows NT 4.0 or later, and must have Microsoft Internet Explorer 3.0 or later installed. In order to view the movies, your system must be capable of playing sound and displaying .AVI movie files.

- **Install versus copy.** Refer to the instructions under "How to Use the CD," on page vi, and ensure that you have properly installed files. In many cases, files which have simply been copied from the CD to your hard drive will not work properly.

- **Version conflicts.** If you have installed an earlier version of the HTML Help Workshop or the Microsoft Internet Explorer, you may need to uninstall it before installing the version on this CD.

- **Known issues.** Any known issues concerning version 1.1 of the HTML Help Workshop are described in the HTML Help Workshop Help file. Look in the **Reference** chapter, in the topic entitled **Readme**.

- **New versions.** The HTML Help Workshop and Microsoft Internet Explorer are both continually being improved. You may find that an update is available to remedy difficulties you encounter. Check for the latest version of the HTML Help Workshop at

  http://www.microsoft.com/workshop/author/htmlhelp/

  Check for updates to Microsoft Internet Explorer at

  http://www.microsoft.com/ie/default.htm

Microsoft Press Support Information

Every effort has been made to ensure the accuracy of the book and the contents of this companion disc. Microsoft Press provides corrections this book through the World Wide Web at

http://mspress.microsoft.com/mspress/products/1408

If you have comments, questions, or ideas regarding the book or this companion disc, please send them to Microsoft Press via e-mail to:

MSPINPUT@MICROSOFT.COM

or via postal mail to:

Microsoft Press
Attn: Official Microsoft HTML Help Authoring Kit Editor
One Microsoft Way
Redmond, WA 98052-6399

Please note that product support is not offered through the above addresses.

HTML Help Support

For support information regarding the Microsoft HTML Help Workshop, you can connect to Microsoft Technical Support on the Web at:

http://www.microsoft.com/support/

or call Microsoft HTML Help Workshop Pay-Per-Incident Support at

(800) 936-5800 or **(900) 555-2300**.

Contents

Introduction

In this introduction we will explore HTML Help's history, some of the compelling reasons to adopt HTML Help as a hypertext authoring and delivery system, why HTML Help will be used for much more than just Help for applications, and who should read this book.

What's in the Introduction

History

HTML, the Early Months

The first time I used a browser I was not impressed. This was in early 1995, and, while the ability to "instantly" access information anywhere in the world was electrifying, the quality of hypertext displayed was disappointing. Coming from a Windows Help background—WinHelp authors can be a pretty snobbish bunch—I was accustomed to a much faster, richer and just plain more fun hypertext system.

By the end of 1995 it was clear that HTML was going to be the standard for hypertext development and delivery. Although I was delighted that the world was starting to embrace the power of publishing reference guides like employee handbooks, procedure manuals, and ISO 9000 documentation online—the WinHelpers have been preaching this use for years—HTML systems just weren't as rich as WinHelp systems. For example, where was the expanding and collapsing table of contents? The keyword index? The ability to easily control window size and placement? The font control? The ability to distill hundreds of pages (or topics) into one, compressed, easy-to-access file?

And where were the popups?

HTML Help to the Rescue

By mid-1996 HTML did look considerably more inviting. Innovations such as cascading style sheets for layout and ActiveX controls to extend basic browser functionality made for rich hypertext systems that offered sophisticated graphics, fancy buttons, sound, video, and interactivity.

However, the capabilities that made WinHelp such a compelling solution still weren't available in HTML. Then Microsoft released the specification for HTML Help.

In August of 1996 I started working with an early alpha release of HTML Help. I was excited. HTML Help doesn't just meet WinHelp's functionality, it exceeds it.

Why I Like HTML Help

The expanding and collapsing table of contents is a lot more useful than the one found in Windows 95 and Windows NT Help. So is the keyword search. And HTML Help introduced a new feature not found in any existing hypertext delivery system: Information Types.

Using Information Types the author can designate topics as conceptual, procedural, advanced, and so on, and the user can apply filters to limit display to topics of certain information types. The author can create an unlimited number of different information types and the user can apply multiple filters so he can just view "Advanced Concepts" or "Beginner Tips" or even "Troubleshooting Procedures for Product A."

And there are popups. While they're not as good as WinHelp popups—yet—at least they're there.

HTML Help Works on Other Platforms

While some of HTML Help's features—such as compression and associative links—are only available to Windows users, some of the best features are available to Macintosh and Unix users. These features include the table of contents and the index. We'll cover distribution on other operating systems in "HTML Help on Other Platforms," on page 251.

HTML Help Is Not Just for "Help"

Some people, when they hear the word "help," think of the little window that appears when they press F1 or click the Help button in a dialog box. While this is certainly *one* use for HTML Help, HTML Help is designed for much more than just online Help. For example, Microsoft will use HTML Help to create and publish all of its online documentation (including the Microsoft Developer Network and Development Studio documentation) as well as commercial reference works, such as Microsoft Encarta.

HTML Help is also the ideal solution for online publication of such reference works as employee handbooks, procedural manuals, and ISO 9000 documentation.

So by all means, use HTML Help to add Help to an application. But you should also consider using HTML Help as a way to improve the content of your intranet.

Who Should Read This Book

While the current Windows Help community is small compared to the general purpose web development community, HTML Help is going to thrust Help authoring into the mainstream. There are just too many needed innovations for HTML Help to be ignored. People who in the past may not have been interested in Windows Help may be very interested in HTML Help.

Who Will Do HTML Help Development?

So who's going to be authoring HTML Help systems? Will it, like WinHelp, be handled primarily by technical writers, documentation specialists, and, in some cases, application developers? Will HTML Help's ability to become a true child of the application and even to be embedded in the application make HTML Help production mostly the responsibility of the application developer, or will the HTML Help content still be driven by the technical writer? Or will the current crop of web experts, with their knowledge of standard HTML and sophisticated image editing tools, rule the HTML Help kingdom?

The answer is all three will be tackling HTML Help, and in this book we will try to meet the needs of, and view things from the perspectives of, these three types of HTML Help producers and their managers.

The Help Author

Perhaps you've used some of the popular commercial tools to create Help systems. If you haven't already experimented with HTML Help, you may be approaching it with some degree of fear and loathing. Maybe you feel that you just got through migrating to Windows 95 Help, and now you have to learn something completely new.

Don't worry. The skills you've mastered will translate very well to developing HTML Help systems. Certainly the tool vendors are working to make sure their tools embrace the new standard while allowing users to leverage their existing skills and work.

Also, Windows 3.1 Help and Windows 95 Help will be around for a long time and will be supported by Microsoft indefinitely. So no one is going to put a gun to your head forcing you to migrate to HTML Help. We think, however, that any possible reluctance you have will be replaced by curiosity and then unbridled enthusiasm. There are so many exciting features in HTML Help, you're going to want to use them, even if Windows Help meets your current needs.

With this book we hope to show you, the Windows Help author, how to leverage your skills and knowledge to create and distribute powerful HTML Help systems.

The Programmer

As a programmer, you probably have at least some idea of how to link an application to a Help system and create "what's this" style Help (but don't worry if you don't). There are a lot of new capabilities in HTML Help that will allow you to greatly enhance the usability of your application's Help system. You may be wondering how you go about adapting your application so that it calls HTML Help instead of WinHelp. Or perhaps you want to know how to take advantage of the HTML Help API so that Help becomes an adjunct of your application.

In this book we will show you, the application developer, both how to link an application to HTML Help and how to seamlessly integrate it into your application.

The Web Author

As a web author, you're probably comfortable using some type of HTML tool. You may also be very adept at using sophisticated image editing tools and may have produced some beautiful web pages.

While you may know what a gaussian blur is, you may not know what a popup is and what constitutes a good keyword search.

In this book we will show you, the web author, how to take a typical web site or intranet and supercharge it with HTML Help capabilities so that your users will be able to access better content more easily.

Managers

Perhaps you won't do any HTML Help development yourself, but you will be responsible for managing an HTML Help development team. What are the issues with which they will have to contend? How difficult will it be? How much time will it take? What communication and collaboration needs to happen between the person writing the content and the person integrating it with the application?

In this book we will show you, the manager, what's involved in creating, maintaining, and distributing both standalone and application-dependent HTML Help systems so that you can manage your staff well.

This Book Will Not Teach You Basic HTML

You don't need to have a thorough understanding of HTML to read this book, which is a good thing, because we're not going to teach you very much of that. If you feel you need to know more about esoteric tags, or want to really understand what's "under the hood" of an HTML page, we suggest that you read either of the following books:

HTML in Action by Scott Isaacs, published by Microsoft Press.

Learn HTML in Two Weeks by Laura Lemay, published by Que.

CHAPTER ONE

Help Systems Past, Present and Future

The potential readership for this book is pretty wide (at least that's what I've been telling my editor). In this chapter we'll attempt to find common ground by comparing different types of Help systems and how they work with a simple program.

For the Help author: We'll show how HTML Help extends and enhances features found in Windows Help.

For the programmer: We'll show different examples of a program linked to a Help system, and how an HTML Help system can be embedded inside a program.

For the web author: We'll show how HTML Help can enhance standard web pages as well as familiarize you with the "vocabulary" of Help authors.

Before You Get Started

If you want to follow along with the examples in this chapter, you will need to make sure the following components have been installed on your computer:

- Windows 95 or later, or Windows NT 4.0 or later.

- Microsoft Internet Explorer 3.*x* or later (Internet Explorer 4.01 is available on the CD that accompanies this book).

- Microsoft HTML Help Workshop 1.1 (available on the CD that accompanies this book).

What Needs to Be Installed

Follow the instructions with included with the CD to install the sample files and folders to a folder called HHKIT on your hard disk.

What's in this Chapter

Tour of Windows 3.1, Windows 95, and HTML Help Systems

In this chapter you will work with ICECREAM.EXE, a simple application designed to show how different Help systems work.

The files you will need for these exercises can be found in HHKIT\ICECREAM.

To Start ICECREAM.EXE

1 Open the folder that contains ICECREAM.EXE and the accompanying Help systems.

2 Double-click ICECREAM.EXE.

The Ice Cream Creation Simulator will appear, as shown below.

"What's This" help is available in Windows 95 and HTML Help modes.

The program can run in four different help modes.

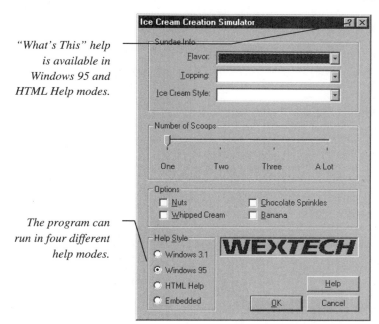

The Ice Cream Creation Simulator.

Exploring Windows 3.1 Help Features

Let's suppose you are a Windows 3.1 user and you're not sure how the controls in a dialog box are used. If the programmer and Help developer have done their jobs, clicking the Help button will display a Help screen (called a Help topic) that explains the different dialog box options.

Let's see how this works.

To Run Windows 3.1-style Help

1   In the Help Style group box, choose **Windows 3.1**.

    Notice that the question mark in the upper right corner of the title bar disappears.

2   Click the **Help** button.

    The Help topic associated with the dialog box appears, as shown below.

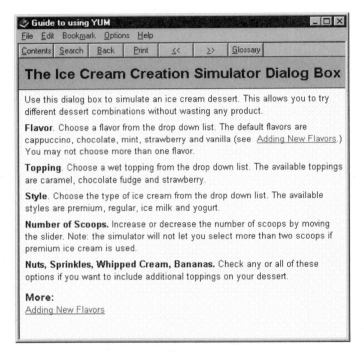

Context-sensitive Help topic under Windows 3.1.

How People Find Things in a Windows 3.1 Help System

With any luck, the Help topic displayed will give you everything you need to know to complete your task.

But suppose the topic doesn't have everything you need? Or suppose you're curious to see what else is in the Help system?

The Contents Topic

In Windows 3.1, your introduction to a particular Help system was usually through the Contents topic. Clicking the **Contents** button displays the Contents topic, as shown below.

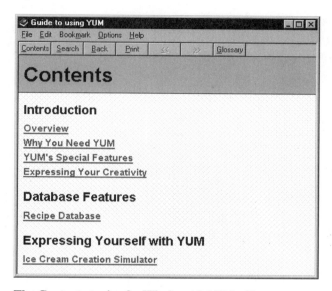

The Contents topic of a Windows 3.1 Help file

While certainly a welcome focal point, the contents screen does not give you complete access to all the topics in the Help system. It also can't show you where you are within the hierarchy of the Help system if you click on a hyperlink.

Let's explore the Help system a little.

Clicking **Overview** (the first hyperlink under the word "Introduction") displays this screen:

Browse forward button

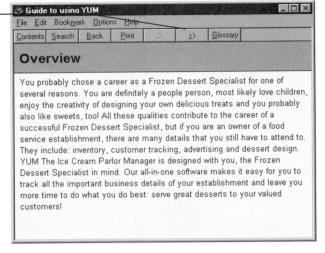

A typical Windows 3.1 Help topic.

Browse Buttons

If you click the Browse forward button twice, you will see this screen:

Clicking the dotted underlined green text displays a popup definition

Windows 3.1 Help topic with a popup.

Popups

Clicking **IICPA** displays this popup:

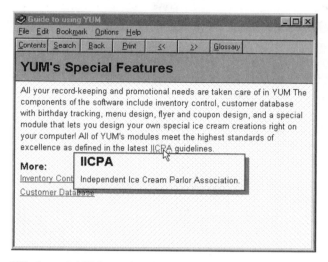

Windows 3.1 Help topic with displayed popup.

Note: One of the most common concerns among Help authors considering migrating to HTML Help is whether they will be able to make popups. The ability to provide an instant definition of a word, phrase or graphic without having to leave the current topic is a great feature of Windows Help, and Help authors will not give it up easily. Fortunately, they won't have to.

Keyword Search

Clicking the **Search** button displays the keyword search dialog box:

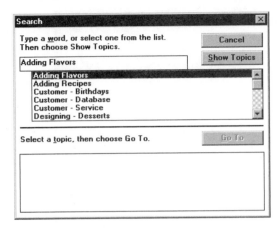

Windows 3.1 Keyword Search dialog box.

Just as people often go first to a printed manual's index to find information, a smart Help user will first employ a keyword search to find information in a Help system. (Unfortunately, most Windows users aren't aware that this keyword search is available.)

While Windows 3.1's keyword search is awkward and doesn't provide support for secondary index entries, it's a huge improvement over the Boolean search engines used to navigate the World Wide Web. With keywords the Help author can take into account the different ways a user may search for information. For example, let's suppose you have a Help file that explains how the exhaust system in a car works. The term "dissipater" is used frequently, while the term "muffler" is never used. A good keyword search would list both terms as well as any other similar terms, and these terms, even if not used in the text, would point the user to the pertinent sections of the Help.

Exploring Windows 95 Help Features

Let's explore some of the features of a Windows 95 Help system.

To Run Windows 95-style Help

1   If it's open, close the Windows 3.1 Help window.

2   In the Help Style group box, choose **Windows 95**.

Notice that a question mark appears in the upper right corner of the title bar.

Context-sensitive Help
in a Windows 95 Help System

Windows 95 provides a facility for displaying field-level Help. To get help about a particular control (field) in a dialog box, click the question mark button at the top of the dialog box, and then click the item you want information about. A popup window will appear, as shown in the sample below.

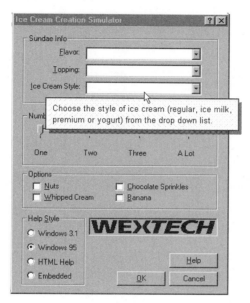

"What's This" style Help in action.

In addition, clicking the **Help** button displays a Help topic about the entire dialog box, just as with Windows 3.1 Help.

Notice that the left-most button is "Help Topics" instead of "Contents."

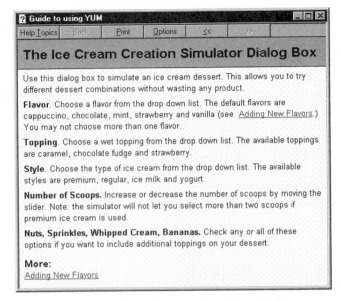

Context-sensitive Help topic under Windows 95/NT.

How People Find Things in a Windows 95 Help System

Clicking the **Help Topics** button displays the Help Topics dialog box:

Help Topics dialog box with Contents tab showing.

The Contents Tab

Windows 95 and NT offer a facility for viewing a Help file using an expandable outline. This hierarchical outline is a big improvement over Windows 3.1's Contents topic, as it allows users to see the structure of the Help file and to access different topics by expanding and collapsing different branches of the outline.

While it's a significant improvement, it still has several drawbacks. The first drawback is that you can't look at your Help file and the outline at the same time. In other words, there's no way to determine "where am I" within the Help system while you're looking at a topic, nor can you randomly access any other topic without closing the outline.

The second drawback is that a heading, containing a collection of subsidiary topics, and shown in the Help Topics dialog box as text next to a book icon, cannot also be a topic to which you can jump. Consider the Help topic shown below.

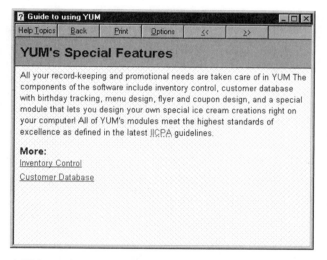

A Help topic that contains information and links to child topics.

Ideally, the outline for this topic and its child topics would look like this:

Partial contents of the sample Help system showing ideal outline.

Since "YUM's Special Features" includes subsidiary topics, the information it contains cannot be accessed. In the Contents tab, only topics without subtopics can be accessed directly.

To allow access to the information contained in the book, the Help author must generate an additional topic. A possible solution is shown below. When viewed, the title for the topic's information would be "About This Topic," and it is equivalent in the hierarchy to the child topics.

Partial contents of the sample Help system showing actual outline.

The Index Tab

A welcome improvement to WinHelp 3.1's keyword search facility is support for secondary index entries. This makes the keyword search dialog box look and behave more like a book index.

In the next example we will use the index tab to search for the keyword "summary."

Finding a Topic Using the Index Tab

1   If you have not already done so, click the **Help Topics** button.

2   Click the **Index** tab. Your screen should look like the one shown below.

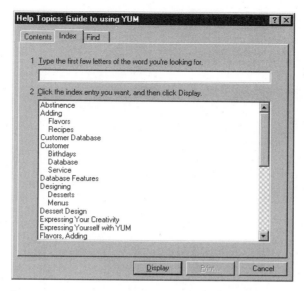

Index tab showing secondary level index entries.

3   Type the first few letters of the word you are trying to find, in this case **summary**.

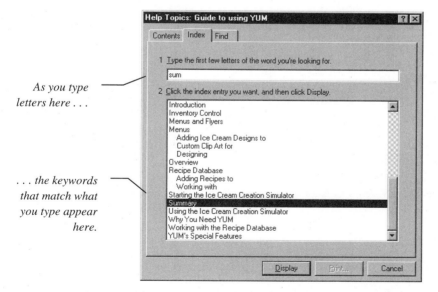

As you type letters here . . .

. . . the keywords that match what you type appear here.

The word wheel in action. A word wheel matches the items as you type.

4   Click the **Display** button.

"Overview"— the topic associated with the keyword "summary"—appears, as shown on the next page.

Note: If more than one topic is associated with the keyword, a dialog box appears from which you can select the topic you want to display.

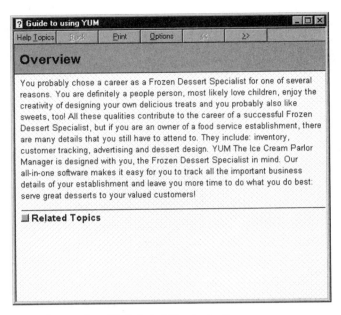

Overview topic with Related Topics button.

Associative Links

An associative link allows a Help author to create jumps to other topics based on shared keywords. In the example shown above, clicking the **Related Topics** button displays the following dialog box:

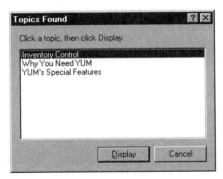

Topics Found dialog box.

The list of topics in the Topics Found dialog box is derived using an A-Link macro. Clicking the Related Topics button launches a search for all topics in the current help file (as well as any other help files included in the contents file) that share an A-Link keyword with the current topic. The related topics are listed in the Topics Found dialog box.

With A-Links, it's the Help engine itself that determines which topics should be displayed when the button is pressed; the Help author doesn't have to hard code any links. This feature is particularly useful for modular Help systems where you may not know which components will be installed. With A-Links (and K-links, which we will discuss later), as more components of the Help are written or installed, more topics may appear in the Topics Found dialog box.

Note: Before continuing, close the Topics Found dialog box.

The Find Tab

You can also add a plain language interface to Windows Help and HTML Help using WexTech Systems' *AnswerWorks*. A plain language interface allows people to query a Help system using everyday language. An example of a plain language interface can be found in Microsoft's *Answer Wizard* and *Office Assistant.*

A lot of fuss has been made over Windows 95 Help's Find tab, which allows people to search through all the text in a Help file and display topics based upon that search.

Getting the Find tab to appear in your Windows Help system is effortless; it appears automatically, even with Windows 3.1 Help files. In fact, because of a bug in the Windows 95 Help engine, you can't get rid of the Find tab, even if you wanted to.

While this new search capability is very welcome, it's no substitute for a good keyword search. Full-text searches tend to find too many instances of a term, and they don't take into account the term someone may use to find a topic. (A full text search for "chocolate" would fail to find possibly relevant materials dealing with "cocoa.")

In the next example we'll use the Find tab to learn how to start the Ice Cream Creation Simulator.

Finding a Topic Using the Find Tab

1   With the Help Topics dialog box on the screen, click the **Find** tab.

2   If this is the first time you are using the Find feature, the Find Setup Wizard will appear. Accept all the defaults and keep clicking **Next** until the Find tab appears.

3   With the Find tab active, type the first few letters of the word you want to find, in this case **Start**.

Your screen will look like the one shown on the next page.

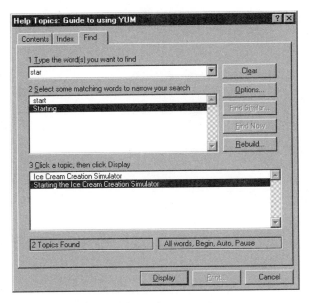

Find tab word wheel in action.

4   Select the topic you want to access, in this case **Starting the Ice Cream Creation Simulator**, and click **Display**.

The following topic appears:

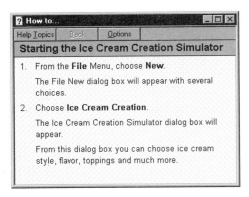

A typical procedural topic in Windows 95 Help.

Procedural Help versus Conceptual Help

Windows 95 Help makes a distinction between conceptual Help and procedural Help. Microsoft recommends displaying procedural Help in a small window that sits on top of the application. The user can proceed stepwise with both the application and the Help visible.

Conceptual Help is typically displayed in a larger window; it is assumed the user does not need to refer back and forth from the Help to the application.

Note: One of the side effects of using an always-on-top window in Windows 95 Help is that it remains on top of all windows, not just the application it's supporting. An HTML Help always-on-top window is by default set to stay on top of only the application it's supporting.

Exploring HTML Help Features

Let's explore some of the features of an HTML Help system.

To Run HTML Help-style Help

1   If it's open, close the Windows 95 Help window.

2   In the Help Style group box, choose **HTML Help**.

Notice that the question mark in the upper right corner of the title bar is still visible.

Context-sensitive Help in an HTML Help System

As with Windows 95, HTML Help provides a facility for displaying field-level Help. To get help about a particular control in a dialog box, click the question mark button at the top of the dialog box, and then click the item you want information about. A popup window will appear.

Introducing the Three-Pane HTML Help Window

Clicking the **Help** button displays a Help topic about the entire dialog box in the HTML Help three-pane window, as shown on the next page.

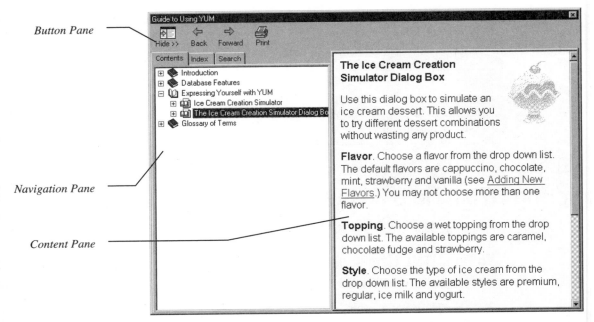

Button Pane

Navigation Pane

Content Pane

Help Topic in the HTML Help three-pane window. The Hide button in the left corner of the Button pane is a toggle. Clicking it hides the navigation pane and displays a Show button in its place. Clicking the Show button redisplays the navigation pane.

A Kinder, Gentler Table of Contents

Notice that the navigation pane displays the Contents tab open to the current topic displayed in the content pane. Unlike the Windows 95 table of contents, the HTML Help table of contents can appear along with the content, *and* it can stay synchronized with the content pane.

Let's see what happens when we click the **Adding New Flavors** hypertext link.

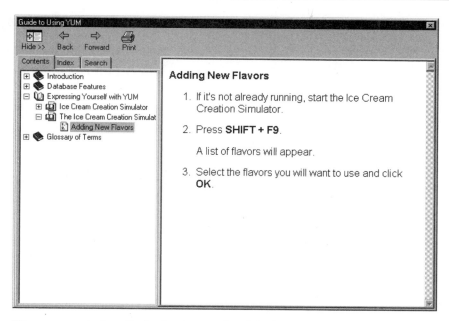

Three-pane window displaying a procedural topic.

Notice that there are different icons to designate different types of information. In contrast to Windows 95 Help, HTML Help lets you use custom icons in the Contents tab, thereby giving the Help user a better idea of the kind of information being offered. For example, the 🖹 icon is used to designate procedural information, while the 🗐 icon is used to designate a page that's both a heading (with a subsidiary topic) and a topic.

In addition to the over 40 icons that come with HTML Help, you can also create your own icons.

Smart Headings

As we mentioned in "The Contents Tab" on page 17, one of the shortcomings of Windows 95 Help is that a heading cannot also be a topic to which you can jump. In HTML Help a heading can also be a topic. Consider what happens when you click **Ice Cream Creation Simulator** in the navigation pane.

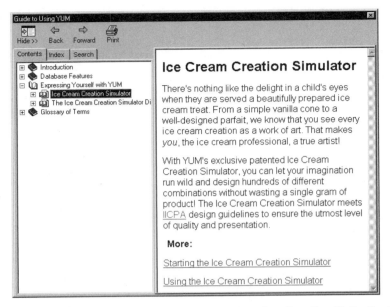

In HTML Help, the contents tab can display a heading (book) that's also a topic to which you can jump.

Popups

If you click IICPA you'll see an HTML Help popup, as shown below.

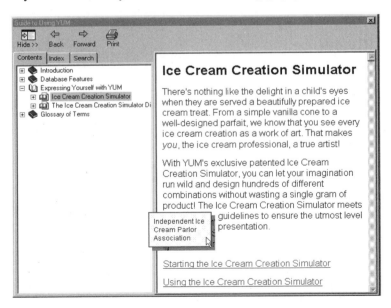

Yes, it's an HTML Help popup!

While the first release of HTML Help only allows you to display text in a popup, HTML Help popups can still be very effective at clarifying information without displaying a completely different topic.

Keyword and Full-Text Search

Both keyword and full-text search capabilities are available in HTML Help. You access the keyword search by clicking the Index tab.

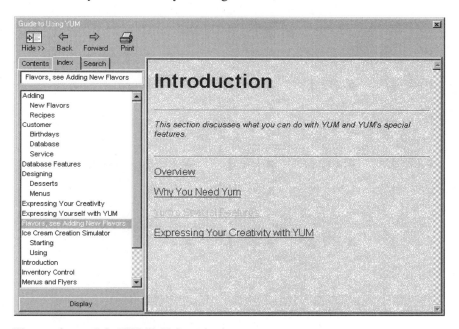

Keyword search in HTML Help.

The keyword search facility is a lot more robust in HTML Help than it is in Windows Help. For example, you can have an unlimited number of index levels, you can define how items are sorted, and you can even have book-like "see-also" entries.

The full-text search facility falls a little short of the Windows 95 full-text search (at least in the initial release of HTML Help). Unlike the word wheel in Windows 95 Help, HTML Help does not display matching topics while you type. You must type in the entire word, and then click the **Display** button.

Information Types

Help authors are always trying to please different audiences. Will advanced users find the information too elementary? Will novices find the material too confusing? Is there a way to let people who simply want to get a task done view just the procedural information?

As we mentioned earlier, one of the most exciting features of HTML Help is the author's ability to designate topics as conceptual, procedural, advanced, and so on, and the user's ability to apply filters to limit display in the table of contents to topics of certain information types.

For this next example, let's see how to make it so that only procedural topics are displayed in the Navigation pane.

To View Procedural Topics

1 Right-click in the Navigation pane.

2 When the popup menu appears, click **Customize**.

3 When the Customize Information dialog box appears, click **Custom** and click **Next**.

4 When the next dialog box appears, de-select Overview and Concept and leave **Procedure** selected, as shown below.

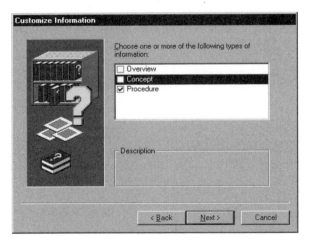

Customize Information dialog box with Procedure selected.

5 Click **Next**, and then click **Finish**.

The table of contents will collapse. Notice that when you click the plus sign to expand books, only procedural topics are displayed, as shown below.

Table of contents showing procedural topics only.

Exploring an Embedded HTML Help System

Up to this point we've looked at Help systems that display information in a separate window. With HTML Help, the online information can be embedded inside the calling application's main window.

Let's explore some of the features of an Embedded HTML Help system.

To Run Embedded HTML Help-style Help

1 If it's open, close the HTML Help window.

2 In the Help Style group box, choose **Embedded**.

The dialog box window expands to display the embedded Help information, as shown below.

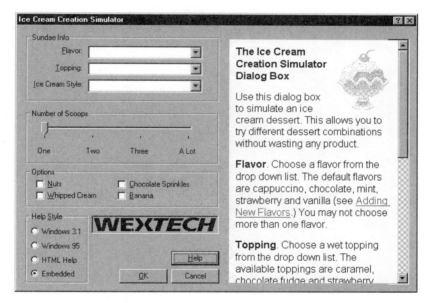

HTML Help embedded inside an application.

The example shown above doesn't provide any navigation features. Clicking the hypertext "Adding New Flavors" jumps the user to the new topic, and there's no way for the user to get back.

We'll address how to add navigation controls to an embedded Help system later in this book.

Comparison of WinHelp, HTML, and HTML Help

The table below compares the features of WinHelp, HTML, and HTML Help.

Feature	WinHelp 3.1	WinHelp 95	HTML	HTML Help
Hierarchical table of contents (TOC)	No	Yes	No	Yes
Customizable TOC	No	No	No	Yes
Synchronized TOC	No	No	No	Yes
Information Types	No	No	No	Yes
Keyword search	Yes	Yes	No	Yes
Multi-level keyword search	No	Yes (a)	No	Yes
Full-text search	No	Yes	No	Yes
Associative links	No	Yes	No	Yes (b)
Advanced formatting	No	No	Yes (c)	Yes (c)
Table borders	No	No	Yes	Yes
Popups	Yes	Yes	No	Yes (d)
Custom buttons	Yes	Yes	Yes	Yes
Shortcuts	Yes	Yes	No	Yes
Multiple windows	Yes	Yes	Yes (e)	Yes
Help can be embedded in or a child of calling application	No	No	No	Yes
Compressed / compiled into one file?	Yes	Yes	No	Optional
Can be displayed on platforms other than Windows	No	No	Yes	Yes (f)
Context-sensitive	Yes	Yes	No	Yes
Field-level	No	Yes	No	Yes

(a) Windows 95 Help is limited to two levels.

(b) With compressed HTML Help only.

(c) With cascading style sheets.

(d) Text only.

(e) Can be achieved by running a new instance of the browser that displays different content.

(f) Not all features are available.

Frequently Asked Questions

Question: *With a Windows Help system, all the topics are compiled into one file. When I do web page development, I notice that I have lots of small .HTM files. Is there a way to combine all the .HTM files into one file using HTML Help?*

Answer: Yes. You can combine all of the .HTM files into a single file that is both compiled and compressed. By default, the HTML Help Workshop assigns this file a .CHM extension.

You can also use HTML Help's Split feature to take a large .HTM file and have the compiler break it up into separate topics (or pages) automatically. The HTML Help Workshop splits the file into smaller files during the compiling process, and then combines all the files into a single .CHM file. This allows you to work with a single .HTM file that has may topics, and display these topics as separate pages (rather than as a long topic through which the user most scroll).

Question: *How big is a compiled HTML Help file when compared with a Windows Help file?*

Answer: A compiled HTML Help file is usually about half the size of a corresponding WinHelp file.

Question: *Where will a compiled HTML Help file live, on the user's hard disk, on a file server, or on the web?*

Answer: It depends. If the HTML Help system is designed to work with a program, you will probably want to install the system on the user's hard disk or on a file server because you don't want the user to have to wait to access timely Help information. For example, a user who has to wait two or three minutes to connect to a web server just to view a "what's this" topic will be a little peeved.

Question: *I'm not sure I like the idea of the Help system living on the user's hard disk. One of the best things about distributing information on the web is having the ability to update it often. How will I be able to update users with timely information?*

Answer: In a future release of HTML Help, when you distribute an HTML Help system the user gets a copy of the same compiler you use to create the Help system. You can put a link in the hard-disk-based Help system that accesses your web site, downloads new information and recompiles the Help system with the new information, all without user intervention.

Note: This feature is not available in HTML Help 1.1.

Question: *I like being able to display procedures in small windows that are set to be always on top. Can I do that in HTML Help?*

Answer: Yes.

C H A P T E R   T W O

The Big Picture—Understanding What's Behind HTML Help

In this chapter we'll examine what components make up an HTML Help system and how the HTML Help engine works. We'll also explore the ActiveX architecture and how HTML Help exploits this architecture to allow you to display HTML Help systems in their own windows without having to use a browser.

Many of the concepts in this chapter are illustrated in the movies that can be found in the MOVIES folder of the accompanying CD.

For the Help author: We'll compare how the WinHelp and HTML Help engines work and discuss what ActiveX is (and why you should care).

For the programmer: If you are already familiar with ActiveX and the Component Object Model (COM), you can skip this chapter. We'll discuss creating context-sensitive Help and the HTML Help API in detail in "Understanding and Creating Context-Sensitive HTML Help," on page 175, and "The HTML Help API," on page 199.

For the web author: We'll explain the relationship between applications, the HTML Help engine, and HTML Help pages and explain how you can exploit Internet Explorer's layout engine to create customized Help systems.

What's in this Chapter

How the WinHelp Engine Works

What happens when you click the Help button in a dialog box? What happens when you choose "What's This" help for a control? What happens when you double-click a Help icon to run a standalone Help system?

The diagram below shows the relationship between a program, the Windows Help engine (WINHELP.EXE or WINHLP32.EXE) and a Help file.

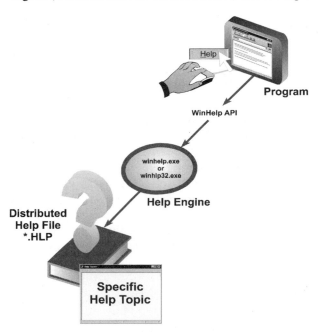

How a program communicates with WinHelp.

Responding to the Help Request

Clicking the Help button in a dialog box initiates a series of events that allows your program to communicate with the Windows Help engine and display a particular topic. Here's a somewhat simplified view of what happens:

1   User clicks the Help button in a dialog box.

2   Program determines the ID of the button that's been clicked.

3   Program determines which Help file contains the Help topic associated with that ID.

4   Program determines how the Help should be displayed (in a window or as a popup) and, if it's to be displayed in a window, which window.

5   Program communicates with the Windows Help engine via the WinHelp API and requests that a particular Help file be opened, and that the Help topic associated with the Help button ID be displayed in a particular window.

Note: While the programmer can specify which window the topic should appear in, the programmer cannot change that window's appearance because these settings are determined by the Help author when the Help file is compiled. In HTML Help, the programmer can choose not to use the settings indicated by the Help author and can instead create his own window and specify its properties programmatically.

What's an API?

An API (Application Program Interface) is just a set of rules that specifies how one program can talk to another program (or library) and get that other program to perform certain tasks or return certain results. For example, WinHelp is capable of displaying the contents tab in the Help Topics dialog box. How does a program request that WinHelp display that tab when the user clicks Help Topics from the Help menu? The WinHelp API provides the programmer with the exact language (or syntax) for making this happen.

What About Standalone Help Systems?

In Windows 95, the program WINHELP.EXE is just a stub file that calls WINHLP32.EXE.

The Windows Help engine is commonly used to display Help systems that complement a program, but it may also be used for distributing reference materials online. In cases such as these, the Help system *is* the application and the only program involved is WINHELP.EXE (or WINHLP32.EXE on 32-bit platforms).

You run a standalone Help system either by double-clicking its icon or by running WINHELP.EXE with command line parameters. Just running WinHelp by itself won't do anything because it won't know which Help system to load.

WinHelp Wasn't Designed to Offer Tight Integration

WinHelp was never designed to offer the level of integration found in HTML Help. For example, a Help file can't be embedded in an application the way an HTML Help system can. Also, since the online Help is not a child of the host application, a Help window will stay open even if you minimize its associated application.

And as we stated earlier, an always-on-top Help window will be on top of all other windows, not just the associated application's window.

Because the HTML Help services are supplied by an ActiveX control (HHCTRL.OCX) and not a program, HTML Help can offer a much tighter level of integration with a calling program.

Before we discuss how the HTML Help engine works, you will need to understand what ActiveX is and how it fits into the picture.

What Is ActiveX?

ActiveX is the name for an ever-growing collection of reusable software building blocks that adhere to certain rules and specifications. The ActiveX specification was created by Microsoft Corporation, but is now maintained by the Open Group, an independent organization.

By using ActiveX components—also called ActiveX controls—software developers can include pre-built software "parts" in their software applications, thereby reducing development costs and shortening time to market.

Many software development environments support ActiveX, including Visual Basic, Visual C++, PowerBuilder and Delphi. Microsoft's Internet Explorer browser also supports ActiveX. One of the reasons Internet Explorer is so flexible is that pre-built ActiveX components can be "plugged into" the browser, thereby making the browser do things it couldn't do when you first installed it.

The developer chooses which ActiveX controls she wants to use in her application or web documents. (Some ActiveX controls come free with popular development tools; others must be purchased separately.) The end user is usually unaware that the application he is using—or the web page he is visiting—is comprised of different controls working in concert. In the same way a friend may not notice or care about what components make up your stereo system (he may say "your stereo system sounds nice"), your users will just think "hey, that's a cool web page."

Of Containers and Controls

In becoming familiar with ActiveX, you will often hear two terms: *control* and *container*.

A *control* is a reusable chunk of pre-built software that can be used to build or enhance an application. A *container* hosts one or more controls. The protocol that permits the controls to "talk" to the container and to each other is called ActiveX and it is based on Microsoft's Component Object Model (COM) for modular software development.

If COM didn't exist—and therefore if you didn't have controls and containers—developing sophisticated applications and web systems would be much harder than it already is.

An Analogy

Let's try to get a better understanding of this by way of an analogy. Take a look at a typical custom stereo system. It usually has an amplifier, a tuner, a CD player, a tape deck and speakers. It's likely that these components were built by different manufacturers, yet the components have no problems "talking" to each other.

Not only do the components work together, but their size and shape are similar, too. If you were outfitting a professional recording studio you would discover that virtually all the components you wanted to buy—tape decks, amplifiers, echo chambers, and so on—were 19 inches wide and fit neatly into a standard rack.

If you have ever shopped for cabinets for your sound system you may have noticed that most stereo cabinets are about the same width and they can all accommodate components that are 19 inches wide and two to eight inches tall.

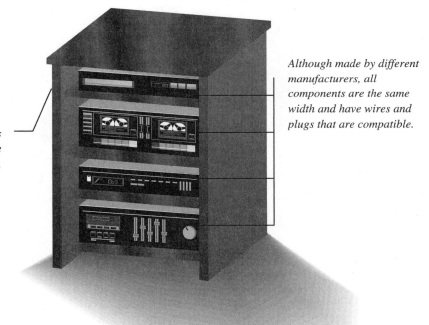

Although made by different manufacturers, all components are the same width and have wires and plugs that are compatible.

All the components can easily fit in the cabinet.

Stereo cabinets are designed to accommodate components that are the same width.

While this is an oversimplification, you can think of the stereo cabinet as being a software container and the stereo components as being controls. Microsoft Visual Basic is a popular container. So are Microsoft Excel and Word.

Microsoft's Internet Explorer browser is also a container. It can host HTML pages. It can also host controls that display animation, live stock quotes, mainframe terminal emulation and more.

Living in Your Browser

In addition to acting as a container for controls, Internet Explorer is also made up of components. The Internet Explorer executable, IEXPLORE.EXE, is very small and provides a frame for the web browser object, SHDOCVW.DLL. The web browser object is in turn a container that hosts MSHTML.DLL, the HTML viewer that contains the code needed to display HTML documents.

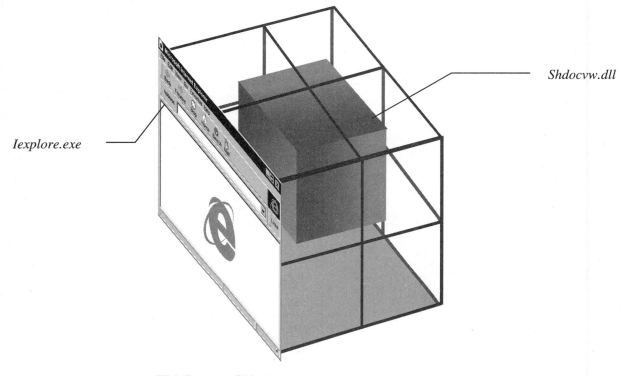

Shdocvw.dll

Iexplore.exe

Web Browser Object.

The web browser object can also host Excel documents, Word documents, and any other type of ActiveX document.[1]

Try loading a Word document or an Excel worksheet into Internet Explorer. Not only can you view the document, but you can edit it as well: Internet Explorer will assume all the capabilities of the program that created the document. This means that you can use your browser to access pages on the web *and* documents on your hard disk.

Goodbye Desktop, Hello Browser

By now you've probably discovered that you spend a lot of time doing work from within your browser. (And if you're not spending time with your browser or you

---

[1] A thorough discussion of Internet Explorer's architecture and ActiveX documents is beyond the scope of this book. To learn more about this, see "ActiveX, the Internet, and the World Wide Web" in David Chappell's *Understanding ActiveX and OLE,* published by Microsoft Press (1996).

don't yet use a browser, you will.) Indeed, with the recent release of Internet Explorer 4.01, the browser is indistinguishable from the desktop.

Well, the things you want to do with your browser may be very different from the things other people want to do. For example, some people need to access timely stock market information from within their browsers, as shown below.

Browser displaying stock market ticker information.

Other people may want to play virtual reality arcade games from within their browsers.

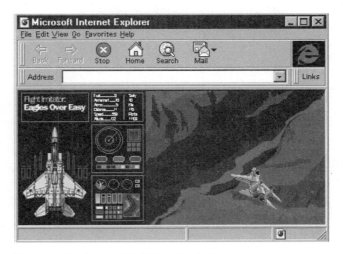

Browser displaying 3D flight simulation game.

You may not be interested in stock quotes and perhaps you don't play arcade games (okay, *maybe* every once in a while). You are, however, very interested in creating and displaying sophisticated Help systems complete with an expanding table of contents, keyword search, shortcuts, and so on, all from within a browser.

A standalone Help system with expandable table of contents and keyword search.

If Internet Explorer did everything everybody wanted it to do, right out of the box, it would be one very large browser. Instead, Internet Explorer has a rich set of basic capabilities, but supports an open architecture—ActiveX—that allows developers to plug in additional components (ActiveX controls) that extend the basic functionality.

Web Pages: What Functionality Is the Help Author Looking For?

Let's focus on how this extensibility affects the Help author. On using a browser for the first time, you may have thought that it looked a lot like Windows Help but was missing some important features of a well-crafted Help system. Yes, there were jumps, and graphics with multiple hotspots and even some great multimedia, but where was the nice hierarchical outline? The keyword search? And even if you had that stuff, how could you link your application to the browser so that a user clicking a Help button saw a particular web page? And how could you create "What's This" Help, as well as all the other WinHelp things you've come to know and love?

Meet HHCTRL.OCX

The way you get this Help functionality is with an ActiveX control called HHCTRL.OCX. With this control loaded, Internet Explorer can now offer Help authors and Help users the services of a sophisticated hypertext delivery system.

At this point, you may be wondering how you get HHCTRL.OCX and how you distribute it to your users. Obtaining it is easy: HHCTRL.OCX comes with the Microsoft HTML Help Workshop as well as with many third-party Help authoring tools. How you distribute this control is another matter and highlights an additional benefit of the ActiveX architecture.

If your HTML Help system gets installed locally on a user's hard disk, you will probably want your program's setup routine to install the ActiveX control to the hard disk as well.

If, however, you elect to have your users access the Help information from a remote site, your users may have to download the ActiveX control from that remote site. Fortunately, ActiveX-enabled browsers, such as Microsoft Internet Explorer, make it very easy for people to do this.

Note: HHCTRL.OCX is only meant to be used in a browser or in conjunction with SHDOCVW.DLL. There is no design-time support that would permit it to be used in development tools that support ActiveX controls such as Visual Basic or Visual C++.

Automatic Installation of Controls

Let's suppose a user accesses the HTML Help system either by clicking "Help Topics" on the Help menu or by clicking a Help button in a dialog box. Performing either of these actions will cause a particular page to be loaded in the web browser. Embedded within this page is a tag—officially it's called an object tag—that in effect says "if it's not already loaded, please load HHCTRL.OCX." The tag could look something like the following.

```
<OBJECT
    id=hhctrl
    type="application/x-oleobject"
    classid="clsid:adb880a6-d8ff-11cf-9377-00aa003b7a11"
    codebase="http://www.myplace.com/goodstuff/hhctrl.ocx"
    width=250
    height=270
    >
    <PARAM name="Command" value="Contents">
    <PARAM name="Item1" value="file:toc.hhc">
</OBJECT>
```

If this is the first time the user has loaded a page that needs HHCTRL.OCX, he will see a dialog box that looks something like this:

Don't worry, this is to be expected. Anytime a user attempts to add functionality to the browser via an ActiveX control, Internet Explorer (IE) is going to ask for confirmation. This is a safety measure to prevent accidentally downloading some virulent add-in from a disreputable source. The authentication certificate provides a way to know that the user is getting a valid control from a reputable source.

Notice the check boxes at the bottom of the dialog box. Selecting the first option tells the browser that it can install any control published by Microsoft Corporation without asking for confirmation. Selecting the second option tells the browser that it can install any control that has been certified by VeriSign.

You can also modify the way IE handles the addition of ActiveX controls (and suppress the authentication dialog box) by changing the browser's security settings. To do this, choose the Options command from the View menu and select the Security tab from the Options dialog box. The Security options are shown below:

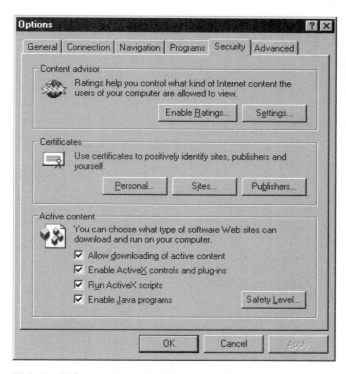

This is all fine and good if the control is already on the user's hard disk, but what if the control hasn't been installed and registered? If you look more closely at the object tag—and the first time you look at one of these things it does seem pretty complicated—you will find an absolutely brilliant provision for this situation. The line

```
codebase="http://www.myplace.com/goodstuff/hhctrl.ocx"
```

tells the browser to look for the control at a remote location—a location where you, the author, know the control can be found—and to download, install and load the control. (By the way, ActiveX controls for the web are smart—they know how to install themselves.)

So just by loading a particular page from your Help system, your users can automatically—and depending on their browsers' security settings, in some cases, transparently—install and load the control they need to turn their browsers into sophisticated Help viewers.

At this point you may be wondering if you have to use Microsoft Internet Explorer to get this functionality. The answer is not only do you not have to use Internet Explorer, you don't have to use any browser at all. Microsoft's architecture for Internet Explorer and HTML Help allows you to use just the browser's layout engine.

We'll discuss how this works in "HTML Help on Other Platforms," on page 251, and "Distributing Compiled HTML Help Systems," on page 274.

How the HTML Help Engine Works

What happens when you click the Help button in a dialog box? What happens when you choose "what's this" help for a control? What happens when you double-click a Help icon to run a standalone Help system?

The diagram below shows the relationship between a program, the HTML Help engine and an HTML Help file.

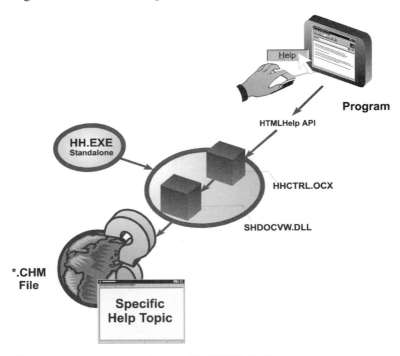

How a program communicates with HTML Help.

Responding to the Help Request

Clicking the Help button in a dialog box initiates a series of events that allows your program to communicate with the HTML Help engine and display a particular topic. Here's a somewhat simplified view of what happens:

1 User clicks the Help button in a dialog box.

2 Program determines the ID of the button that's been clicked.

3 Program determines which HTML Help file contains the Help topic associated with that ID.

4 Program determines how the Help should be displayed (in a window or as a popup) and, if it's to be displayed in a window, which window.

5 Program communicates with HHCTRL.OCX via the HTML Help API and requests that a particular HTML Help file be opened, and that the topic associated with the Help button ID be displayed in a particular window.

Note: At no point is the HTML Help executable, HH.EXE, being called.

The HTML Help Engine Is Accessed through a Dynamic Link Library

While there is an HTML Help executable which is used for displaying standalone HTML Help systems, all the real work of displaying topics, popups, table of contents, and so on, is handled by HHCTRL.OCX. Because all the heavy lifting is done by a DLL and not an executable, the programmer has much more control over how the Help system is integrated with the calling program. For example, with WinHelp it's the Help author who defines the appearance of Help windows. In HTML Help the programmer has the option of defining his own window and populating it with his own buttons. In addition, the programmer can take a window type defined by the Help author and modify it dynamically to suit the needs of the calling program, for example, setting its position, its width and height, and so forth.

With WinHelp, a Help topic is displayed in a separate window. In HTML Help the programmer has the option of embedding the Help inside the calling application.

No one is going to force you to take advantage of this extended functionality. Just having Information Types may be enough reason for you to embrace HTML Help as your preferred Help delivery system. If you are, however, interested in how you can better integrate a program with HTML Help, see "Understanding and Creating Context-Sensitive HTML Help," on page 175, and also "The HTML Help API," on page 199.

Standalone HTML Help Systems

There are two ways you can distribute standalone HTML Help systems. The first is as an uncompiled collection of related web pages stored on a web server. This is the way people distribute standard web documents now. People will be able to access your pages from their browsers, although not all HTML Help functionality will be available to them because certain features, such as associative links and full text search, require the HTML Help system to be compiled (see "What Works with What," on page 47).

The second is to create a compiled HTML Help system (a .CHM file) and access it with HH.EXE, the HTML Help executable. In this scenario, HH.EXE functions like WINHELP.EXE except that HH.EXE is really just hosting a browser window. That is, unlike WINHELP.EXE, where the "smarts" live in the executable, HH.EXE is just a shell that uses the HTML Help API.

HTML Help on Other Platforms: a Preview

So far our discussion has centered on using Internet Explorer's layout engine and the HTML Help API to create HTML-based Help systems. While the layout engine and its supporting components can be distributed freely, there may be reasons why you may not want to pursue a "browserless" solution. Maybe you don't want to require that additional components get installed on a user's system. Or perhaps your Help system has to run under the Unix or Macintosh operating systems. Or maybe you just like displaying information in a browser.

You are in luck. While some of the features of HTML Help are only available under Windows 95 and Windows NT, many of the features work fine using any browser under any operating system. For example, the expanding table of contents and the keyword search will work with Netscape Navigator running under Unix.

To create HTML Help systems that run on different platforms you will need to distribute a Java applet instead of HHCTRL.OCX. We'll discuss how you do this in "HTML Help on Other Platforms," on page 251.

What Works with What

The table below summarizes which HTML Help features are available under Windows NT and Windows 95 and which features are available under other platforms.

Feature	Windows 95/NT	Other Platforms (including Unix, Windows 3.1, and Macintosh)
Expanding and collapsing TOC	Yes	Yes
Keyword search	Yes	Yes
Full text search	Yes*	No
Information Types	Yes	No
Compression/Compilation	Yes	No
HTML Help API	Yes	No
Shortcuts	Yes	No
Related Topics (author defined)	Yes	Yes
Related topics (determined at runtime based on common keywords)	Yes*	No
Splash screen	Yes	No
Popups	Yes	No

* Requires compilation

What's Next?

So far we've explored what you can do with HTML Help and what's behind the HTML Help engine. In the next chapter we will get down to the business of making an HTML Help system using the HTML Help Workshop.

Frequently Asked Questions

Question: *Do I have to use Internet Explorer to view a compiled HTML Help file?*

Answer: No, you don't have to use Internet Explorer. You must, however, have at least some parts of Internet Explorer installed because the HTML Help engine uses the Internet Explorer layout engine (see "Distributing Compiled HTML Help Systems," on page 274).

Question: *Do I have to use Internet Explorer to view a non-compiled HTML Help System?*

Answer: No, as long as you don't need to take advantage of certain features that are only available with a compiled HTML Help system, you can view an HTML Help system on any ActiveX or Java-enabled browser.

Question: *Can I distribute a compiled HTML Help system to Windows 3.1 users?*

Answer: No, compiled HTML Help systems use the HTML Help API which is only available to Windows 95 and Windows NT users.

Question: *Will I have to re-write a lot of my application so that it calls HTML Help instead of WinHelp?*

Answer: It depends on what development tool you use to create your application. In many cases, updating your application will be very simple because the HTML Help API has been modeled on the WinHelp API. See "Understanding and Creating Context-Sensitive HTML Help," on page 175 and "The HTML Help API," on page 199, for more information.

C H A P T E R   T H R E E

Creating a Simple HTML Help System

In this chapter we'll discuss the components you need to assemble to create an HTML Help system and how these components differ depending on whether you want to display your Help system in a browser or as a compiled file in the three-pane window. We'll also work through step-by-step procedures for creating a simple HTML Help system using Microsoft's HTML Help Workshop.

For the Help author and web author: We'll examine the pieces that comprise an HTML Help system and work with the HTML Help Workshop to create a table of contents, index, and compiled HTML Help system.

For the programmer: If you're not going to be doing any HTML Help development, you can probably skip this chapter, but you may want to review the information presented on pages 51 through 59.

What's in this Chapter

Making an HTML Help System: Concepts and Procedures

This chapter is divided into two parts. The first part, "Conceptual Framework for Creating an HTML Help System," on page 51, discusses the concepts involved in creating both compiled HTML Help systems and browser-based HTML Help systems. The second part, "Procedures for Creating a Simple HTML Help System," on page 60, presents the steps needed to create an HTML Help system using the Microsoft HTML Help Workshop.

HTML Help Workshop vs. Commercial Tools

The Microsoft HTML Help Workshop is an authoring tool that comes on the CD that accompanies this book. While a serviceable tool, it does not offer the ease of use and sophistication of third-party authoring tools. If you will be doing any volume of HTML Help authoring, I would urge you to consider purchasing a more sophisticated tool. (Okay. My company makes a popular Help authoring tool called Doc-To-Help, but even if we didn't, I would encourage you to consider purchasing a third-party tool.)

If you will not be using the HTML Help Workshop as your authoring tool, you can skip the second part ("Procedures for Creating a Simple HTML Help System," on page 60).

Important Note: Microsoft HTML Help is under constant refinement. To access the latest version of HTML Help and the HTML Help Workshop, visit this web site:

   http://www.microsoft.com/workshop/author/htmlhelp/

In addition, updates to this book can be found at this location:

   http://mspress.microsoft.com/mspress/products/1408

Make Sure You Understand the Concepts

Whatever tool you use, the theory underlying the creation of an HTML Help system is the same, so get comfortable with the concepts presented in this chapter before proceeding.

Conceptual Framework for Creating an HTML Help System

We'll start by looking at developing a compiled HTML Help system that is displayed in a three-pane window, and then we'll see how to display the same system as a collection of uncompiled files in a web browser.

Creating a Compiled HTML Help System

The diagram below shows the components that comprise a simple compiled HTML Help system.

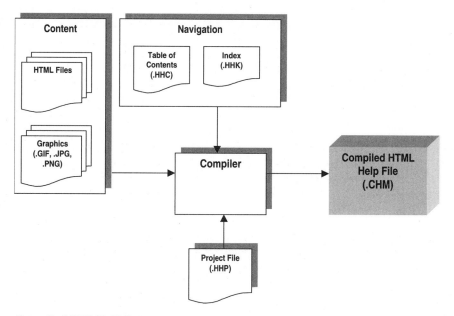

Compiled HTML Help components.

You Need Lots of HTML Files

You *can* create a web page that contains more than one topic, but the user may have to scroll to get to adjacent topics. This structure is similar to using intratopic jumps in a WinHelp project.

Perhaps the biggest difference between a WinHelp system and an HTML system is the number of HTML files that you will need to create compared to the number of RTF files you need for a WinHelp system. Unlike a WinHelp system (where each topic is separated by a hard page break, and a single RTF file can contain hundreds of topics), each HTML "topic," or page, is stored in a separate HTM file. This means if you want to have 500 topics, you will need to create 500 separate HTM files.

The reason for breaking a system down into lots of small files is to minimize download time. Only the pages a user visits get downloaded from a web site.

Note: If you know for a fact that you will be compiling your HTML Help system, you can combine multiple topics into a single .HTM file and let the compiler do the work of splitting them into individual files using HTML Help's Split feature. (For more information, see the HTML Help Workshop's online Help.)

Compiled HTML Files Take up Much Less Disk Space

In addition to the easier file management that comes from distributing a single compiled file instead of hundreds of separate files, compiled HTML files require much less disk space. For one thing, compiled HTML files are also compressed, so the size of the single compiled file is much smaller than the sum of the individual files.

Compiled HTML files also overcome the minimum file size that plagues many computer users (specifically those who don't use the FAT32 or NTFS file systems). While you may think each of your web pages takes up only two or three kilobytes (KB) of space, many hard disks are formatted so that every file—no matter how small—takes up at least 32 KB and in many cases 64 KB.

Where Will the Compiled HTML Help File Be Stored?

If the Help system you are creating is designed to complement an application (as opposed to a standalone Help system where the Help system *is* the application), you will probably want to store the Help system on the user's hard disk or on a file server, because an end user is not going to want to deal with a long wait to access the web just so she can display context-sensitive Help.

Why Users Won't Like Accessing the Web for Context-Sensitive Help

Consider the following example. A user is flummoxed by the choices in a dialog box, so she clicks the Help button or right-clicks a control to get "What's This" help. Instead of being rewarded instantly with a useful Help topic, she instead hears her modem dialing into the Internet. About a minute later, a web page with applicable information is displayed.

Unfortunately, by the time the topic has displayed she will have called the Help desk or asked a colleague for assistance.

Updating Users Who Store Their Compiled HTML Help Files Locally

For those in the business of disseminating information, the advent of the web has streamlined the challenge of distribution and keeping information current. Multiple users can simultaneously access information on a web server. The originator of the information need only update, revise, correct, etc. in one place once for all users to have access to the new information.

In the compiled HTML Help scenario, the Help system lives locally and not on a web server. So how are you going to update your users when you have new information to share with them? Are they supposed to download the entire compiled HTML file whenever it's updated?

Fortunately, with an upcoming release of HTML Help, you will be able to have your cake and eat it too. With this new release, users will be able to download updates from your web site and assimilate them into their local compiled HTML files. The assimilation consists of downloading the new information, decompiling the existing file, and then recompiling with the updated information. The process is reasonably fast, and more important, it's transparent to the user.

Note: The ability to transparently update a compiled HTML Help system is not available in HTML Help 1.1, but is expected to be available in mid-1998.

Creating an HTML Help System for Display in a Browser

The diagram below shows the components that comprise a simple HTML Help system that will be displayed in a browser.

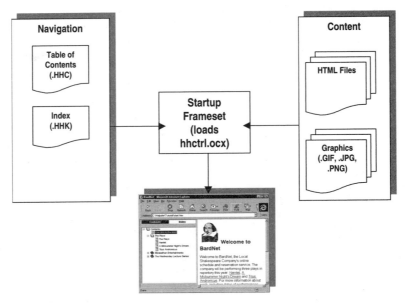

Components of a browser-based HTML Help system.

The Framework for Framesets

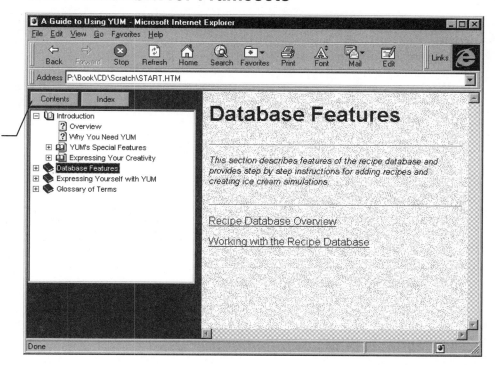

A simple VB script generates these buttons.

HTML Help system in a browser showing navigation controls in the left frame and content in the right frame.

While it is not our goal to discuss or dig into HTML coding, having a quick look at the code that displays frames will help you better understand how the navigation controls are displayed in the left side of a browser window and how content is displayed in the right side.

To divide your screen into frames you need to load a startup HTML file that specifies how many frames you want to have, their shape, and what content to display in those frames.

Here's the code for creating the frameset shown on the previous page.

```
<!DOCTYPE HTML PUBLIC "-//W3C//DTD HTML 3.2//EN">
<HTML>
<HEAD>
<TITLE>Guide to Using YUM</TITLE>
</HEAD>
<FRAMESET COLS="260,100%" framespacing=0  frameborder=0>
   <FRAME SRC="hh_toc.htm" name="left" scrolling="no">
   <FRAME SRC="main.htm" name="right" scrolling="yes">
</FRAMESET>
```

Understanding the Code

The line

```
<FRAMESET COLS="260,100%" framespacing=0  frameborder=0>
```

tells your browser to create two frames. The first frame should be 260 pixels wide and the second frame should take up whatever space is left in the browser window. Also, there should be no space or border between the frames.

The line

```
<FRAME SRC="hh_toc.htm" name="left" scrolling="no">
```

tells the browser to display the file HH_TOC.HTM in the first frame, name that first frame "left," and not to permit users to scroll in the frame.

The line

```
<FRAME SRC="main.htm" name="right" scrolling="yes">
```

tells the browser to display the file MAIN.HTM in the second frame, name the second frame "right," and to allow scrolling.

What's in the Table of Contents and Index Files?

So now we know that HH_TOC.HTM should be loaded into the left frame. Just what's in this file and what makes it display the expanding and collapsing table of contents?

What's in HH_TOC.HTM?

The source for HH_TOC.HTM is shown below.

```
<SCRIPT LANGUAGE=VBScript>
</SCRIPT>
</HEAD>
<BODY TOPMARGIN=0 LEFTMARGIN=0>
<TABLE>
<TR>
<TD><FORM ACTION=POST><INPUT TYPE=BUTTON VALUE="Contents"
ONCLICK="location = 'hh_toc.htm'" NAME="Help
Topics"></FORM></TD>

<TD><FORM ACTION=POST><INPUT TYPE=BUTTON VALUE="Index"
ONCLICK="location = 'hh_index.htm'" NAME="Index"></FORM></TD>
</TR>

<P>

<OBJECT id=hhctrl type="application/x-oleobject"
        classid="clsid:adb880a6-d8ff-11cf-9377-00aa003b7a11"
        codebase=
"http://www.myplace.com/stuff/hhctrl.ocx#Version=4,71,1111,0"
        width=250
        height=270
>
    <PARAM name="Command" value="Contents">
    <PARAM name="Item1" value="icecream.hhc">
</OBJECT>
```

Understanding the Code

The lines

```
<TD><FORM ACTION=POST><INPUT TYPE=BUTTON VALUE="Contents"
ONCLICK="location = 'hh_toc.htm'" NAME="Help
Topics"></FORM></TD>

<TD><FORM ACTION=POST><INPUT TYPE=BUTTON VALUE="Index"
ONCLICK="location = 'hh_index.htm'" NAME="Index"></FORM></TD>
</TR>
```

are responsible for displaying the buttons at the top of the left frame. Clicking the left button (the one labeled "Contents") loads HH_TOC.HTM while clicking the right button (the one labeled "Index") loads HH_INDEX.HTM.

The lines

```
<OBJECT id=hhctrl type="application/x-oleobject"
        classid="clsid:adb880a6-d8ff-11cf-9377-00aa003b7a11"
        codebase=
"http://www.myplace.com/stuff/hhctrl.ocx#Version=4,71,1111,0"
```

will make the browser load the ActiveX control HHCTRL.OCX. If the control is not on the user's hard disk—or if the version of the control is older than the one specified in the codebase statement—Internet Explorer will offer to download the control for you.

The lines

```
width=250
height=270
```

indicate that the space occupied by the control in the left frame should be 250 units wide and 270 units high.

The lines

```
<PARAM name="Command" value="Contents">
    <PARAM name="Item1" value="icecream.hhc">
</OBJECT>
```

indicate that HHCTRL.OCX should be called upon to display a table of contents and that the instructions that describe how that table of contents should be displayed can be found in ICECREAM.HHC. We'll examine the contents of this file in the next chapter.

What's in HH_INDEX.HTM?

The source for HH_INDEX.HTM is shown below.

```
<SCRIPT LANGUAGE=VBScript>
</SCRIPT>
</HEAD>
<BODY TOPMARGIN=0 LEFTMARGIN=0>
<TABLE>
<TR>
<TD><FORM ACTION=POST><INPUT TYPE=BUTTON VALUE="Contents"
ONCLICK="location = 'hh_toc.htm'" NAME="Help
Topics"></FORM></TD>

<TD><FORM ACTION=POST><INPUT TYPE=BUTTON VALUE="Index"
ONCLICK="location = 'hh_index.htm'" NAME="Index"></FORM></TD>
</TR>

<P>
<OBJECT id=hhctrl type="application/x-oleobject"
        classid="clsid:adb880a6-d8ff-11cf-9377-00aa003b7a11"
        codebase=
"http://www.myplace.com/stuff/hhctrl.ocx#Version=4,71,1111,0"
        width=248
        height=275

>

    <PARAM name="Command" value="Index">
    <PARAM name="Item1" value="IceCream.hhk">
</OBJECT>
```

Everything is the same as with HH_TOC.HTM, except that the width and height of the control is different and, instead of displaying a table of contents, these instructions call for the display of an index, ICECREAM.HHK.

As with the table of contents, we'll examine the contents of ICECREAM.HHK in the next chapter.

Procedures for Creating a Simple HTML Help System

In the next series of examples and exercises we will work with Microsoft's HTML Help Workshop. The HTML Help Workshop contains tools for creating a table of contents and an index, defining window attributes, and so on. It also contains a very simple, yet adequate, editor for inserting HTML tags.

As with HTML Help itself, the Workshop is under constant refinement, so you should visit **www.microsoft.com/workshop/author/htmlhelp** to see if there is a newer version of the authoring environment (a true WYSIWYG editor is scheduled to replace the text editor in mid-1998).

Why We're Not Going to Use the Tag Editor

While you can create content using the simple text editor, we will not do so in this book (although we may do some simple editing from time to time). There are just too many free, yet robust, tools available for creating high quality HTML content. For example, most of the HTM files that we'll look at in this chapter were created and edited using Word for Windows 97's Save as HTML feature.

Procedures for Creating a Compiled HTML Help System

In this next series of examples we will take several existing HTML files and create a simple compiled HTML Help system with a simple table of contents and a simple index.

Here is a summary of the steps we'll take to create a compiled HTML Help system.

1   Start the HTML Help Workshop

2   Create a new project

3   Specify files to compile

4   Create a window definition

5   Create a Contents file

6   Add headings and pages to Contents

7   Create an Index file

8   Reorganize and test the contents and index

9   Compile

The files you will need for these exercises can be found in HHKIT\CHAP03.

The completed examples can be found in HHKIT\CHAP03\FINISHED.

To Start the HTML Help Workshop

1 Click the **Start** button.

2 Choose **Programs**.

3 Choose the **HTML Help Workshop** program group.

4 Choose **HTML Help Workshop**.

The HTML Help Workshop will load.

To Create a New Project

1 From the **File** menu, choose **New**.

The New dialog box will appear.

2 Choose **Project** and click **Next**.

The New Project wizard will appear.

3 Make sure Convert WinHelp project is *not* selected and click **Next**.

4 When asked to create a name for you project, type **ICECREAM.HHP** and save the file in the **CHAP03** folder underneath the HHKIT folder.

5 When asked to specify existing files, click **Next**.

6 Click **Finish**. Your screen should look like the one shown on the next page.

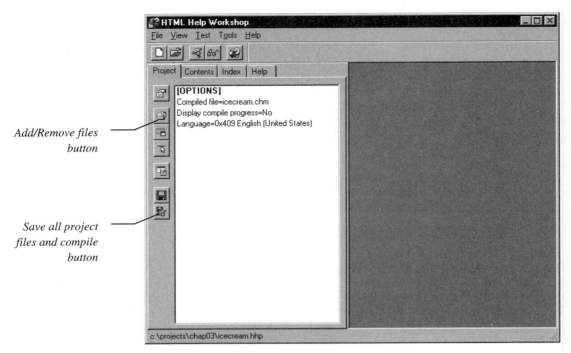

Add/Remove files button

Save all project files and compile button

The HTML Help Workshop. By default, the compiled HTML Help file will be called ICECREAM.CHM.

Adding Files

Before the HTML Help Workshop can create a compiled HTML Help file, you will need to specify which files to compile. You won't need to list every file that will comprise your system as the compiler will automatically include all referenced files and graphics when it compiles your system.

For example, the file MAIN.HTM contains links to INTRO.HTM, DATABASE.HTM and EXPRESS.HTM. Each of these files in turn contains links to all the other files in the Help system.

In this case, the compiler only needs to know about MAIN.HTM to be able to figure out which files should be included in the compiled system.

Important note: If want to see a list of all the page titles in your project when you create a table of contents, you will need to specify all the files you want to include in the compiled HTML Help file.

Specifying Files to Include

1   Click the **Add/Remove** files button.

2   When the Topics Files dialog box appears, click **Add**.

You can select more than one file at a time by holding down the SHIFT key.

3   Select the files you want to include, in this case all of the .HTM files in the CHAP03 folder, and click **OK**.

Your screen should look like the one shown below.

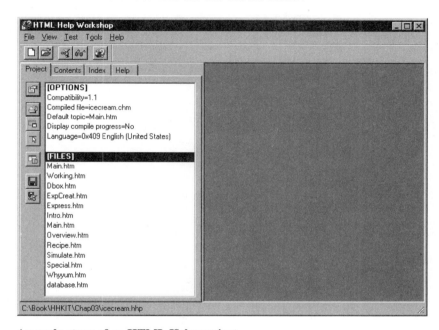

An early stage of an HTML Help project.

A Preview of Compiling

There's still a lot we should do to create a *good* HTML Help system, but we have specified enough to be able to create a compiled HTML Help system that works. In this next exercise we compile the HTML Help file.

To Compile the Project and View the Results

1   Click the **Save all project files and compile** button.

The "meat grinder" will appear and the HTML Help Workshop will display a compilation log in the right pane.

2   Click the **View compiled HTML Help file** button.

3   Specify the file you want to view, as shown on the next page.

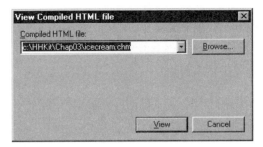

4 Click **View**.

The compiled HTML Help file, ICECREAM.CHM, will appear.

A compiled HTML Help file in its own window. The program HH.EXE is hosting SHDOCVW.DLL and HHCTRL.OCX to display ICECREAM.CHM (see "How the HTML Help Engine Works," on page 44).

Making a *Useful* Compiled HTML Help File

While appealing, this compiled HTML Help system isn't particularly useful. Without any navigation aids, the user will quickly hit a dead end within the system because there isn't a way to navigate back to a previous screen.

In the next series of exercises, we will create a window definition, a table of contents, and an index so that the compiled HTML Help file will help, rather than frustrate, a user.

Creating a Window Definition

1 Click the **Add/Modify window definitions** button in the HTML Help Workshop.

2 Type a name for the window, in this case **Main**.

The Window Types dialog box will appear, as shown below.

3   In the Title bar text edit box, type **Guide to Using YUM**.

4   Click the **Navigation Pane** tab.

5   Select **Window with navigation pane, topic pane and button bar**.

6   Make sure the **Auto sync** and **Add Search tab** options are selected, as shown below.

For a search tab to appear, the Compile Full-Text Search option in the Project Options dialog box must be turned on. If you turn the Add Search Tab option on without having set the project options, the Resolve Windows Inconsistencies dialog box will appear.

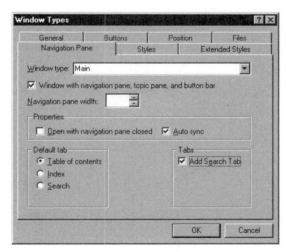

7   Click **OK**.. The Resolve Window Inconsistencies wizard will appear.

8   Click **Next**.

9   Make sure **Search Tab** and **Compile Full-text Search Information** are both selected, and click **Next**.

10 Click **Finish**.

Creating a Contents File

With the window definition set, we're now ready to create a table of contents. We'll do this by creating a new .HHC file, setting its properties, and adding headings and pages. In contrast to a WinHelp table of contents derived automatically from the Help file's own hierarchy, the table of contents for a simple HTML Help system must be explicitly assembled. There is no hierarchy until it is created by specifying the order that .HTM are listed in the table of contents.

Creating a New Table of Contents File

1 Click the **Contents** tab.

   A dialog box appears warning that there is no table of contents associated with this project.

2 Choose **Create a new contents file** and click **OK**.

3 When asked to specify a file name, type **ICECREAM.HHC** and click **OK**.

Setting Contents Properties

1 Click the **Contents Properties** button.

2 Make sure Use Folders Instead Of Books is turned off, as shown below.

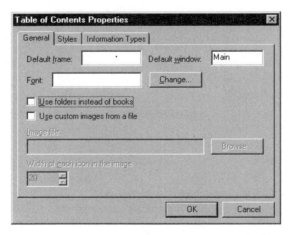

The Table of Contents Properties dialog box. Notice that you can change the font.

3 Click **OK**.

Adding Headings

1   Click the **Insert a Heading** button.

2   In the Entry title edit box, type **Introduction**.

3   Click the **Add** button.

4   In the Path or URL dialog box, select the title you want to associate with this heading, in this case **Introduction**, as shown below.

Make sure the project file (icecream.hhp) is specified.

5   Click **OK**.

6   Click **OK** again.

Practice Exercise

On your own, follow the steps outlined above and add a heading for **Database Features** (DATABASE.HTM) and **Expressing Yourself with YUM** (EXPRESS.HTM). When you are finished your screen should look like the one shown below.

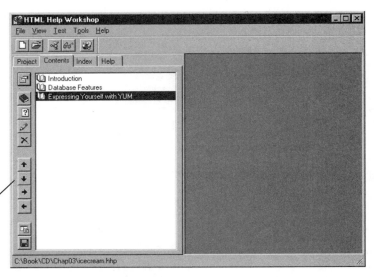

Use these buttons to reorganize headings and pages

The early stages of a Contents (.HHC) file. You change the order of items by selecting an item and clicking one of the arrow buttons on the left side of the window.

Adding Pages

1 Click the heading under which you want the first page to appear, in this case "Introduction."

 2 Click the **Insert a page** button.

3 When asked if you want to insert the entry at the beginning of the table of contents, click **No**.

4 In the Entry title edit box, type **Overview**.

5 Click the **Add** button.

6 In the Path or URL dialog box, choose **Overview**.

7 Click **OK** to close the dialog box.

8 Click **OK**. Your screen should look like the one shown below.

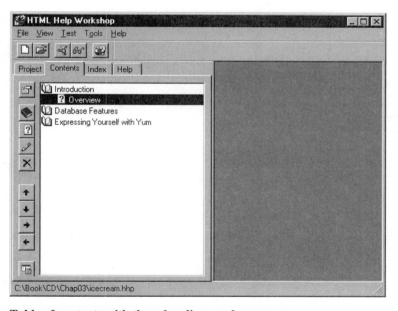

Table of contents with three headings and one page.

Practice Exercises

On your own, do the following:

- Underneath "Overview," add the pages "Why You Need YUM," "YUM's Special Features," and "Expressing Your Creativity."

- Underneath "Database Features," add the pages "Recipe Database" and "Working with the Recipe Database."

- Underneath "Expressing Yourself with YUM," add the pages "Ice Cream Creation Simulator" and "Ice Cream Creation Simulator Dialog Box."

- Save the file.

When you are finished, your screen should look like the one shown below.

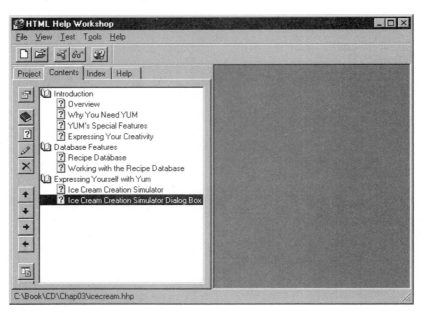

A more robust table of contents.

Creating a Keyword Search

There are two ways you can create a keyword search list in HTML Help. The first method involves inserting keyword object tags into each .HTM file and letting the HTML Help Workshop compiler assemble these keywords into an index file (.HHK file). This method only works if you will be compiling your HTML Help system and will not work if you want to display the system in a browser.

The second method involves directly editing the index file.

There are two advantages to inserting object keywords into the source .HTM files:

- You can insert the keywords while you create and edit the content; and

- You can take advantage of HTML Help's associative linking feature to create links to other topics that share similar content. (We'll explore how to do this in "Associative Links: Concepts," on page 146.)

Since we want the keyword search to work in both the browser-based and compiled HTML Help system, we'll use the second method in the next series of examples.

Creating a New Index File

1   Click the **Index** tab.

A dialog box appears warning that there is no index associated with this project.

2   Choose **Create a new index file** and click **OK**.

3   When asked to specify a file name, accept the default of **INDEX.HHK** and click **OK**.

Adding a Keyword that Links to One Title

 1 Click the **Insert Keyword** button.

2 In the Keyword edit box, type **Introduction** and click the **Add** button.

The Path or URL dialog box will appear, as shown below.

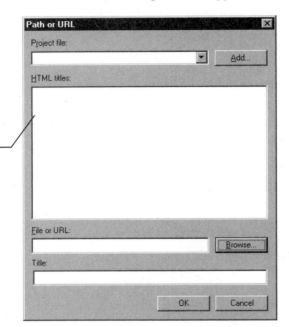

The HTML Titles list will be empty until you select a Project file from the drop-down list box.

3 From the Project file drop-down list, choose the project file with which you are working, in this case **ICECREAM.HHP**.

This populates the HTML titles list.

4 Choose the title you will want to appear when the keyword "Introduction" is selected, in this case **Introduction**.

5   Click **OK**. Your screen should look like the one shown below.

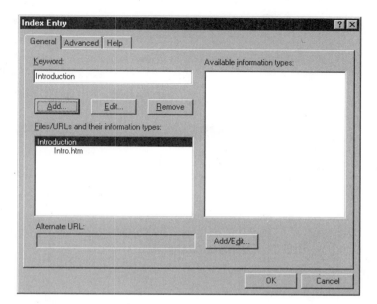

When the user selects "Introduction" from the keyword list, INTRO.HTM will be
displayed.

6   Click **OK**.

Practice Exercise

On your own, create a keyword "Basic Concepts" that when clicked accesses the
topic called "Overview."

Adding a Keyword that Links to Several Titles

You can design your system so that clicking a keyword presents the user with
several topics from which to choose. In this next example we'll associate a
keyword with two topics.

1   Click the **Insert keyword** button.

2   In the Keyword edit box, type **Features** and click the **Add** button.

The Path or URL dialog box will appear.

3   From the Project File drop-down list, choose the project file with which you
are working, in this case **ICECREAM.HHP**.

This populates the HTML titles list.

4   Choose the first title you will want to appear when the keyword "Features" is
selected, in this case **Database Features**, and click **OK**.

5   Click the **Add** button again.

6   From the Project file drop-down list, choose the project file with which you are working, in this case **ICECREAM.HHP**.

7   Choose the second title you will want to appear when the keyword "Features" is selected, in this case **YUM's Special Features**, and click **OK**.

    Your screen should look like the one shown below.

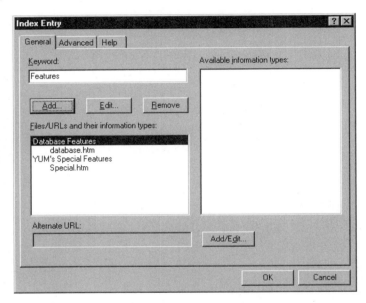

The single keyword "Features" will give the user the choice of two topics to jump to.

8   Click **OK**.

Creating Second-Level Keyword Entries

As with WinHelp, you can create secondary-level index entries (in fact, you can go as many levels deep as you want). In this next example, we'll create a second-level keyword, "Overview," that is a child of the keyword "Features."

1   Click the keyword under which you want the second-level entries to appear, in this case **Features**.

   2   Click the **Add Keyword** button.

3   In the Keyword edit box, type **Overview**.

4   Click the **Add** button.

5   From the Project file drop-down list, choose the project file with which you are working, in this case **ICECREAM.HHP**.

6 Select the title you will want to appear when the "Overview" keyword is selected, in this case **Database Features**, and click **OK**.

7 Click **OK** again.

8 Click the **Move Selection Right** button.

Your screen should look like the one shown below.

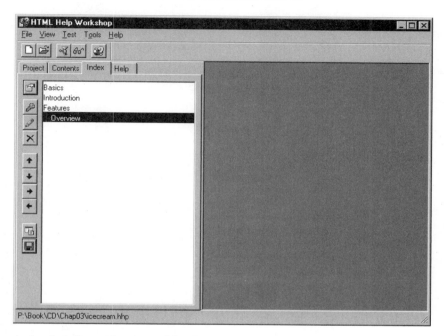

A simple index with a second-level entry.

Practice Exercise

Create a second-level keyword "Special" under the keyword "Features" that when selected displays "YUM's Special Features."

Reorganizing and Testing the Contents and the Index

You may have noticed that the index we've created is not alphabetized. The HTML Help workshop comes with several tools that allow you to examine, test and reorganize your contents and index.

In this next series of exercises, we will change the order of the index, view the HTML source for an index entry, and view that HTM file in a window.

Changing the Order of Keywords

1   Click the keyword you want to change, in this case **Features**.

  2   Click the **Move Selection Up** button.

Your screen should look like the one shown below.

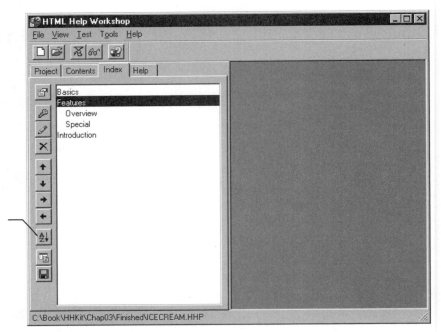

You can also click the Sort button to sort the entire index.

Moving the primary keyword (Features) up also moved the secondary keywords.

Viewing Topics Associated with a Keyword

1 In the HTML Help Workshop, double-click the keyword whose associated title you want to examine, in this case **Features**.

Since there are two titles associated with this keyword, the Topics Found dialog box will appear, as shown below.

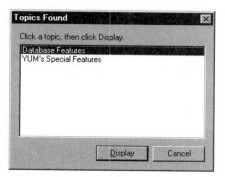

2 Choose the topic you want to examine, in this case **Database Features**, and click **Display**.

Your screen should look like the one shown below.

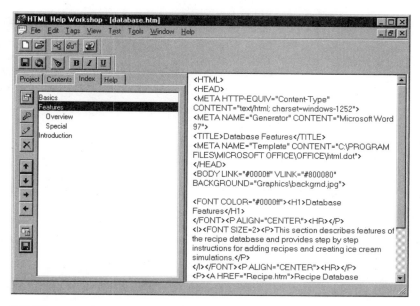

HTML source for DATABASE.HTM. A future release of HTML Help Workshop will display the source in a WYSIWYG editor.

Note: You can edit the HTML source from within the HTML Help Workshop. We'll do this in "Editing the Startup Files," on page 83.

Examining an HTM File in a Browser Window

▸ With the source for the HTM file you want to examine in the right pane of the HTML Help workshop, click the **View In Browser** button.

The HTM file will be displayed in a browser window, as shown below.

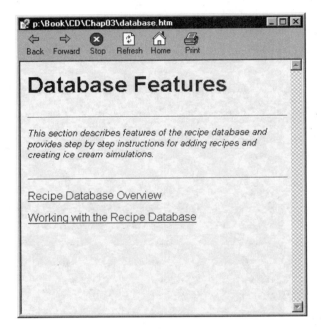

HTM file viewed in a browser window.

Setting Project Options and Recompiling

Before recompiling and viewing, let's change some of the project options so that

- the compiled HTML Help file appears in the window we created (Main),

- a title appears in that window (Guide to Using YUM),

- the .HHC and .HHK files are included in the compiled file, and

- full-text search information is included in the compiled file.

To Set the Project Options

1 Click the **Project** tag.

2 Click the **Change Project Option**s button.

3 Change the title to **Guide to Using YUM** and the default window to **Main,** as shown below.

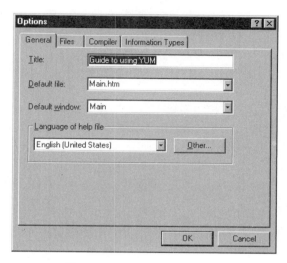

4 Click the **Files** tab.

5 Make sure the Contents file is ICECREAM.HHC and the Index file is INDEX.HHK, as shown below.

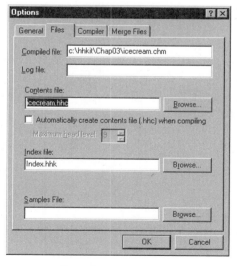

6 Click the **Compiler** tab.

7   Make sure **Compile Full-Text Search Information** is turned on.

8   Click **OK**.

Recompiling and Viewing the Results

 1   Click the **Save All Project Files And Compile** button.

The "meat grinder" will appear and the HTML Help Workshop will display a compilation log in the right pane.

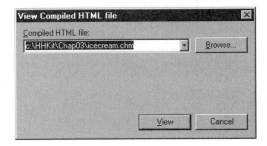 2   Click the **View Compiled HTML Help File** button.

3   Specify the file you want to view, as shown below.

4   Click **View**.

The recompiled HTML Help file, ICECREAM.CHM, will appear, as shown on the opposite page.

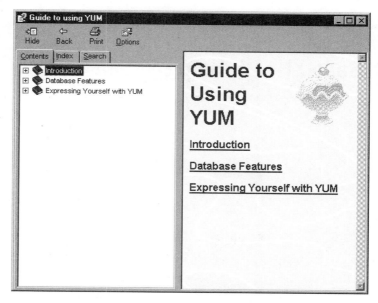

Compiled HTML Help file with a table of contents.

Procedures for Creating a Browser-Based HTML Help System

The steps needed to create a browser-based HTML Help system are almost the same as those needed to create a compiled HTML Help system. The only difference is that instead of compiling and displaying in the three-pane window we will create a startup frameset and display the system in a browser.

Here is a summary of the steps required to create a browser-based HTML Help system.

1   Start the HTML Help Workshop

2   Create a new project

3   Specify files to include

4   Create a Contents file

5   Add headings and pages to Contents

6   Create an Index file

7   Reorganize and test the contents and index

8   Create a startup frameset and startup files

9   Edit the contents file (ICECREAM.HHC) and index (INDEX.HHK) so that topics accessed from either appear in the right frame.

10   View the startup file in a browser

At this point we've done everything except create the startup frameset (START.HTM), the files that get loaded by the startup frameset (HH_TOC.HTM and HH_INDEX.HTM), and edit the .HHC and .HHK files.

Creating a Startup Frameset

To create the startup files we will "borrow" some files that have already been created for you. Specifically, we will

1   Copy the startup frameset and startup files from the template folder of the CD to the current project folder.

2   Edit these files so that they refer to the contents files and index files you have already created.

Copying Startup Files from the Template Folder

▶ Copy the files START.HTM, HH_TOC.HTM and HH_INDEX.HTM from the template folder (HHKIT\TEMPLATE) to the current project folder (HHKIT\CHAP03).

Editing the Startup Files

1 Using the Microsoft HTML Help Workshop, open **START.HTM.**

   Your screen should look like the one shown below.

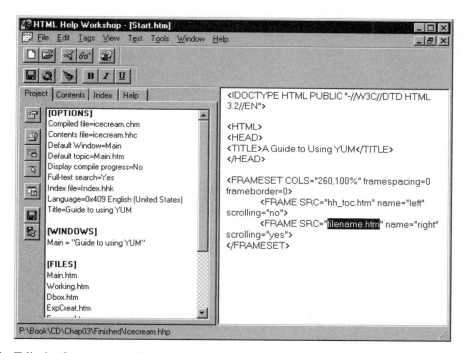

MAIN.HTM is the file that will be displayed in the content frame when the system is first loaded.

2 Edit the frame source for the right frame so that it is **MAIN.HTM** instead of FILENAME.HTM, as shown below:

```
<FRAME SRC="main.htm" name="right" scrolling="yes">
```

3 Save the file.

4 Open **HH_TOC.HTM.**

5 Locate the PARAM name="Item1" entry and change the file name to **ICECREAM.HHC,** as shown below.

```
PARAM name="Item1" value="icecream.hhc">
```

6 Save the file.

Note: HH_INDEX.HTM already refers to the correct index file, INDEX.HHK, so we don't need to edit it.

Editing the Contents and Index Files

1 Click the **Contents** tab.

2 Click the **Properties** button.

3 In the Default frame edit box, type **right**.

4 Click **OK**.

5 Click the **Index** tab.

6 Click the **Properties** button.

7 In the Default frame edit box, type **right**.

8 Click **OK**.

Displaying the HTML Help System in a Browser

From the Internet Explorer, open **HHKIT\START.HTM**. Your screen should look like the one shown below.

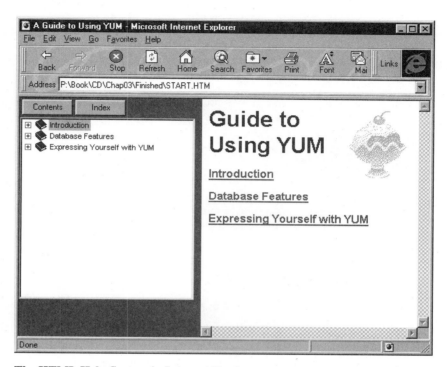

The HTML Help System in Internet Explorer.

What's Next?

In this chapter we've looked at what it takes to create a simple HTML Help system with a table of contents and an index. In the next chapter we'll explore what's behind the table of contents and the index, and we'll work with Information Types.

Frequently Asked Questions

Question: *Can I use framesets with compiled HTML Help files?*

Answer: Yes. Any valid HTML construct will work in a compiled HTML system.

Question: *I have some existing WinHelp projects. Instead of starting from scratch, is there any way to convert them to HTML Help?*

Answer: Yes. We'll look at how to do this in "Other HTML Help Workshop Tools," on page 276.

Question: *Do I have to use the HTML Help Workshop to create .HHC and .HHK files?*

Answer: No. In fact, you can create these files using a simple text editor, like Notepad. You will, however, spend a lot more time than you need to if you don't use a tool that facilitates creating these files. We'll look at what's inside these files in the next chapter.

Question: *Can I customize the appearance of the table of contents?*

Answer: Yes. We'll look at how to do that in the next chapter.

CHAPTER FOUR

Navigation and Information Types

In this chapter we'll further explore HTML Help's navigation features and we'll explain how you can use Information Types to display different content to different audiences. We'll also work through step-by-step procedures for creating sophisticated tables of contents that support Information Types.

For the Help author and web author: We'll examine the advanced functionality available using Information Types with HTML Help's table of contents and index. We will then see how to use the HTML Help Workshop to create a compiled HTML Help system that uses Information Types.

For the programmer: If you're not going to be doing any HTML Help development, you can probably skip this chapter, but you may want to review the information presented on pages 88 through 108.

What's in this Chapter

Navigation and Information Types: Concepts

Whether you are a technical writer, a Help author, or a web expert, there are three questions you should ask yourself whenever you create HTML Help systems:

1. How do I explain things so that people will understand them?

2. How do I make sure people can find the information they need?

3. How do I present different information to different audiences?

The first item is beyond the scope of this book. We will, however, show you state-of-the-art techniques for making sure people will be able to find the information you write.

For item two, we'll look at HTML Help's built-in table of contents, keyword search (index), and full-text search, as well as WexTech's Systems' AnswerWorks natural language interface technology.

For item three, we'll look at what is arguably HTML Help's most innovative feature: Information Types.

Table of Contents

I've recently attended Windows Help conferences where a noted hypertext and usability expert stated that very few people use the Windows 95 table of contents. This presenter explained that most people rely on context-sensitive Help to get them where they want to be, or that they randomly click the Index and Find tabs, not knowing exactly what distinguishes these two search options.

What the presenter failed to mention was *why* no one uses the table of contents. Is it that *any* table of contents is inherently limited, or is it just that *Windows 95's* table of contents is inherently limited?

I feel strongly that the problem is not the concept of a table of contents, but its implementation.

Why I Don't Like the Windows 95/NT Help System Table of Contents

As we saw in "The Contents Tab," on page 17, there are many drawbacks to the Windows 95 and NT table of contents. The table below summarizes these shortcomings.

Problem	Description
Help Topics are displayed in a modal dialog box.	User can't look at Help topics and the outline at the same time.
Table of contents does not synchronize with Help system.	User can't use the outline to determine where she is within the hierarchy of the Help system.
Can't jump to a heading; "books" can only be opened or closed.	A heading cannot also be a topic to which you can jump.
Book and topic icons cannot be customized.	Author can't provide visual cues as to what type of information (procedure, concept, tip, and so on) is available when the user displays a particular topic.

The HTML Help Table of Contents

As we saw in "Introducing the Three-Pane HTML Help Window," on page 23, The HTML Help table of contents overcomes the shortcomings listed above.

The table below summarizes the features of the HTML Help table of contents.

Feature	Description
Simultaneous display of table of contents and topics	Using frames or the three-pane window, the table of contents is visible when you're viewing topics.
	The three-pane window's Hide button is a toggle. Clicking it hides the navigation pane and displays a Show button in its place. Clicking the Show button redisplays the navigation pane.
Synchronization	Table of contents dynamically updates as you access other topics so you always know where you are within the hierarchy of the Help system.
"Smart" headings	A heading can be a topic to which you can jump.
Different icons	Different icons can be used to designate different types of information. For example, the 📄 icon is used to designate procedural information, while the 📑 icon is used to designate a page that's both a heading and a topic.
	In addition to the icons that come with the HTML Help Workshop, you can also create your own icons. You can make these icons larger than the default icons.

Labeling and Other Visual Cues

The ability to label information using custom icons is a very welcome addition and should not be buried in the "well, I'll never use that feature" dust bin. Users like to know ahead of time what they are likely to find when they make a selection, and anything that prepares a user for what's ahead will make your Help system more usable.

Consider the table of contents shown below.

Table of contents with different icons.

The ☁ icon next to "What's New" indicates that the topic lives on a web server and that the user can expect a bit of a delay when he accesses it. The ▦ icon next to "Overview" indicates that the topic contains a video.

Index

The index, or keyword search, should be the primary means for users to find information in your HTML Help system. Any user who knows how to use Windows Help or who knows how to look up information in a reference guide will first see if she can find the information in the index before resorting to a full text search.

Creating a good index requires a lot of work, because you must anticipate all the different terms a user may use when he's trying to find something. For example, in a Help system for a spreadsheet program there will probably be a topic that explains how to insert rows. A user may try to find this topic using any of the following keywords:

Insert
Add
Rows
Put in

The indexer needs to anticipate the keywords users will use to find information and include those keywords in the index.

Creating a good index takes time and skill. Unfortunately, most Help authors wait until the very end of their projects to create the index (which is ironic, given that most Help users go to the index first).

New Features in the HTML Help Index

The HTML Help Index adds three new capabilities to WinHelp's index. The first new feature is that you can have an unlimited number of index levels, versus the two levels available in Windows Help. To be honest, I don't know why you would need more than two levels of index entries, but this feature usually generates some applause when it is demonstrated at Help conferences.

The second feature is the ability to add book-like cross references and "see-also" entries. Consider the example shown below.

A cross reference in an HTML Help index.

Double-clicking this entry will jump to a different entry in the Index, as shown below.

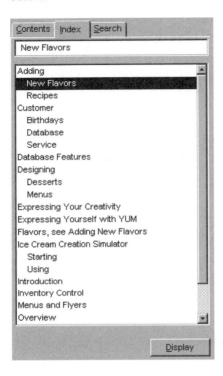

Full Text Search

I've never been a fan of full text search, and HTML Help's implementation has done little to win me over. If, however, I can't find what I need through the index or table of contents, I will certainly give the full text search a try.

Full-text searches tend to find too many instances of a term and they don't take into account the term someone may use to find a topic. For example, a Help system may have topics in which the words "gold," "silver," and "platinum" appear, but may not reveal any topics when the word "metals" is typed into the full text search edit box. (A good index, on the other hand, would contain entries for all of these terms.)

HTML Help Full Text Search vs. Windows Help Full Text Search

Unlike the Windows Help full text search engine, the HTML Help full text search engine does not provide any feedback as you type a word into the search edit box. With the Windows Help full text search engine, items appear dynamically as you type, so you know whether the item is contained in the list or not. With the HTML Help engine you must click the List Topics button to find out whether or not there is a hit.

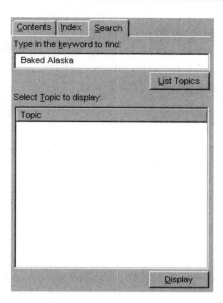

In HTML Help 1.x there is no word wheel; you must click the List Topics button to see if there are any matches.

Boolean Search

The HTML Help full text search engine does allow you to perform simple Boolean searches. For example, typing

Software and errors

in the search edit box will display only the topics that contain both the words "software" and "errors," while typing

Software or errors

in the search edit box will display all topics that contain the word "software" and all topics that contain the word "errors."

Information Types

As we mentioned earlier, perhaps the most exciting innovation in HTML Help is Information Types. Using Information Types the author can designate topics as conceptual, procedural, advanced, and so on, and the user can apply filters to limit display in the table of contents to topics of certain information types. The author can create an unlimited number of different information types and the user can apply multiple filters so he can just view "Advanced Concepts" or "Beginner Tips" or even "Troubleshooting Procedures for Product A (French)."

When to Use Information Types

Assigning information types to topics is a helpful way to get relevant information to different audiences. Here are some examples of how you might use information types:

Experience Level. You can identify topics as being geared towards novice, intermediate, or advanced users.

Different Products. Perhaps you are writing documentation for several different products. Some of the information pertains to all of the products, while other information is specific to a particular product. Using Information Types you can specify which topics pertain to all products and which topics pertain to a particular product.

Job Description. You can designate topics as being for managers, vice presidents, directors, sales clerks, and so on.

Language. Perhaps your online documentation needs to be available in English, French, and German. Using Information types, all of the documentation can be stored in one HTML Help system and the user can specify which language she wants to see.

An Example of Information Types

Consider the example shown below which is the new, improved documentation for the Ice Cream Creation Simulator.

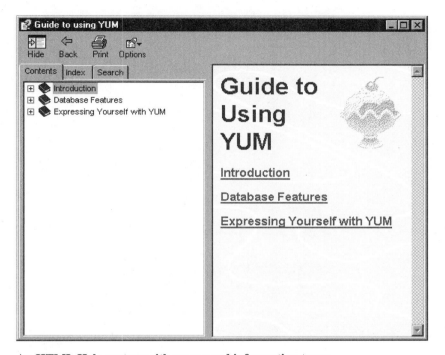

An HTML Help system with compound information types.

The online documentation contains information about both the standard and the deluxe models, and you just want to see procedures for the deluxe model. Here's how you would apply a filter so you just see the information you want.

1   Click **Options** and select **Customize**.

   The Customize Information wizard will appear.

2   Make sure **Custom** is selected and click **Next**.

3   Make sure only **Procedure** is selected as shown on the next page.

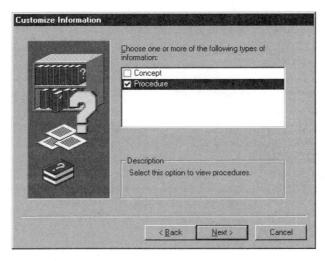

Check boxes for this Information category allow you to select concepts, procedures, or both.

4   Click **Next**. The dialog box will change, as shown below.

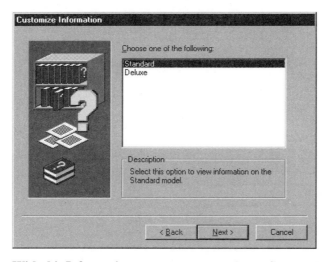

With this Information category you can choose Standard or Deluxe, but not both.

5   Select **Deluxe** and click **Next**.

6   Click **Finish**.

You will now only be able to access procedures for the deluxe model from the table of contents and from the index. To gain access to all the topics, choose Customize from the Options menu and select All.

Exclusive and Inclusive Information Types

Notice that in the previous example the user is able to choose Concept, Procedure, or both. This is because the HTML Help author defined that Information category as being **inclusive**, meaning the user can choose more than one type of Information Type from that category.

On the other hand, the user can choose either the Deluxe or Standard model, but not both. This is because the HTML Help author defined that Information category as being **exclusive**.

Guidelines and Restrictions for Creating
Inclusive and Exclusive Information Types

How you define your information categories is up to you, although categories such as language seem better suited to be exclusive information types (for example, it's unlikely that a user would want to see Help topics in both German and English).

Note: The ability to filter information using the index and full text search is not available in HTML Help 1.1 (you can, of course, filter information from the table of contents). This feature should be available in HTML Help 1.2, scheduled for release in early 1998.

One to Many Relationships

Note: This feature is not working correctly in HTML Help 1.1, but is expected to function properly in HTML Help 1.2, which is slated for release in early 1998. While you can author for this feature now, end users will not be able to take advantage of this until an updated version of the HTML Help ActiveX control, HHCTRL.OCX, is available.

One of the more important ramifications of Information Types is that a single table of contents entry can link to more than one topic. Consider the example shown below.

Adding New Flavors

If the user has indicated that he wants to see information on the Standard model, this topic will be displayed.

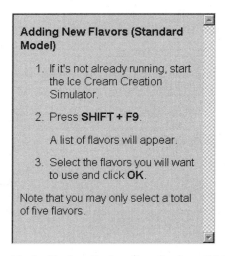

Topic displayed when Standard model is selected.

But if the user indicated he wanted to see information on the Deluxe model, the following topic will be displayed.

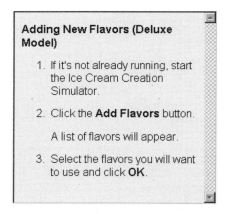

Topic displayed when Deluxe model is selected.

Local versus Remote Links

In addition, a single table of contents entry can specify both a local target and a remote (web-based) target. Suppose you plan for your HTML Help system to be composed of several modules and that a topic in one module may contain a link to a topic in another module. Now further suppose that the user clicks that link, but that the other module has not been installed. Being able to specify an alternative target—in this case a target on a web site that you know exists—the user will access the topic on the remote site instead of seeing an error message indicating that the target topic does not exist.

Issues with Information Types

There are several issues with which you will have to contend in implementing Information Types with HTML Help 1.1. The most important of these are

- conditional linking

- user interface, and

- initialization.

Conditional Linking

While HTML Help's table of contents has a facility for jumping to a different topic based on which Information Type has been selected, its linking facility provides no such feature.

Consider the example shown below.

Clicking this link should display one topic if the Information Type is "standard" and a different topic if the Information Type is "deluxe."

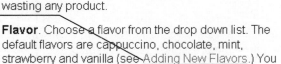

The Ice Cream Creation Simulator Dialog Box

Use this dialog box to simulate an ice cream dessert. This allows you to try different dessert combinations without wasting any product.

Flavor. Choose a flavor from the drop down list. The default flavors are cappuccino, chocolate, mint, strawberry and vanilla (see Adding New Flavors.) You may not choose more than one flavor.

Topping. Choose a wet topping from the drop down list. The available toppings are caramel, chocolate fudge and strawberry.

Style. Choose the type of ice cream from the drop down list. The available styles are premium, regular, ice milk and yogurt.

Number of Scoops. Increase or decrease the number of scoops by moving the slider. Note: the simulator will not let you select more than two scoops if premium ice cream is used.

A link that should be conditional.

Notice the link "Adding New Flavors." If standard is selected, clicking this link should display the standard set of instructions, but if deluxe is selected, the deluxe instructions should be displayed.

In a future release of HTML Help, the related topic feature (which we will discuss in Chapter Six) will provide a simple means for creating a conditional link. In the meantime you can work around this problem by doing either of the following:

- Make sure that general topics (like the one above) do not contain links to Information Type-specific topics.

- Create Information Type-specific general topics. For example, have a "standard" version of the topic shown above that contains a link to the standard "Adding New Flavors" topic and a "deluxe" version of the topic that contains a link to the deluxe "Adding New Flavors" topic.

Coming Soon: Better User Interface

HTML Help 1.1 does not provide a way for the author to define a more friendly and intuitive way for the end user to filter information using Information Types. In addition to not providing a simpler method for applying Information Types, the Customize feature is buried under a menu.

HTML Help 1.2 is expected to provide a better end user interface. In addition, the HTML Help author will be able to create **Information Subsets**. A subset is a pre-defined setting for multiple filters. This means you can present the user with several "canned" settings where multiple filters will be applied automatically.

Note: Microsoft is actively improving and refining HTML Help. Go to **www.microsoft.com/workshop/author/htmlhelp** to download the latest version. You can also visit **http://mspress.microsoft.com/mspress/products/1408** to view updates to this book.

Initialization

HTML Help 1.1 does not provide a way to pre-set Information Type settings. Ideally, a facility would exist that displays certain Information Types automatically, based upon a user's log-in. For example, a network administrator could work with a Help author so that when a particular user accesses an HTML Help system, only certain topics would be available to that user.

The HTML Help 1.2 API is slated to have this capability, so a programmer will be able to load an HTML Help system with certain Information Types turned on as well as dynamically change Information Type settings.

Looking Under the Hood: Understanding Sitemaps

Information that governs the display of your Help system's table of contents and index are stored in the .HHC and .HHK files respectively. These files are examples of **sitemap** files. A sitemap describes the structure of a web site or HTML Help system. The ActiveX control HHCTRL.OCX and the Java applet HHCTRL.CLASS interpret the sitemaps and display them in a manner that can be easily interpreted by the user. The format of these sitemap files adheres to specifications developed by Microsoft and proposed to the World Wide Web Consortium (W3C) as an Internet standard.

Sitemap files are text files that can be edited using a text editor, such as Windows Notepad. While it is unlikely that you will ever need to directly edit or view these files, in the next section we will examine how the code in these files affects the functionality of your table of contents and index.

Understanding What's in a Table of Contents Sitemap File

For this example we'll look at the sitemap file that produced the table of contents samples shown earlier in this chapter. A modified version of this file can be found in HHKIT\CHAP04\FINISHED\ICECREAM.HHC.

A portion of the sitemap is shown below.

```
<!DOCTYPE HTML PUBLIC "-//IETF//DTD HTML//EN">
<HTML>
<HEAD>
<meta name="GENERATOR" content="Microsoft&reg; HTML Help Workshop 4.00">
<!-- Sitemap 1.0 -->
</HEAD><BODY>
<OBJECT type="text/site properties">
    <param name="WindowName" value="Main">
    <param name="Category" value="Type of Info">
    <param name="CategoryDesc" value="Choose the type of information you
want to view.">
    <param name="Type" value="Concept">
    <param name="TypeDesc" value="Select this option to view concepts.">
    <param name="Type" value="Procedure">
    <param name="TypeDesc" value="Select this option to view
procedures.">
    <param name="Category" value="Product">
    <param name="CategoryDesc" value="Select the model you are using.">
    <param name="TypeExclusive" value="Standard">
    <param name="TypeDesc" value="Select this option to view information
on the Standard model.">
    <param name="TypeExclusive" value="Deluxe">
```

```
        <param name="TypeDesc" value="Select this option to view information
on the Deluxe model.">
        <param name="Window Styles" value="0x800025">
</OBJECT>
<UL>
    <LI> <OBJECT type="text/sitemap">
        <param name="Name" value="Introduction">
        <param name="Type" value="Type of Info::Concept">
        <param name="Local" value="Intro.htm">
        <param name="URL" value="http://www.goodstuff.com/intro.htm">
        </OBJECT>
    <UL>
        <LI> <OBJECT type="text/sitemap">
            <param name="Name" value="Overview">
            <param name="Type" value="Type of Info::Concept">
            <param name="Local" value="Overview.htm">
            <param name="ImageNumber" value="11">
            </OBJECT>
        <LI> <OBJECT type="text/sitemap">
            <param name="Name" value="Why You Need YUM">
            <param name="Type" value="Type of Info::Concept">
            <param name="Local" value="Whyyum.htm">
            <param name="ImageNumber" value="11">
            </OBJECT>
        <LI> <OBJECT type="text/sitemap">
            <param name="Name" value="YUM's Special Features">
            <param name="Type" value="Type of Info::Concept">
            <param name="Local" value="Special.htm">
            <param name="ImageNumber" value="11">
            </OBJECT>
        <LI> <OBJECT type="text/sitemap">
            <param name="Name" value="Expressing Your Creativity">
            <param name="Type" value="Type of Info::Concept">
            <param name="Local" value="ExpCreat.htm">
            <param name="ImageNumber" value="11">
            </OBJECT>
    </UL>
    <LI> <OBJECT type="text/sitemap">
        <param name="Name" value="Database Features">
        <param name="Local" value="database.htm">
        </OBJECT>
    <UL>
        <LI> <OBJECT type="text/sitemap">
            <param name="Name" value="Recipe Database">
            <param name="Type" value="Type of Info::Concept">
            <param name="Local" value="Recipe.htm">
            <param name="ImageNumber" value="11">
            </OBJECT>
        <LI> <OBJECT type="text/sitemap">
            <param name="Name" value="Working with the Recipe Database">
            <param name="Type" value="Type of Info::Concept">
```

```
                        <param name="Local" value="Working.htm">
                        <param name="ImageNumber" value="21">
                        </OBJECT>
            <UL>
                <LI> <OBJECT type="text/sitemap">
                    <param name="Name" value="Adding Recipes">
                    <param name="Type" value="Type of Info::Procedure">
                    <param name="Type" value="Product::Standard">
                    <param name="Local" value="addrec.htm">
                    <param name="Type" value="Type of Info::Procedure">
                    <param name="Type" value="Product::Deluxe">
                    <param name="Local" value="addrec_deluxe.htm">
                    <param name="ImageNumber" value="35">
                    </OBJECT>
            </UL>
        </UL>
        ...
...
</BODY></HTML>
```

General Properties

The lines

```
<OBJECT type="text/site properties">
  <param name="WindowName" value="Main">
  <param name="Category" value="Type of Info">
  <param name="CategoryDesc" value="Choose the type of information you
want to view.">
  <param name="Type" value="Concept">
  <param name="TypeDesc" value="Select this option to view concepts.">
  <param name="Type" value="Procedure">
  <param name="TypeDesc" value="Select this option to view procedures.">
  <param name="Category" value="Product">
  <param name="CategoryDesc" value="Select the model you are using.">
  <param name="TypeExclusive" value="Standard">
  <param name="TypeDesc" value="Select this option to view information
on the Standard model.">
  <param name="TypeExclusive" value="Deluxe">
  <param name="TypeDesc" value="Select this option to view information
on the Deluxe model.">
  <param name="Window Styles" value="0x800025">
</OBJECT>
```

establish the general properties of the appearance and functionality of the table of contents.

The line

```
  <param name="WindowName" value="Main">
```

indicates that all topics accessed from the table of contents should be displayed in the Main window.

The lines

```
<param name="Category" value="Type of Info">
<param name="CategoryDesc" value="Choose the type of information you
want to view.">
<param name="Type" value="Concept">
<param name="TypeDesc" value="Select this option to view concepts.">
<param name="Type" value="Procedure">
<param name="TypeDesc" value="Select this option to view procedures.">
<param name="Category" value="Product">
<param name="CategoryDesc" value="Select the model you are using.">
```

establish the inclusive Information Types "Concept" and "Procedure." TypeDesc and CategoryDesc define the descriptive text that appears when the user is presented Information Types from which to choose, as shown below.

The TypeDesc information appears here.

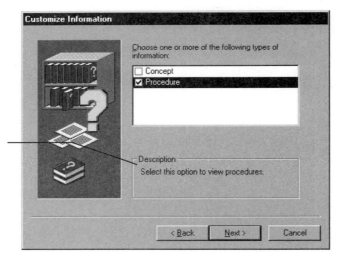

Customize Information dialog box with a description.

The lines

```
<param name="TypeExclusive" value="Standard">
<param name="TypeDesc" value="Select this option to view information
on the Standard model.">
<param name="TypeExclusive" value="Deluxe">
<param name="TypeDesc" value="Select this option to view information
on the Deluxe model.">
```

establish the exclusive Information Types of "Standard" and "Deluxe," while the line

```
<param name="Window Styles" value="0x800025">
```

establishes the appearance of the contents pane.

The Outline

The lines

```
<UL>
    <LI> <OBJECT type="text/sitemap">
        <param name="Name" value="Introduction">
        <param name="Type" value="Type of Info::Concept">
        <param name="Local" value="Intro.htm">
        <param name="URL" value="http://www.goodstuff.com/intro.htm">
        </OBJECT>
    <UL>
```

display the first item in the hierarchy, in this case "Introduction." This item has been assigned the Information Type "concept" under the "Type of Info" category. When the user selects this, the topic "intro.htm" will be displayed from the local HTML Help system. If that topic cannot be found, the topic located at http://www.goodstuff.com/intro.htm will be displayed.

The lines

```
    <LI> <OBJECT type="text/sitemap">
        <param name="Name" value="Overview">
        <param name="Type" value="Type of Info::Concept">
        <param name="Local" value="Overview.htm">
        <param name="ImageNumber" value="11">
        </OBJECT>
    <LI> <OBJECT type="text/sitemap">
        <param name="Name" value="Why You Need YUM">
        <param name="Type" value="Type of Info::Concept">
        <param name="Local" value="Whyyum.htm">
        <param name="ImageNumber" value="11">
        </OBJECT>
    <LI> <OBJECT type="text/sitemap">
        <param name="Name" value="YUM's Special Features">
        <param name="Type" value="Type of Info::Concept">
        <param name="Local" value="Special.htm">
```

```
      <param name="ImageNumber" value="11">
      </OBJECT>
<LI> <OBJECT type="text/sitemap">
    <param name="Name" value="Expressing Your Creativity">
    <param name="Type" value="Type of Info::Concept">
    <param name="Local" value="ExpCreat.htm">
    <param name="ImageNumber" value="11">
    </OBJECT>
</UL>
```

display the next four entries (Overview, Why You Need YUM, YUM's Special Features, and Expressing Your Creativity). Each of these entries has been assigned the Information Type "concept."

The line

```
<param name="ImageNumber" value="11">
```

specifies that instead of letting HTML Help determine the best icon to display for this topic, the eleventh icon in the set of 42 default icons available through the HTML Help Workshop should be displayed.

The lines

```
<LI> <OBJECT type="text/sitemap">
    <param name="Name" value="Database Features">
    <param name="Local" value="database.htm">
    </OBJECT>
<UL>
    <LI> <OBJECT type="text/sitemap">
        <param name="Name" value="Recipe Database">
        <param name="Type" value="Type of Info::Concept">
        <param name="Local" value="Recipe.htm">
        <param name="ImageNumber" value="11">
        </OBJECT>
    <LI> <OBJECT type="text/sitemap">
        <param name="Name" value="Working with the Recipe Database">
        <param name="Type" value="Type of Info::Concept">
        <param name="Local" value="Working.htm">
        <param name="ImageNumber" value="21">
        </OBJECT>
    <UL>
        <LI> <OBJECT type="text/sitemap">
            <param name="Name" value="Adding Recipes">
            <param name="Type" value="Type of Info::Procedure">
            <param name="Type" value="Product::Standard">
            <param name="Local" value="addrec.htm">
            <param name="Type" value="Type of Info::Procedure">
            <param name="Type" value="Product::Deluxe">
            <param name="Local" value="addrec_deluxe.htm">
```

```
            <param name="ImageNumber" value="35">
            </OBJECT>
      </UL>
```

are responsible for displaying this part of the table of contents tree:

- Database Features
  - Recipe Database
  - Working with the Recipe Database
    - Adding Recipes

The lines

```
<param name="Name"  value="Adding Recipes">
<param name="Type"  value="Type of Info::Procedure">
<param name="Type"  value="Product::Standard">
<param name="Local"  value="addrec.htm">
<param name="Type"  value="Type of Info::Procedure">
<param name="Type"  value="Product::Deluxe">
<param name="Local"  value="addrec_deluxe.htm">
<param name="ImageNumber"  value="35">
```

indicate that the topic "Adding Recipes" is a procedure and that if the "Standard" Information Type setting is in place, then the topic "addrec.htm" should be displayed; otherwise, if "Deluxe" has been selected, the topic "addrec_deluxe.htm" should be displayed.

Finally, the line

```
<param name="ImageNumber"  value="35">
```

indicates that a procedural icon (that is, the thirty-fifth icon in HTML Help's icon gallery) should be displayed instead of a standard icon.

Procedures for Adding
Navigation and Information Types

In this next series of examples we will take an existing HTML Help project and refine it so that it uses visual cues and Information Types to help a user find the information she needs.

Here is a summary of the steps we'll take to modify the HTML Help system.

1   Open an existing project.

2   Add two Information Categories ("Topic Type" and "Model").

3   Add four Information Types ("Concepts" and "Procedures", which will be associated with Topic Type, and "Standard" and "Deluxe", which will be associated with Model).

4   Designate certain topics as Procedural and others as Conceptual.

5   Designate certain topics as Standard and others as Deluxe.

6   Change the icon associated with certain topics.

7   Designate a topic as new.

8   Compile.

The files you will need for these exercises can be found in HHKIT\CHAP04.

The completed examples can be found in HHKIT\CHAP04\FINISHED.

To Open an Existing Project

1   If it's not already running, start the HTML Help Workshop.

2   From the **File** menu, choose **Open**.

3   In the File Open dialog box, browse to the file you want to open, in this case **ICEREAM.HHP** (located in the HHKIT\CHAP04 folder).

4   Click the **Contents** tab.

Your screen should look like the one shown on the following page.

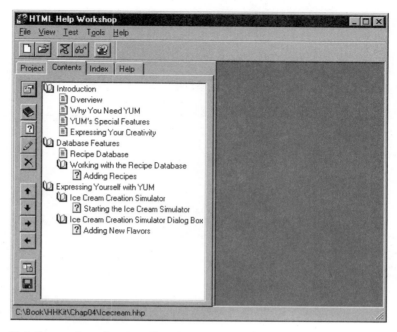

Existing project showing Contents tab

Categories and Information Types

As we mentioned earlier, HTML Help 1.1 only allows you to have one category of Information Types, where the category could be experience, job description, product type, and so forth.

In this next series of steps, we will create two categories: "Topic Type" and "Model."

To Create Two Categories

1   With the Contents tab selected, click the **Contents Properties** button.

The Table of Contents Properties dialog box will appear.

2   Click the **Information Types** tab.

3   Click the **Add** button.

4   In the Category Name edit box, type **Topic Type.**

5   In the Category Description edit box, type **Select the type of information you want to view**.

The dialog box should look like this:

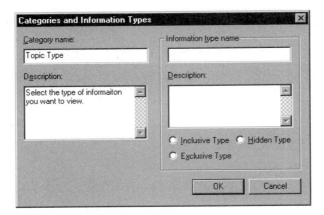

6   Click **OK**.

7   Click the **Add** button..

8   In the Category Name edit box, type **Model**.

9   In the Category Description edit box, type **Select the model you use.**

10 Click **OK**.

Note: Do not close the Table of Contents properties dialog box. The HTML Help Workshop will not record the category information until you have created information types.

To Create Four Information Types

1 With the two categories (Topic Type and Model) now created, click the **Add** button again.

2 In the Information Type name dialog box, type **Concepts**.

3 In the Description edit box, type **Select this to view concepts**.

4 Select **Inclusive**.

The dialog box should look like the one shown below.

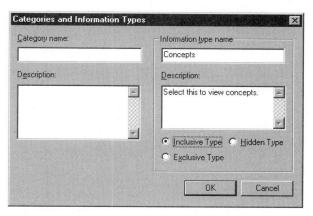

5 Click **OK**.

6 Click the **Add** button again.

7 Fill in the dialog box as shown below, and click **OK**.

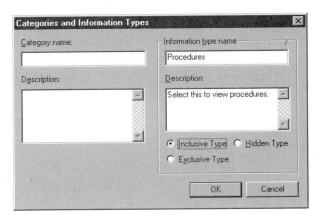

8 Click the **Add** button again, fill in the dialog box as shown below, and click **OK**.

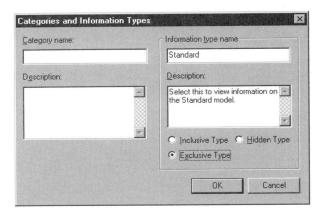

Notice that Exclusive Type has been selected.

9 Click the **Add** button again, and fill in the dialog box as shown below.

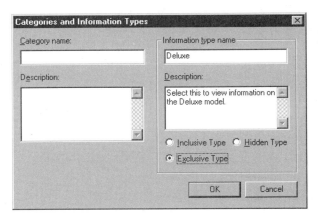

10 Click **OK**.

The dialog box should look like the one shown below.

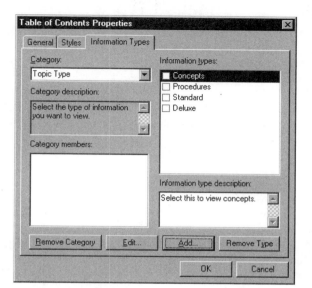

We are now ready to associate the information types "Concepts" and "Procedures" with the category "Topic Type", and the information types "Standard" and "Deluxe" with the category "Model."

To Associate Information Types with Categories

1   With the Category Topic Type selected, click **Concepts** and click **Procedures** from the Information Types list.

2   From the Category drop down list, choose **Model**.

3   Click **Standard** and click **Deluxe**.

4   Click **OK**.

Applying Information Types

Once you have created your Categories and Information Types, you can apply Information Types to your topics.

In the next exercise, we will mark the topics "Adding Recipes," "Starting the Ice Cream Creation Simulator," and "Adding New Flavors" as Procedural.

To Apply an Information Type

1 With the Contents visible, select the topic you want to mark, in this case **Adding Recipes**.

 2 Click the **Edit Selection** button.

3 In the Table of Contents Entry dialog box, select **Procedures**, as shown below.

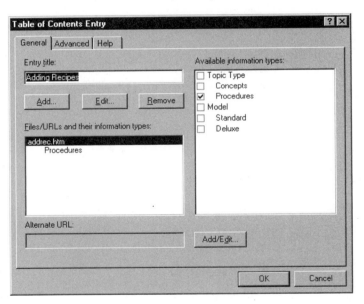

4 Repeat steps 2 and 3 for the other procedural topics.

Practice Exercise

On your own, mark "Why You Need Yum," "Yum's Special Features," "Expressing Your Creativity," and "Recipe Database" as Concepts.

Applying Exclusive Information Types

As we saw in "One to Many Relationships," on page 97, it is possible to have a single table of contents entry that displays a different topic based on the Information Type setting.

In the next example, we will change the properties of the Adding Recipes topic so that it displays a different topic if the Deluxe model is selected. In particular, we will design it so that the topic ADDREC.HTM is displayed if Standard is selected and ADDREC_DELUXE.HTM is displayed if Deluxe is selected.

To Apply an Exclusive Information Type

1   With the Contents tab selected, choose the topic entry you want to edit, in this case Adding Recipes.

2   Click the **Edit Selection** button.

3   Click **Standard**.

4   Click the **Add** button.

5   In the File or URL edit box, type **ADDREC_DELUXE.HTM** and click **OK**.

6   In the Files/URLs and their information types list box, select **ADDREC_DELUXE.HTM**.

7   Click **Procedures** and click **Deluxe**.

The dialog box should look like the one shown below.

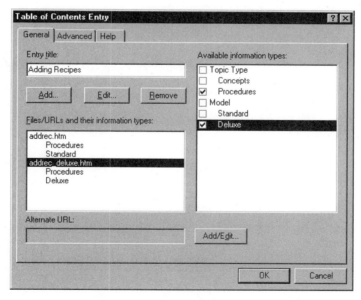

The Adding Recipes contents entry now has two possible targets.

8   Click **OK**.

Practice Exercise

Using the techniques shown above, edit the "Starting the Ice Cream Creation Simulator" and "Adding New Flavors" contents entries so that they display the topics STARTING.HTM and ADDING.HTM if Standard is selected, and STARTING_DELUXE.HTM and ADDING_DELUXE.HTM if Deluxe is selected.

Assigning Different Icons to Topics in the Table of Contents

While we have now marked some topics as procedures and others as concepts, we've done nothing to label these topics so that the user knows ahead of time what type of information they contain.

In the next series of examples we will see how to assign different icons to topics as well as see the convention used to specify that topics are new.

To Change a Table of Contents Icon

1 Select the topic you want to change, in this case "Adding Recipes."

 2 Click the **Edit Selection** button.

3 When the Table of Contents Entry dialog box appears, click the **Advanced** tab.

4 Change the Image Index to **35**, as shown below.

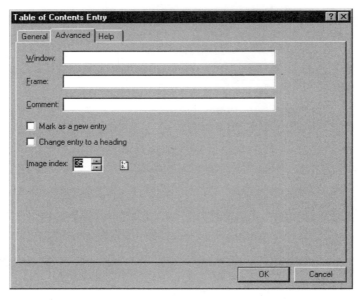

HTML Help 1.1 comes with 42 pre-defined images. We'll see how to create custom images in Chapter Six.

5   Click **OK**.

6   Repeat Steps 4 and 5 for "Starting the Ice Cream Creation Simulator" and "Adding New Flavors." When you are finished, your screen should look like the one shown below.

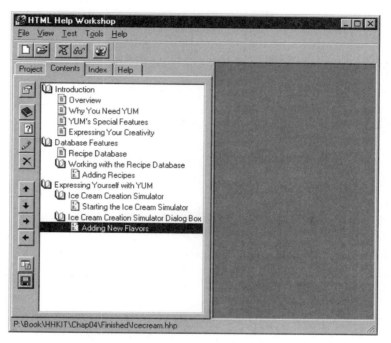

Table of Contents with procedures marked with different icons.

Practice Exercise

Change the image index to 21 for the topics "Working with the Recipe Database," "Ice Cream Creation Simulator," and "Ice Cream Creation Simulator Dialog Box."

Marking Topics as New

HTML Help uses a red asterisk to indicate that a topic is new, that is, a topic that the author has added to the system since the last time the system was distributed.

The ability to apply this visual cue will be particularly useful in an upcoming version of HTML Help which allows the user to download incremental updates to his Help system.

To Mark a Topic as New

1   Select the topic you want to change, in this case "Working with the Recipe Database."

2 Click the **Edit Selection** button.

3 When the Table of Contents Entry dialog box appears, click the **Advanced** tab.

4 Change the Image Index to **22**, as shown below.

The Mark as New Entry check box only works if the Image Index is set to Auto.

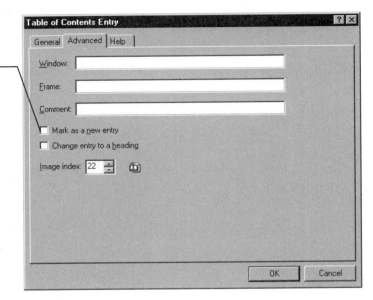

5 Click **OK**.

To Recompile and View the Results

1 Click the **Project** tab.

 2 Click the **Save all project files and compile** button.

3 After the project is finished compiling, click the **View Compiled HTML Help File** button.

4 When the View Compiled Dialog Box appears, click **View**.

5 With the compiled HTML Help system on the screen, click the **Options** button and choose **Customize.**

6 When the Custom Information dialog box appears, choose **Custom** and click **Next**.

7   Indicate that you only want to view **Concepts** and **Procedures**, as shown below.

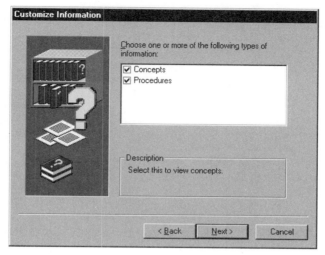

8   Click **Next**.

9   Indicate that you want to view topics for the **Deluxe** model, as shown below.

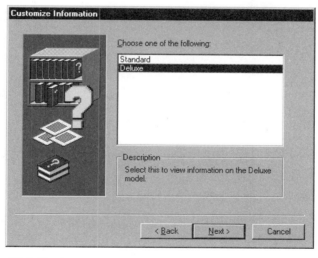

10 Click **Next**.

11 Click **Finish**.

You will now only be able to access Procedural topics from the table of contents.

What's Next?

In this chapter we've looked at what's behind the table of contents and index and how to work with Information Types. In the next chapter we'll explore HTML Help's architecture for creating compiled Help systems and how we can exploit it to create modular Help systems.

Frequently Asked Questions

Question: *What's the difference between an Information Type and a Category?*

Answer: A Category is a group of related Information Types. For example, you may define a Category called "User Level" that contains the Information Types "Beginner," "Intermediate," and "Advanced." Another Category might be called "Job Description" with the Information Types "Secretary", "Manager," "Engineer," and so on.

Question: *Can I define as many Categories as I want?*

Answer: With HTML Help 1.1 you can only define one Category. HTML Help 1.2, slated for release in early 1998, is supposed to allow an unlimited number of Categories.

Question: *What is a Subset (and when can I buy one)?*

Answer: A Subset is a pre-defined view of the HTML Help system. For example, instead of the user having to specify that she only wants to see advanced concepts for managers working in the textile division, a pre-defined collection of Category settings—or a Subset—can be used.

Subsets are expected to be available in HTML Help 1.2.

Question: *This seems like a lot of work. Do I have to use Information Types?*

Answer: No one is going to put a gun to your head and make you use Information Types. Like a table of contents and an index, Information Types make your Help system more accessible. They also allow you write for multiple audiences without alienating an audience.

Question: *This still seems like a lot of work. Do I have to mark all of the topics?*

Answer: No. Topics not designated as being of a particular Information Type will appear only if the user indicates he wants to see all topics in the Help system.

Question: *Can I make the icons in the table of contents larger?*

Answer: A table of contents icon can be a maximum of 20 x 20 pixels. Microsoft recommends that each icon be 16 pixels high. We'll see how to create custom icons in "Custom Icons for the Table of Contents," on page 149.

Question: *When I created Windows 95 Help I made sure that conceptual information appeared in one kind of window and procedural information appeared in a smaller, always-on-top window. Is there a way to do this with HTML Help? Should I be doing this?*

Answer: HTML Help does allow you to create secondary windows and you can make it so that a particular topic appears in a particular window (this feature is accessible from the Advanced tab in the Table of Contents Entry dialog box). As with Windows 95 Help, you can define up to 255 secondary windows and display nine at one time.

However, unlike Windows 95 Help, HTML Help 1.1 does not provide a way for the Help author to close a window when another window is displayed, so you may have trouble using this feature. A programmer, however, can open and close windows using the HTML Help API (see "The HTML Help API," on page 199).

C H A P T E R   F I V E

Creating Modular
HTML Help Systems

In this chapter we'll examine HTML Help's architecture for creating modular Help systems. We'll see how modular Help systems work under HTML Help and we'll work through step-by-step procedures for linking the components of a large Help system.

For the Help author and web author: We'll examine the elements that comprise a modular Help system, explain why modular development is worthwhile, and work through the procedures needed to create a modular Help system.

For the programmer: If you're not going to be doing any HTML Help` development, you can probably skip this chapter, but you may want to review the information presented on pages 124 through 134.

What's in this Chapter

Modular Help Systems: Concepts

If your Help system contains more than 300 topics or so, you will probably want to divide it into a collection of linked .CHM files instead of having one large .CHM file, because it's a lot easier to maintain several small Help files than one large Help file.

There is absolutely no downside to building a Help system in small pieces. Users can't tell the Help they're looking at is built from several linked Help files instead of one big Help file.

Modular Help for Modular Software

Suppose you are responsible for creating the HTML Help for a new accounting system. Users of the system can purchase different modules, but as a Help author you won't be able to know ahead of time which modules they buy, with the exception of the main module, which must be installed for the system to work.

For example, you know that the buyer will purchase the General Ledger component (the system won't work without it), but you can't be sure if he'll buy the modules for Accounts Receivable, Accounts Payable, Payroll, and so on. As new modules are installed, the Help for these modules should be integrated with the Help for the main module so that:

- A unified table of contents provides access to all the modules' Help.

- A unified index provides access to all the modules' Help.

- One full text search searches across all the Help files.

- If a module is removed the Help still works and the user doesn't see any error messages indicating that a file is missing.

Modular Help Allows You to Plan Ahead

Suppose your company's plans call for releasing a product over a 12-month period. As the year progresses, more features are added to the product and more modules are added to the software. As more modules are added, more Help is added, and you want that Help to become seamlessly integrated with the main Help that has already been distributed. Using HTML Help's modular Help feature, you can design your Help systems to include modules that don't yet exist.

For example, let's suppose you know that when the whole system is finished, it will be comprised of the following five Help files:

- MAIN.CHM

- MOUSE.CHM

- INTERNET.CHM

- BACKUP.CHM

- ADVANCED.CHM

When the system is first deployed, only MAIN.CHM and BACKUP.CHM will be finished. Yet, if the Help author specifies ahead of time that the completed system will consist of these five .CHM files, the topics contained in the other three files will automatically appear—and appear in just the right place with just the right hierarchy—as soon as they get installed on the user's machine.

Let's examine a Windows 95 modular Help system and an HTML Help modular Help system.

Modular Help in Windows 95 and NT

Windows 95 Help introduced the concept of a modular Help system. In Windows 95 Help you could create a Help system that appeared to the end user as a single comprehensive system but was in fact several smaller Help files seamlessly linked together.

Consider the Help for Windows 95, shown below:

The Windows 95 Help System.

The Help for Windows 95 is composed of over a dozen separate .HLP files, yet it appears to be one unified Help system. There's no way to tell that you're looking at "MOUSE.HLP" versus "NETWORK.HLP." As far as the end user is concerned, it's just the Help you see when you click Help from the Start button.

This seamless modularity extends to the keyword search and the full text search as well. When you enter a word to find from the Find tab or a keyword from the Index tab, Windows Help searches through all of the linked Help files.

Modular HTML Help

In a correctly designed modular Help system, the table of contents tab, keyword search tab and full text search tab will automatically reflect new topics as new modules are added to the system.

Modular Help and the Table of Contents

Consider the HTML Help system for a fictitious accounting software program, shown below.

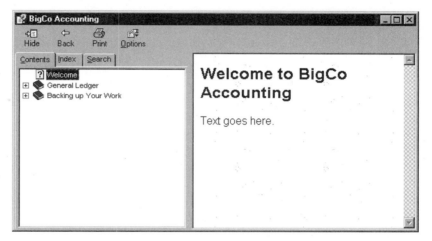

Help system for BigCo Accounting when only the General Ledger module has been installed.

In this example only the General Ledger module—and its associated Help file GLEDGER.CHM—have been installed. GLEDGER.CHM is composed of two major sections: "General Ledger" and "Backing up Your Work."

If the Accounts Receivable and the Accounts Payable modules are purchased later, the installation routine for these modules adds two more Help files—ACCREC.CHM and ACCPAY.CHM—to the same folder where GLEDGER.CHM is kept. Without any additional intervention, the Help system looks like this the next time a user accesses it:

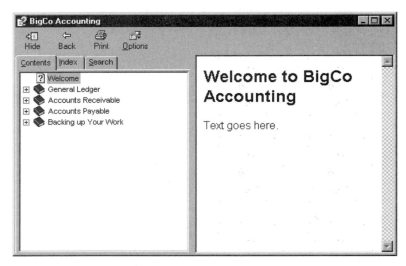

BigCo Accounting Help with General Ledger, Accounts Receivable, and Accounts Payable modules installed.

Modular Help and the Index

If the user clicks the Index tab with only the General Ledger module installed, he will see the following entries:

Index tab when only the General Ledger module is installed.

But if the Accounts Receivable and Accounts Payable modules are installed, the index will look like this:

Index tab when three modules are installed.

Test-Driving Modular Help

A completed modular Help system can be found in HHKIT\CHAP05\FINISHED. If you move the files ACCREC.CHM and ACCPAY.CHM to a different folder and open GLEDGER.CHM, your screen should look like the one shown below.

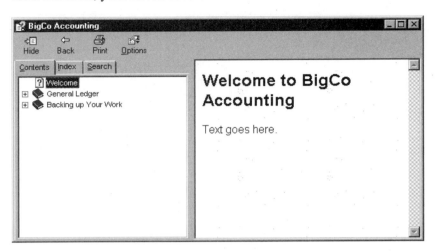

BigCo Accounting Help main file GLEDGER.CHM when no other modules are present.

Now close GLEDGER.CHM, move the other .CHM files back into the HHKIT\CHAP05\FINISHED folder and open GLEDGER.CHM again. Notice that the table of contents now contains additional entries.

No Alterations Necessary (If You Plan Ahead)

It's important to note that all that is required for the modular system to recognize the new Help files is that the .CHM files get copied into the same folder as the main Help system. In this case, ACCREC.CHM and ACCPAY.CHM just need to get copied to wherever GLEDGER.CHM is stored. The installation program does *not* need to make any changes to GLEDGER.CHM.

For this to all work, however, the Help author must know ahead of time which modules might be installed on the system. The main Help's project (.HHP) file must include references to all the other .CHM files in its [MERGE FILES] section. This ensures that the keyword and full text searches reflect the contents of all the Help files. The main Help's contents (.HHC) file must include references to all the other .HHC files. We'll see how to make these changes in the following pages.

Framework for a Modular Help System

The diagram below shows the framework for the BigCo Accounting system
HTML Help.

Gledger.chm

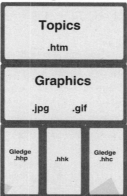

```
[MERGE FILES]
AccRec.chm
AccPay.chm
Payroll.chm
Inventory.chm
```

```
    <LI> <OBJECT type="text/sitemap">
         <param name="Name" value="Organizing Your Accounts">
         <param name="Local" value="GLtopic3.htm">
         </OBJECT>
    </UL>
    </UL>
</UL>
<OBJECT type="text/sitemap">
  <param name="Merge" value="AccRec.chm::\AccRec.hhc">
</OBJECT>
<OBJECT type="text/sitemap">
  <param name="Merge" value="AccPay.chm::\AccPay.hhc">
</OBJECT>
<OBJECT type="text/sitemap">
  <param name="Merge" value="Payroll.chm::\Payroll.hhc">
</OBJECT>
<OBJECT type="text/sitemap">
  <param name="Merge" value="Inventory.chm::\Inventory.hhc">
</OBJECT>
<UL>
```

AccRec.chm

AccPay.chm

Payroll.chm

Inventory.chm

Framework of the BigCo HTML Help System.

When it's first released, BigCo's Help consists of three modules: GLEDGER.CHM, ACCREC.CHM, and ACCPAY.CHM. Eventually the system will also include PAYROLL.CHM and INVENTORY.CHM. Only GLEDGER.CHM is required; purchase and installation of the others is optional.

Merge Files for Integrated Index and Full Text Search

The contents of the project file (GLEDGER.HHP) for GLEDGER.CHM are shown below.

```
[OPTIONS]
Compiled file=GLedger.chm
Contents file=GLedger.hhc
Default Window=Tripane
Default topic=BigCo.htm
Display compile progress=No
Full-text search=Yes
Index file=GLedger.hhk
Language=0x409 English (United States)
Title=BigCo Accounting

[WINDOWS]
Tripane="BigCo Accounting" , "GLedger.hhc" , "GLedger.hhk" ,
"BigCo.htm",,,,,,0x2520,,0x3006,,,,,0,,,

[FILES]
GLtopic3.htm
GLtopic2.htm
GLtopic1.htm
Backup1.htm
Backup2.htm

[MERGE FILES]
AccRec.chm
AccPay.chm
Payroll.chm
Inventory.chm
```

The [MERGE FILES] section of the .HHP file indicates that when the user clicks either the Index tab or the Find tab, the files listed in this section should also be included when displaying the index and find lists. If these .CHM files don't exist—either because they have not been installed or because they are not yet finished—the HTML Help engine will just display the topics that are in the main Help file (GLEDGER.CHM).

Including External .HHC Files in the Main Module's .HHC File

As we saw earlier, when the end user clicks the Contents tab of a modular Help system, she sees a fully populated table of contents. Upon close examination of the underlying .HHC file, you will see that only some of the entries that comprise the table of contents are contained in GLEDGER.HHC. Most of the entries will in fact be found in the .HHC files for the other modules; references to these .HHC files appear in the main module.

The contents of the GLEDGER.HHC file are shown below.

```
<!DOCTYPE HTML PUBLIC "-//IETF//DTD HTML//EN">
<HTML>
<HEAD>
<meta name="GENERATOR" content="Microsoft&reg; HTML Help Workshop 4.1">
<!-- Sitemap 1.0 -->
</HEAD><BODY>
<OBJECT type="text/site properties">
    <param name="WindowName" value="Tripane">
    <param name="Window Styles" value="0x800025">
</OBJECT>
<UL>
    <LI> <OBJECT type="text/sitemap">
        <param name="Name" value="Welcome">
        <param name="Local" value="BigCo.htm">
        </OBJECT>
    <LI> <OBJECT type="text/sitemap">
        <param name="Name" value="General Ledger">
        <param name="Local" value="GLedger.htm">
        </OBJECT>
    <UL>
        <LI> <OBJECT type="text/sitemap">
            <param name="Name" value="Overview">
            <param name="Local" value="GLtopic1.htm">
            </OBJECT>
        <LI> <OBJECT type="text/sitemap">
            <param name="Name" value="Using the GL Package">
            <param name="Local" value="GLtopic2.htm">
            </OBJECT>
        <LI> <OBJECT type="text/sitemap">
            <param name="Name" value="Creating a Chart of Accounts">
            <param name="Local" value="Chart.htm">
            </OBJECT>
        <UL>
            <LI> <OBJECT type="text/sitemap">
                <param name="Name" value="Organizing Your Accounts">
                <param name="Local" value="GLtopic3.htm">
                </OBJECT>
        </UL>
    </UL>
</UL>
<OBJECT type="text/sitemap">
    <param name="Merge" value="AccRec.chm::\AccRec.hhc">
</OBJECT>
<OBJECT type="text/sitemap">
    <param name="Merge" value="AccPay.chm::\AccPay.hhc">
```

```
</OBJECT>
<OBJECT type="text/sitemap">
    <param name="Merge" value="Payroll.chm::\Payroll.hhc">
</OBJECT>
<OBJECT type="text/sitemap">
    <param name="Merge" value="Inventory.chm::\Inventory.hhc">
</OBJECT>
<UL>
    <LI> <OBJECT type="text/sitemap">
        <param name="Name" value="Backing up Your Work">
        <param name="Local" value="Backup.htm">
        </OBJECT>
    <UL>
        <LI> <OBJECT type="text/sitemap">
            <param name="Name" value="Overview">
            <param name="Local" value="Backup1.htm">
            </OBJECT>
        <LI> <OBJECT type="text/sitemap">
            <param name="Name" value="To Back Up Your Work">
            <param name="Local" value="Backup2.htm">
            <param name="ImageNumber" value="35">
            </OBJECT>
    </UL>

</UL>
</BODY></HTML>
```

Understanding the Merge Statement

The lines

```
<OBJECT type="text/sitemap">
    <param name="Merge" value="AccRec.chm::\AccRec.hhc">
</OBJECT>
<OBJECT type="text/sitemap">
    <param name="Merge" value="AccPay.chm::\AccPay.hhc">
</OBJECT>
<OBJECT type="text/sitemap">
    <param name="Merge" value="Payroll.chm::\Payroll.hhc">
</OBJECT>
<OBJECT type="text/sitemap">
    <param name="Merge" value="Inventory.chm::\Inventory.hhc">
</OBJECT>
```

indicate that when displaying the table of contents, the HTML Help engine should also display the table of contents information that has been compiled into ACCREC.HHC, ACCPAY.HHC, PAYROLL.HHC, and INVENTORY.HHC.

Note: The HTML Help viewer will search for the referenced .CHM files in the same folder as the main .CHM file and then in the \WINDOWS\HELP folder.

Procedures for Linking Modular HTML Help Systems

In this next series of examples we will take an existing HTML Help project, GLEDGER.CHM, and modify it so that it will automatically incorporate information found in other, related, .CHM files.

Here is a summary of the steps we'll take to modify the HTML Help system.

1   Open the GLEDGER.HHP project file

2   Add the Merge Files information to the project file

3   Edit the main .HHC file so that it references information from other .HHC files

4   Recompile and display GLEDGER.CHM

The files you will need for these exercises can be found in HHKIT\CHAP05.

The completed examples can be found in HHKIT\CHAP05\FINISHED.

To Open the General Ledger Project File

1 If it's not already running, start the HTML Help Workshop.

2 From the **File** menu, choose **Open**.

3 In the File Open dialog box, browse to the file you want to open, in this case **GLEDGER.HHP** (located in the HHKIT\CHAP05 folder).

4 Select the file and click **OK**. Your screen should look like the one shown below.

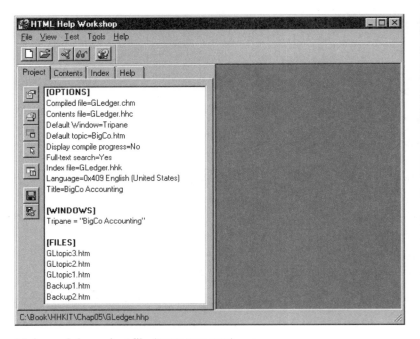

Main module project file (GLEDGER.HHP).

Adding the Merge File Information

In the next series of steps we'll use the Merge Files dialog box to add the additional compiled HTML Help files to our system. This list of files is compiled into GLEDGER.CHM. When the Help is displayed and the index or find tab is selected, this list of files to merge "tells" the HTML Help viewer to assimilate index and full text information from the other files.

To Add Merge File Information

 1   With the Project tab selected, click the **Change Project Options** button.

The Options dialog box will appear.

2   Click the **Merge Files** tab.

3   Click the **Add** button.

4   In the Add Merge Files dialog box, type the name of the file you want to merge, in this case **accrec.chm**.

5   Repeat steps 3 and 4 and add **accpay.chm, payroll.chm,** and **inventory.chm** to the list, as shown below.

Options dialog box with Merge Files tab selected.

6   Click **OK**.

Editing the Contents File to Include External Contents Files

In the next series of steps we'll edit the contents file (GLEDGER.HHC) so that it includes information from contents files contained in other compiled HTML Help files. In this case, we want the references to the external contents files to appear between the "General Ledger" and "Backing up Your Work" headings.

To Include External Files in the Contents File

1   Select the **Contents** tab.

2   Select the item under which you will want the external contents entry to appear, in this case **Organizing Your Accounts**, as shown below.

3   Right-click the entry and choose **Insert File** from the popup menu.

The Include Files dialog box will appear.

The file we want to include is ACCREC.HHC, but it's been compiled into ACCREC.CHM.

4   Type the name of the contents file you want to include, in this case **accrec.chm::/accrec.hhc**.

The HTML Help Workshop will display a dialog box indicating that it cannot find the specified file.

5   When asked if you want to include the file anyway, click **Yes**.

6 Repeat steps 3, 4, and 5 to include the following entries:

accpay.chm::\accpay.hhc
payroll.chm::\payroll.hhc
inventory.chm::\inventory.hhc

Your screen should look like the one shown below.

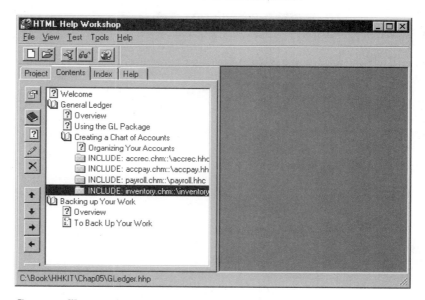

Contents file containing multiple include statements.

Note: Including the contents files for PAYROLL.CHM and INVENTORY.CHM is done in anticipation of these files eventually being written and incorporated into the Help system.

Adjusting the Heading Levels and Recompiling

At this point, all we have left to do is adjust the heading levels of the Include entries so that they are at the same level as "General Ledger" and "Backing up Your Work," and recompile.

To Adjust the Heading Level of the Include Entries

1 Select the first Include entry, in this case **Include: accrec.chm::\accrec.hhc**.

2 Click the **Move Selection Left** button twice.

3 Adjust the other Include entries as needed.

To Recompile and View the Project

1 Click the **Project** tab.

2 Click the **Save All Project Files And Compile** button.

3 Click the **View Compiled HTML Help File** button.

4 When the View dialog box appears, click **View**.

Advanced Features and Design Issues

Decompiling

One of the best ways to learn how to do something is to study how others do it. Nowhere is this technique more popular than with web design.

The Microsoft HTML Help Workshop includes a decompiler so you can examine the source files for any compiled HTML Help system.

You can access the decompiler in the HTML Help Workshop by opening the **File** menu and selecting **Decompile**.

Labeling Modules

We may have gone a little overboard in trying to hide the BigCo Accounting Help system's modularity from users: Except for the topic highlighting in the table of contents, there's no way for users to know which module they are in. In some cases, this may be desirable, but for our sample accounting package the user would probably welcome knowing that he's looking at Help for "Accounts Receivable" versus "Payroll."

Letting the user know where he is could be as simple as changing the title bar or using different colors. For example, instead of the title bar being "BigCo Accounting," it could be "BigCo Accounting – Inventory" or "BigCo Accounting – Payroll," depending on the module that's being displayed.

You could also change the background color or employ a background image to clue the user to where she is in the Help system.

Linking Across Files

One of the biggest challenges of creating a modular Help system is not knowing whether a module will be installed when authoring hypertext links. For example, let's say you are authoring a topic in the General Ledger module and know that there is related information in the Payroll module. You cannot simply create a link from the General Ledger module to the Payroll module because you can't be sure if the Payroll module will be installed, and creating this link will yield an error message if the user clicks it and the Payroll module is not installed.

Fortunately, as with Windows 95 Help, there is a provision in HTML Help that allows you to create links that are evaluated for their integrity at runtime. We'll see how to do this in "Associative Links: Concepts," on page 146.

Client-side Compiling

One of the best things about distributing information on the web is how easy it is to distribute updates. If a user wants the latest and greatest, she need only visit your web site.

But how, you may ask, are you going to be able to publish timely updates if you distribute a compiled HTML Help system that lives on the user's hard disk or file server, and not on the web?

A future release of HTML Help will allow client-side compiling (not available in HTML Help version 1.1). With this future release of HTML Help, when you distribute an HTML Help system the user will also get a copy of the same compiler you use to create the Help system. You will be able to put a Link in the hard-disk-based Help system that accesses your web site, downloads new information and recompiles the Help system with the new information, all without user intervention.

This feature is slated to be available in mid-1998.

What's Next?

In this chapter we've looked at modular Help systems and how to create them with the HTML Help Workshop. In the next chapter we'll see how to create a more refined HTML Help system that uses associative links (links that are interpreted and resolved at runtime), popups, custom icons in the table of contents, and splash screens.

Frequently Asked Questions

Question: *Can I open a page of a compiled HTML Help file in my browser?*

Answer: You can open to a page of a compiled HTML Help file in either Internet Explorer 3.*x* or 4.*x*.

- To open to a specific page in Internet Explorer 3.*x*, use this syntax to specify the URL, filling in the specific names of the .CHM and .HTM files:

  mk:@MSITStore:filename.chm::\page.htm

- To open to a specific page in Internet Explorer 4.*x*, use this syntax to specify the URL, filling in the specific names of the .CHM and .HTM files:

  its:filename.chm::\page.htm

Question: *I noticed that after working with the examples in this chapter, there's a file called GLEDGER.CHW in HHKIT\CHAP05. How did this file get there, and do I need it?*

Answer: A .CHW file gets created automatically by the HTML Help engine when you click the Index tab in a modular Help system. The .CHW file is a type of internal binary index file that assembles the index information from all the .CHM files that make up your Help system. If you delete this file, it will get created again the next time you click the Index tab.

Question: *Can I have nested Include statements in a contents file? That is, can I insert an Include statement to an external .HHC file that in turn contains an Include statement to another .HHC file?*

Answer: Yes.

C H A P T E R   S I X

Refining Your HTML Help System

In this chapter we'll explore some of the more sophisticated HTML Help features that make HTML Help such a compelling hypertext delivery system. In particular, we'll examine HTML Help's associative linking feature, the ability to use custom icons in a table of contents, popups, and shortcuts that run other programs.

For the Help author and web author: We'll examine the underlying principles that make these features work (and make them useful), and then we'll work through the procedures needed to create ALinks and KLinks, custom icons, popups, and shortcuts.

For the programmer: If you're not going to be doing any HTML Help development, you can probably skip this chapter, but you may want to review the information presented on pages 146 through 152.

What's in This Section

Topic	See Page
Associative Links: Concepts	146
Custom Icons for the Table of Contents: Concepts	149
Shortcuts: Concepts	150
Popups: Concepts	152
Procedures for Creating Associative Links	156
Procedures for Using Custom Icons in the Contents File	166
Procedures for Creating a Shortcut	169
Procedure for Creating Popups	173
Frequently Asked Questions	174

Associative Links: Concepts

WinHelp authors can provide their readers with automatically generated lists of topics related to the current topic. Now, HTML Help authors can, too. Instead of hard-coding jumps to other topics, you can let the HTML Help engine create and display a list of all topics that include information related to the current topic. This list is based on associative links that you, the Help author, create.

Associative links allow a Help author to create jumps to other topics based on shared keywords, ALink names, or both (we'll discuss what ALink names are in a moment). Consider the example shown below, where clicking the Related Topics button displays the Topics Found dialog box.

With HTML Help, the Topics Found lists can appear in a dialog box (as shown here) or in a popup menu.

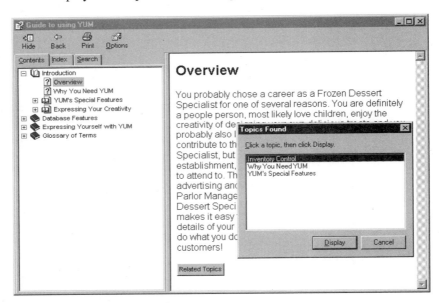

Clicking the Related Topics button displays the Topics Found dialog box.

An ALink is a hidden keyword that the Help author uses to create links between topics. We discuss the differences between ALinks and keyword links in "ALinks," below.

The list of topics in the Topics Found dialog box is derived using ALink names embedded in topic files. Clicking the Related Topics button launches a search for all topics in the current Help file (as well as any other Help files included in the contents file) that share an ALink name with the current topic. The related topics are listed in the Topics Found dialog box.

With ALinks and keyword links, it's the Help engine itself that determines which topic titles should be displayed when the button is pressed; the Help author doesn't have to hard-code any links. This feature is particularly useful for modular Help systems where you may not know which components will be installed. With ALinks (and keyword links, which we will discuss in a moment), as more components of the Help are written or installed, more topics may appear in the Topics Found dialog box.

KLink and ALink jumps are only available in compiled HTML Help systems.

To use this associative linking feature you will need to edit the .HTM files directly to add keywords, ALink names, or both. Up until this point we've been able to take .HTM files created using any HTML tool and use them in our HTML Help systems without modification. To take advantage of associative links, we will have to edit these .HTM files so that they contain information the compiler can use to create a link index. With the HTML Help Workshop, you do this using the **Edit Compiler Information** dialog box.

Inserting Keywords into Your .HTM Files

There are two ways to create a keyword index in HTML Help. The first way (which we looked at in Chapter Three) is to create a separate Index file (.HHK file) containing a list of all the project's keywords and their associated .HTM files. The second method, which is only available if you will be compiling your HTML Help system, is to embed keywords in each of your Help system's .HTM files and have the HTML Help compiler create a comprehensive keyword list automatically. This is similar to the way a keyword list is created in WinHelp: The Help compiler assigns to each topic a K footnote that contains keywords associated with that topic.

Once keywords have been inserted into your .HTM files, you can create keyword search links, or KLinks, by inserting a keyword search object tag into the .HTM files where you want the links to appear.

ALinks

An ALink jump looks to the user just like a KLink jump, but the list of topics found is based on ALink names (not index keywords) inserted into the .HTM files. Unlike keywords (which will populate the Index tab's dialog box), ALink entries are hidden from the user. They never manifest themselves and are only used to create associations among topics in the HTML Help system; the user never sees the ALink names that make up that association.

Why Use ALinks?

You may be wondering why you would ever bother to insert ALink information into your .HTM files and create ALink jumps if you have already gone to the trouble of inserting keyword entries. There are several reasons for using ALinks:

- You have already created an index by building an .HHK file and don't want to take the time to extract this information and embed it into individual .HTM files.

- You don't want, or don't have time, to create an index.

- You have a reason to associate a particular topic with a keyword for the display in the index tab, but you don't want that topic displayed in the Topics Found dialog box when you create a KLink jump.

- You will be translating your HTML Help system into another language, and you'd like the associations that exist in the English HTML Help system to carry over automatically to the translated system without having to translate the object tags that establish these associations. For example, any keywords embedded into your .HTM files must be translated because the end user will see these words when she clicks the Index tab in the three-pane window. But ALink information doesn't need to be translated because the end user will never see it.

Custom Icons for the Table of Contents: Concepts

As we discussed earlier, HTML Help's ActiveX control contains 42 built-in icons from which you can choose to change the appearance of the icon for a table of contents entry. You can also use your own custom images, as shown here.

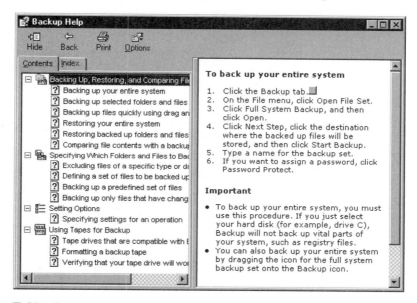

Table of contents with custom icons for the headings.

By using custom icons, you can give your users a visual cue about the topic associated with the icon. For example, the icon associated with the heading "Using Tapes for Backup" looks like a tape cartridge (although it is pretty hard to convey lots of meaning in an icon that's only 16 by 16 pixels).

Restrictions and Design Issues with Custom Icons

You Can Only Use One Set of Images at a Time

All of the icons you can use for a particular project must be stored in a single .BMP or .GIF file. This means you cannot use built-in icons and icons from a custom file at the same time. You can, however, edit the built-in icon file and add more icons to it. You'll find a copy of the built-in images in HHKIT\TEMPLATE\CNTIMAGE.BMP and HHKIT\TEMPLATE\CNTIMAGE.GIF.

Image Files Do Not Get Compiled

The custom image file does not get compiled into its associated .CHM file, so you must distribute the image file with your .CHM file or make sure the referenced image file can be found at a URL that the user can access.

Think "16"

The icons contained in image files must be no taller than 16 pixels. We have found that keeping the width at 16 pixels works best.

The image file must be saved as a 16-color image.

Shortcuts: Concepts

Windows 95 Help allows a Help author to create hotspots that launch other programs or take the user to a particular tab in a dialog box. In HTML Help, both of these capabilities are accessed using the Shortcut command, which is available thanks to the ActiveX control HHCTRL.OCX.

The figure below shows an HTML Help version of a page from the Help system for the Backup program that comes with Windows 95.

We created this HTML Help system by converting the existing WinHelp Backup Help system using a conversion utility that comes with the HTML Help Workshop. We'll discuss this and other Workshop tools in "Other HTML Help Workshop Tools," on page 276.

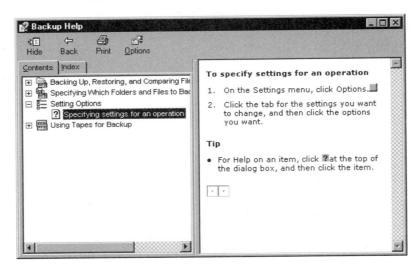

HTML Help topic with a shortcut.

Step 1 includes a shortcut button to perform the described actions. Clicking this shortcut button not only launches backup.exe, but also displays the Settings dialog box, as shown below.

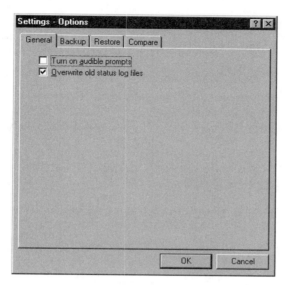

Results of clicking the shortcut.

Restrictions on Shortcuts

Keep in mind these restrictions on shortcuts:

- Shortcuts only work with compiled Help systems.

- If you want to employ a custom image or have an icon appear on a pushbutton, that image or icon must be distributed along with your Help system. Custom icons and images will not get compiled into the .CHM file (and would not get read from the .CHM file even if you were clever enough to figure out a way to get them in).

Popups: Concepts

As we mentioned earlier, one of the most common concerns among Help authors migrating to HTML Help is whether they will be able to make popups. The ability to provide an instant definition of a word, phrase or graphic without having to leave the current topic is a great feature of Windows Help, and Help authors will not give it up easily.

The good news is that you can have popups in HTML Help. The bad news is that these popups cannot contain formatted text, links to other topics, or graphics. Yet even with these restrictions, popups can still do a lot to make your Help systems more usable.

How to Make a Popup

As we've seen before, the best way to figure out how to do something in an HTML Help system is to look under the hood and see how someone else did it.

Consider the example shown below.

You can find this example in HHKIT\CHAP06\FINISHED\BACKUP.CHM.

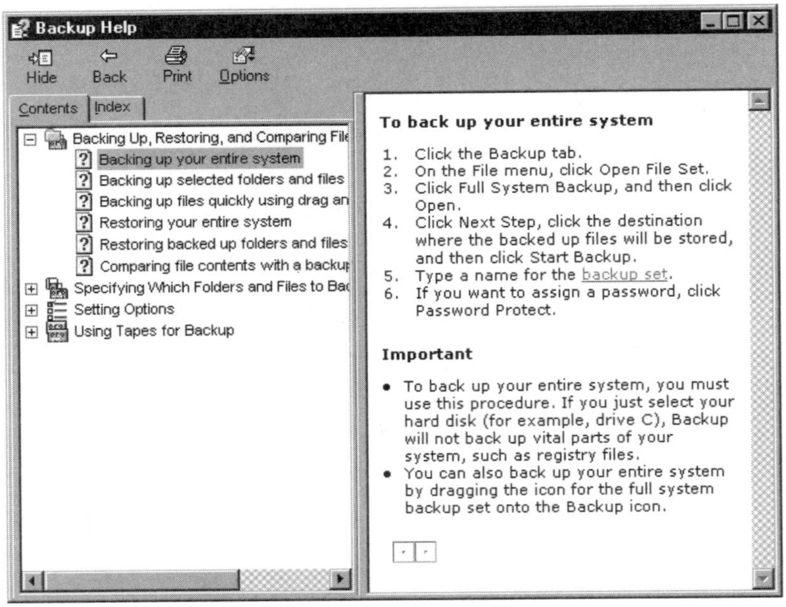

HTML Help topic with a link to a popup.

Clicking the link "backup set" will display the following popup window.

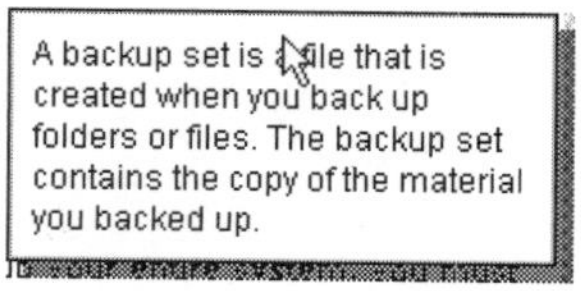

A backup set is a file that is
created when you back up
folders or files. The backup set
contains the copy of the material
you backed up.

An HTML Help popup.

If you right-click the content window and choose **View source** from the popup menu, the HTML Help source will be loaded into Notepad. The source is shown below.

```
<Title>To Back Up Your Entire System</Title>
<HEAD>
<META HTTP-EQUIV="Content-Type" CONTENT="text/html; charset=windows-
1252">
<META NAME="Generator" CONTENT="Microsoft Word 97">
<META NAME="Template" CONTENT="C:\PROGRAM FILES\MICROSOFT
OFFICE\OFFICE\html.dot">
<link rel="stylesheet" type="text/css" href="backup.css"></HEAD>
<BODY TEXT="#000000" LINK="#0000ff" VLINK="#800080" BGCOLOR="#ffffff">

<P><!DOCTYPE HTML PUBLIC "-//W3C//DTD HTML 3.2 Final//EN"></P>

<B><P>To back up your entire system</P>
<OL>

</B><LI>Click the Backup tab.</LI>

<SCRIPT>
PopupValue = "A backup set is a file that is created when you back up
folders or files. The backup set contains the copy of the material you
backed up."
</SCRIPT>

<LI>On the File menu, click Open File Set.</LI>
<LI>Click Full System Backup, and then click Open.</LI>
<LI>Click Next Step, click the destination where the backed up files
will be stored, and then click Start Backup.</LI>
<LI>Type a name for the <A
HREF=javascript:hhctrl.TextPopup(PopupValue,"Arial,9",
10,10,10,10)>backup set</A>.</LI>
<LI>If you want to assign a password, click Password Protect. </LI>
</OL>
<B><P>Important</P>
<UL>
</B><LI>To back up your entire system, you must use this procedure. If
you just select your hard disk (for example, drive C), Backup will not
back up vital parts of your system, such as registry files.</LI>
```

```
<LI>You can also back up your entire system by dragging the icon for the
full system backup set onto the Backup icon.</LI></UL>

<OBJECT id=hhctrl type="application/x-oleobject"
        classid="clsid:adb880a6-d8ff-11cf-9377-00aa003b7a11"
        codebase="hhctrl.ocx#Version=4,72,7322,0"

>
    <PARAM name="Command" value="HH Version">
</OBJECT>
</HTML>
```

Understanding the Popup Source Code

The lines

```
<SCRIPT>
PopupValue = "A backup set is a file that is created when you
back up folders or files. The backup set contains the copy of
the material you backed up."
</SCRIPT>
```

create a JavaScript variable called PopupValue that contains the text value contained between the quotes. The line

```
<LI>Type a name for the
<A HREF=javascript:hhctrl.TextPopup(PopupValue,"Arial,9",
10,10,10,10)>backup set</A>.</LI>
```

indicates that the term "backup set" should be a hotspot that when clicked will invoke the TextPopup method of the ActiveX control HHTRCL.OCX, passing it the parameters for the text to be displayed (the variable PopupValue), the font (Arial, 9 point), and the margins for the popup, (left margin of 10 pixels, right margin of 10 pixels, top margin of 10 pixels, and bottom margin of 10 pixels).

The lines

```
<OBJECT id=hhctrl type="application/x-oleobject"
        classid="clsid:adb880a6-d8ff-11cf-9377-00aa003b7a11"
        codebase="hhctrl.ocx#Version=4,72,7292,0"

>
    <PARAM name="Command" value="HH Version">
</OBJECT>
```

invoke the ActiveX control HHCTRL.OCX, which contains the program code for displaying popups.

Note: The reference to the command "HH Version" in the hhctrl object tag is made even though we have no intention of displaying the HTML Help Version dialog box. We do, however, need to have the ActiveX control referenced in this topic, so we have to insert a valid object tag and we have to include something for the command parameter, even if we never invoke that particular command.

Procedures for Creating Associative Links

In this next series of examples we will take an existing HTML Help project, BACKUP.CHM, and modify it so that it has a rich index and contains associative links between topics based on keywords and ALink names.

Here is a summary of the steps we'll take to modify the HTML Help system.

1 Open the BACKUP.HHP project file.

2 Insert keyword object tags into .HTM files using the Edit Compiler Information command.

3 Insert ALink names into .HTM files using the Edit Compiler Information command.

4 Insert an ALink using the HTML Help ActiveX wizard.

5 Insert a keyword link (KLink) using the HTML Help ActiveX wizard.

The files you will need for these exercises can be found in HHKIT\CHAP06.

The completed examples can be found in HHKIT\CHAP06\FINISHED.

To Open the Tape Backup Project

1 If it's not already running, start the HTML Help Workshop.

2 From the **File** menu, choose **Open**.

3 In the File Open dialog box, browse to the file you want to open, in this case **BACKUP.HHP** (located in the HHKIT\CHAP06 folder).

4 Select the file and click **OK**. Your screen should look like the one shown below.

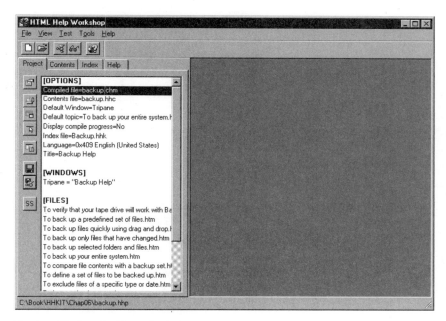

Project file for the Tape Backup Help system.

Embedding Keywords into an .HTM File

In this next example we will embed keyword information into an .HTM file. This information will be read by the HTML Help Compiler and incorporated into an index for BACKUP.CHM.

To Add Keywords to an .HTM File

1 With BACKUP.HHP open, click the **Contents** tab.

2 Double-click the item you want to edit, in this case **Backing up your entire system.**

This will load the .HTM file associated with the contents entry into the right side of the Workshop, as shown below.

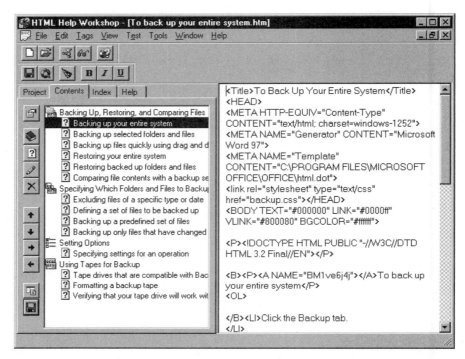

Project file with Contents in left pane and .HTM file we will edit in the right pane.

3 Place your insertion pointer at the end of the file.

4 From the **Edit** menu, choose **Compiler Information**.

5 When the Compiler Information dialog box appears, make sure the **Keywords** tab is selected, and click **Add**.

6 In the Add Keyword dialog box, type the following:

You certainly don't have to enter all of these terms, although doing so will result in a better index.

backing up files;backing up files, selecting folders and files to back up;backup sets;backup sets, creating for a partial system backup;documents;documents, backing up selected documents;files;files, backing up selected files;folders;folders, backing up selected folders;password for backup set;starting a backup

7   Click **OK**. Your screen should look like the one shown below.

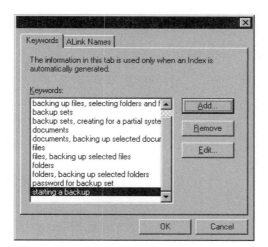

Words that appear after the comma will be indented under the word that appears before the comma in the index list.

8   Click **OK**.

9   From the **File** menu, click **Save File**.

Note: The process for entering ALink names (from the ALink Names tab) is identical.

Automatically Compiling Keywords

As we mentioned earlier, you can have the HTML Help Workshop automatically assemble the keywords from your .HTM files into a comprehensive index for your project. This can be done instead of, or In addition to, creating and editing an .HHK file (see "Creating a Keyword Search," on page 71).

To Set the Compiler to Automatically Assemble Keywords

1   With BACKUP.HPP open, click the **Project** tab.

2   Click the **Change Project Options** button.

3 When the Options dialog box appears, click the **Files** tab.

4 Make sure **Include Keywords From HTML Files** is selected, as shown below.

Notice that an .HHK file is specified.

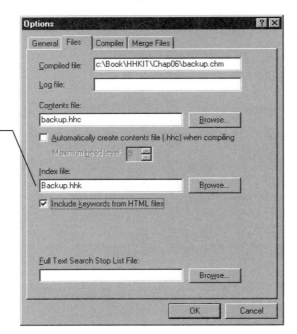

5 Click **OK**.

Note: If you were to save and recompile your project, the Index tab would be populated with keywords. Please note that keywords and ALink names have already been inserted into the other .HTM files.

Bug

At the time of this writing, you had to specify an index file (in this case BACKUP.HHK) even if you wanted the HTML Help compiler to assemble the keyword list automatically from keyword information embedded in each .HTM file. This index file can be empty.

Inserting ALinks and KLinks

In this next series of examples we will insert ALink and KLink jumps into .HTM files using the Workshop's Insert HTML Help ActiveX Control wizard.

To Insert an ALink that Produces a Popup Menu

1   Click the **Contents** tab.

2   Double-click the item you want to edit, in this case **Backing Up Selected Folders And Files**.

3   Scroll down in the file, and select the text "Insert ALink Here," as shown below.

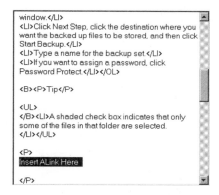

```
window.</LI>
<LI>Click Next Step, click the destination where you
want the backed up files to be stored, and then click
Start Backup.</LI>
<LI>Type a name for the backup set.</LI>
<LI>If you want to assign a password, click
Password Protect.</LI></OL>

<B><P>Tip</P>

<UL>
</B><LI>A shaded check box indicates that only
some of the files in that folder are selected.
</LI></UL>

<P>
Insert ALink Here

</P>
```

4   Click the **Insert HTML Help ActiveX Control** button.

The HHCTRL Command and ID dialog box will appear.

5   From the Specify the Command drop-down list, choose **ALink Search**, as shown below.

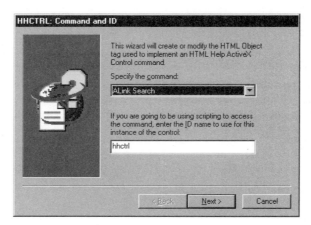

6   Click **Next**.

7   Fill in the dialog box as shown below, and then click **Next**.

Choosing **Display in a popup menu** makes the list of related topics appear in a small popup menu next to the mouse pointer instead of in a dialog box.

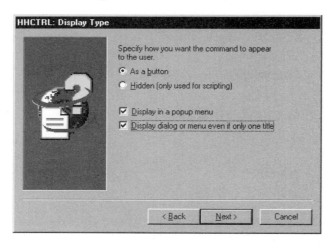

8   Fill in the dialog box as shown below.

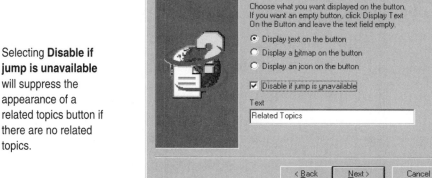

Selecting **Disable if jump is unavailable** will suppress the appearance of a related topics button if there are no related topics.

9   Click **Next**. The ALink Search dialog box will appear.

10   Click **Add**. The Add/Edit ALink Name dialog box will appear.

11   In the ALink Name edit box, type the following:

A_BACKUP_FULLSYS; A_BACKUP_OPTIONS_GENERAL

12   Make sure the **Multiple ALink Names (Separated By Semicolon)** check box is selected and click **OK**.

The dialog box should look like the one shown below.

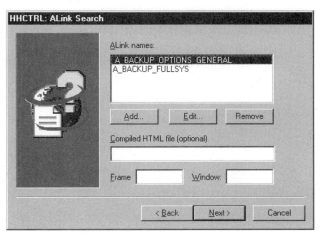

13   Click **Next,** then click **Finish**.

14   From the **File** menu, choose **Save File**.

To Insert a Keyword Link

1 With the **Contents** tab selected, double-click the item you want to edit, in this case **Backing up files quickly using drag and drop**.

2 Scroll down in the file, and select the text "Insert KLink here."

3 Click the **Insert HTML Help ActiveX Control** button.

   The HHCTRL Command and ID dialog box will appear.

4 From the Specify The Command drop-down list, choose **Keyword Search** and click **Next**.

5 Fill in the dialog box as shown below, then click **Next**.

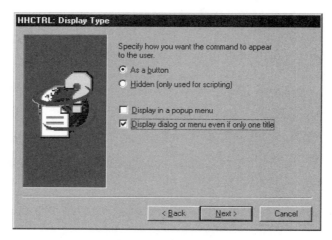

6 Fill in the dialog box as shown below.

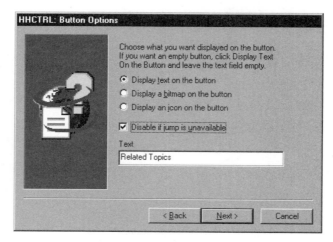

7 Click **Next**. The Keyword Link Search dialog box will appear.

8   Click **Add**. The Add/Edit Keyword dialog box will appear.

9   In the Keyword edit box, type the following:

backing up files; backing up files, using drag and drop; drag and drop options, changing; dragging file sets onto the Backup icon; options, setting; settings; settings, drag and drop options

10   Make sure the **Multiple Keywords (Separated By Semicolon)** check box is selected and click **OK**.

11   Click **Next** and click **Finish**.

12   From the **File** menu, choose **Save File**.

Recompiling and Viewing

Recompile the project by clicking the **Project** tab and clicking the **Save All Project Files And Compile** button.

When you view the compiled HTML Help file, note the following:

- The index tab is populated with a rich keyword list.

- At the bottom of the topic "Backing up selected folders and files," there is a Related Topics button that, when clicked, displays a popup menu of related topics.

- At the bottom of the topic "Backing up files quickly using drag and drop," there is a Related Topics button that, when clicked, displays a Topics Found dialog box.

Procedures for Using Custom Icons in the Contents File

In this next series of examples we will take an existing HTML Help project, BACKUP.CHM, and modify it so that the table of contents uses custom icons instead of the icons that come with HTML Help.

Here is a summary of the steps we'll take to modify the HTML Help system.

1 Open the BACKUP.HHP project file.

2 Change the Contents properties so that icons stored in an external file are used. For this example, we'll use the file ICONS.BMP, which contains several custom icons.

3 Edit content entries so that a different custom icon is associated with each major heading in the project.

The files you will need for these exercises can be found in HHKIT\CHAP06.

The completed examples can be found in HHKIT\CHAP06\FINISHED.

To Use a Custom Image File

1 If it's not already running, load the HTML Help Workshop and open BACKUP.HHP.

2 Click the **Contents** tab.

3 Click the **Contents Properties** button.

4 In the General table, select **Use Custom Images From A File.**

5 In the Image file edit box, type the name of the file you want to use, in this case **ICONS.BMP,** as shown below.

We recommend that the custom image file be saved in the same folder as the .CHM file. Remember, you will need to distribute the custom image file along with the .CHM file.

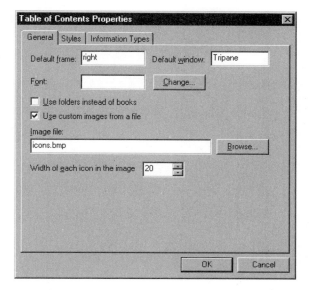

6   Click **OK.**

7   From the **File** menu, choose **Save Project.**

8   Close and reopen the project.

Note: At the time of this writing it was necessary to close and reopen the project so that the HTML Help Workshop contents editor would "look" in the custom image file for which icons to use. This may have been fixed by the time you try this.

To Apply a Custom Icon to a Contents Entry

1   With BACKUP.CHM open, click the **Contents** tab.

2   Click the item whose icon you wish to change, in this case the heading **Backing Up, Restoring and Comparing Files**.

3   Click the **Edit Selection** button.

4   Click the **Advanced** tab.

5 Change the image index to **15**, as shown below.

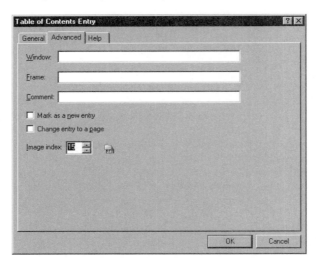

6 Click **OK**.

Practice

On your own, apply images 16, 17, and 18 to the remaining three headings. When you are finished, your screen should look like the one shown below.

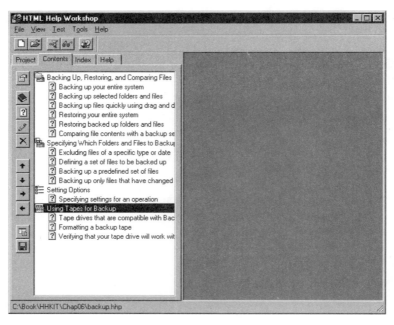

Contents entries with custom icons.

Procedures for Creating a Shortcut

In this next series of exercises we will add a shortcut to a topic. When this shortcut is clicked it will launch Notepad (if it's not already open) and display the Find dialog box.

Here is a summary of the steps we'll take to modify the HTML Help system.

1   Open the NOTEPAD.HHP project file.

2   Use the HTML Help ActiveX Wizard to insert a shortcut into an .HTM file.

3   Recompile and view the project.

The files you will need for these exercises can be found in HHKIT\CHAP06.

The completed examples can be found in HHKIT\CHAP06\FINISHED.

To Insert a Shortcut into an .HTM file

1   If it's not already running, start the HTML Help Workshop and load NOTEPAD.HHP.

2   Click the **Contents** tab.

3   Double-click the contents entry for the file you want to edit, in this case **To find specific characters and words**.

This will load the associated .HTM file, NOTEPAD1.HTM, into the right pane.

4   Place your insertion point where you want the shortcut to appear, in this case after the step "On the Search menu, click Find," as shown below.

Place the insertion point here.

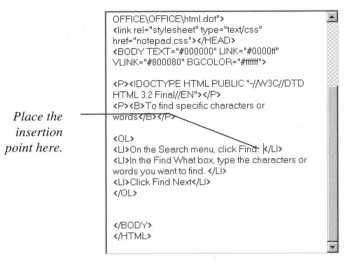

```
OFFICE\OFFICE\html.dot">
<link rel="stylesheet" type="text/css"
href="notepad.css"></HEAD>
<BODY TEXT="#000000" LINK="#0000ff"
VLINK="#800080" BGCOLOR="#ffffff">

<P><!DOCTYPE HTML PUBLIC "-//W3C//DTD
HTML 3.2 Final//EN"></P>
<P><B>To find specific characters or
words</B></P>

<OL>
<LI>On the Search menu, click Find: </LI>
<LI>In the Find What box, type the characters or
words you want to find. </LI>
<LI>Click Find Next</LI>
</OL>


</BODY>
</HTML>
```

5   Click the **Insert HTML Help ActiveX Control** button.

6   Choose **ShortCut** from the Specify The Command drop-down list and click **Next.**

7   Choose **As A Button** and click **Next**.

8   Choose **Display A Bitmap On The Button** and specify that the bitmap you want to use is called **shortcut,** as shown below.

To take advantage of HTML Help's built-in shortcut icon, just type **shortcut** without a .BMP extension.

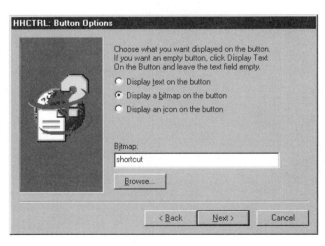

9   Click **Next**.

10 Fill in the dialog box as shown below, and click **Next**.

The programmer you are working with can supply you with the name of the Window class for the program, or you can use a spy utility to determine this and other settings you may need to know.

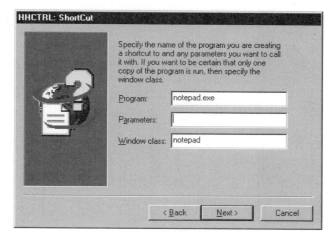

11 Fill in the dialog box as shown below.

Notice that you can specify a topic to display if Notepad cannot be run.

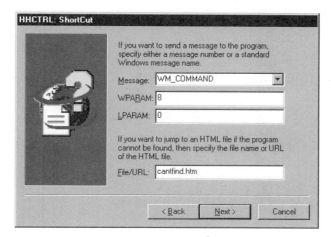

12 Click **Next**, and then click **Finish**.

13 From the **File** menu, choose **Save File.**

Practice

On your own, click the Project tab, click the **Save Project And Compile** button, and view the compiled file. Your Help system should look like the one shown below.

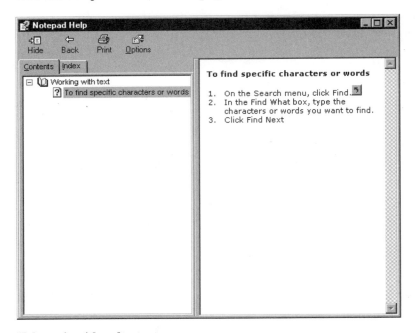

Help topic with a shortcut.

Procedure for Creating Popups

The best way to create a popup in HTML Help is to find a topic that already has a popup in it and copy the code that creates the popup into the topic where you want a new popup to appear. You will find a popup in the first topic of BACKUP.CHM.

To access the source to this topic, right-click and choose **View Source**. This will load the source into Notepad.

You will need to copy and adapt these elements from the source:

The JavaScript variable

```
<SCRIPT>
PopupValue = "Your popup goes here."
</SCRIPT>
```

The hhctrl object tag

```
<OBJECT id=hhctrl type="application/x-oleobject"
        classid="clsid:adb880a6-d8ff-11cf-9377-00aa003b7a11"
        codebase="hhctrl.ocx#Version=4,72,7292,0"
>
    <PARAM name="Command" value="HH Version">
</OBJECT>
```

The <A HREF> link statement

```
Regular text then
<A HREF=javascript:hhctrl.TextPopup(PopupValue,"Arial,9",
-1,-1,-1,-1)>Hotspot text</A>.
```

What's Next?

In this chapter we've looked at refining an HTML Help system by adding associative links, a table of contents with custom icons, shortcuts, and popups. In the next chapter, we'll see how to link a Help system to a program.

Frequently Asked Questions

Question: *Can I open a page of a compiled HTML Help file in my browser?*

Answer: You can open to a page of a compiled HTML Help system in either Internet Explorer 3.*x* or 4.*x*.

- To open to a specific page in Internet Explorer 3.*x*, use this syntax to specify the URL:

   mk:@MSITStore:filename.chm::\page.htm

- To open to a specific page in Internet Explorer 4.*x*, use this syntax to specify the URL:

   its:filename.chm::\page.htm

Question: *I noticed that after working with the examples in this chapter there's a file called Gledger.chw in HHKIT\CHAP05. How did this file get there, and do I need it?*

Answer: A .CHW file gets created automatically by the HTML Help engine when you click the Index tab in a modular Help system. The .CHW file is a type of internal binary index file that assembles the index information from all the .CHM files that comprise your Help system. If you delete this file, it will get created again the next time you click the Index tab.

CHAPTER SEVEN

Understanding and Creating Context-Sensitive HTML Help

Windows applications are typically supplied with online Help. Traditional online Help exposes a table of contents and index to allow a user to find topics of interest. Context-sensitive Help assists the user further by taking her directly to topics relevant to the currently active part of the application. In other words, the choice of which topic to display is sensitive to the context within which help is requested.

For the Help author: We'll discuss the different types of context-sensitive Help and how to author them. If you won't be authoring help specifically for Windows applications, you can skip this chapter. Otherwise, you'll probably want to read everything except the sections titled "What a Visual C++ Programmer Needs to Know and Do," on page 182, and "What a Visual Basic Programmer Needs to Know and Do," on page 188.

For the programmer: We'll cover some conceptual material that you may already know, and then we'll get into how to organize your application development to accommodate context-sensitive HTML Help. Finally, we'll discuss exactly what you need to know and do in order to implement context-sensitive Help in your application. These details assume some familiarity with material covered in "The HTML Help API," starting on page 199.

What's in this Chapter

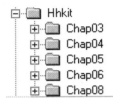

The sample code for both this chapter and Chapter 8 can be found in HHKIT\CHAP08.

Overview of Context-Sensitive Help

Context-sensitive Help comes in a couple of different flavors from the user's point of view: Help buttons and "What's This" Help. For programmers and Help authors, there is an almost dizzying variety of implementation possibilities. The most appropriate techniques for your application will depend on your choice of development tool(s), the roles of programmer and Help author in your development team (particularly if they are the same person), and personal preference.

Help Buttons

The simplest form of context-sensitive Help is the Help button—a regular button with the word "Help" on it. A Help button is a common feature of Windows dialog boxes. Typically, clicking the Help button displays a Help topic in an external Help window that gives an overview of how to use the dialog box.

"What's This" Help

Windows 95 introduced the concept of "What's This" Help, which provides a brief but focused popup topic to describe an individual element of a dialog box or other window.

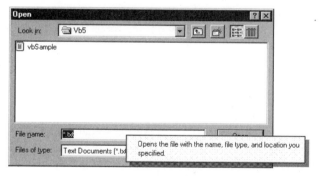

The standard Windows File Open dialog box with "What's This" Help displayed for its Open button.

"What's This" Help looks very similar to tooltips, the brief popup hints that appear when you hold your mouse pointer over an item for a second or two. Generally speaking, tooltips are much shorter than "What's This" Help—one or two words only—and are intended to identify items such as graphical toolbar buttons that do not have text labels.

Tooltips are in the domain of application programmers rather than Help authors. Since they aren't part of a Help system, we won't be discussing tooltips any further in this book.

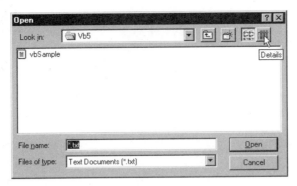

The standard Windows File Open dialog box with a tooltip displayed.

The "What's This" Button

On the Windows CE platform, the "?" button is known as the Help button and behaves as described under "Help Buttons" above.

When a dialog box or other window provides "What's This" Help, a question mark ("?") button appears in the upper-right corner of the window, just to the left of the close button (the one with the "X" on it). Not surprisingly, this is known as the "What's This" button. The mechanism for enabling the "What's This" button depends on your choice of development tool, but in any case you cannot have a "What's This" button at the same time as either a minimize button or maximize button. This is a limitation imposed by Windows itself.

An application may also support alternate ways of accessing "What's This" Help, in addition to the "What's This" button. These include pressing the F1 key to get Help on the item which currently has the focus, and right-clicking an item to display its popup context menu, on which there can be a "What's This?" menu command. If a given item does not have a context menu, Windows may display "What's This" Help immediately in response to a right-click. This is the default behavior if you choose to have HTML Help handle the right-click event on your behalf.

It's important to note that in HTML Help, "What's This" topics are not authored in the same manner as normal Help topics. "What's This" topics are called "text popups" and are completely different from normal HTML Help topics. As their name suggests, text popups are not HTML: They are plain text, and cannot contain HTML tags, graphics, or anything else. We will discuss how to author text popups later in this chapter.

Topic Ids and Map Numbers

When an application implements context-sensitive Help, it needs a way to refer to the HTML Help topics to display. HTML Help topics have a couple of different identifiers associated with them that an application can use to request context-sensitive Help. These identifiers include topic Ids and map numbers.

A topic ID is a name that uniquely identifies a Help topic within a given project. In Windows 95 Help, a topic ID is arbitrarily assigned by the Help author (or Help authoring tool) as a "#" footnote to the topic. In HTML Help, a topic ID is the name of the HTML file that contains the topic—except in the special case of text popup topics, for which the topic ID is just a symbolic name. If an HTML file is stored in a subfolder, the folder name(s) are included in its topic ID: for example, "/MyTopics/Default.htm". Topic Ids are not case-sensitive; the previous example could also be referred to as "/mytopics/default.htm".

Map numbers give Help authors a way to associate a numeric value with any topic ID. This association is called aliasing. An application can use map numbers in conjunction with the HTML Help API to display context-sensitive Help. Map numbers provide a more efficient way for applications to refer to a given topic.

What Happens When a User Asks for Help

A user's request for Help follows a somewhat tortuous path through application code and HTML Help itself before the appropriate topic is eventually displayed. Furthermore, the path differs depending on which method the user chose to request Help in the first place.

Help Button

The most straightforward Help request occurs when a user clicks the Help button in a dialog box. The application responds to this click by telling HTML Help to display the topic with a particular context map number. HTML Help uses aliases provided by the Help author to determine which HTML topic corresponds to the map number. Finally, the topic is displayed to the user.

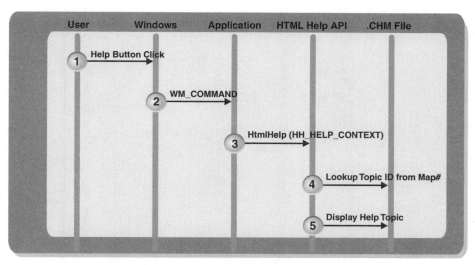

A look under the hood of the Help button in a dialog box.

"What's This" Button

When a user clicks the "What's This" button in a dialog box, Windows changes the mouse pointer and waits for the user to click something or press the ESC key. If the user clicks anywhere within the dialog box, Windows sends a message (WM_HELP) to the application. This message includes information about which element of the dialog box the user clicked.

In response to the WM_HELP message, the application makes a call to HTML Help. This call instructs HTML Help to display a text popup topic from a specific text file stored in a compiled HTML Help file. Included in this call is information about which element was clicked and a complete list of all elements in the dialog box that have Help topics, with the corresponding map numbers of those topics. This list is called a control ID map.

HTML Help examines the control ID map to see if the clicked element has a corresponding context map number. If it does, this map number is looked up in the aliases provided by the Help author. The aliased topic ID is located in the text popup topic file, and then the text popup is extracted. Finally, the text popup topic is displayed to the user.

If there is no context map number for the element that the user clicked, HTML Help displays a generic topic indicating that no Help is available.

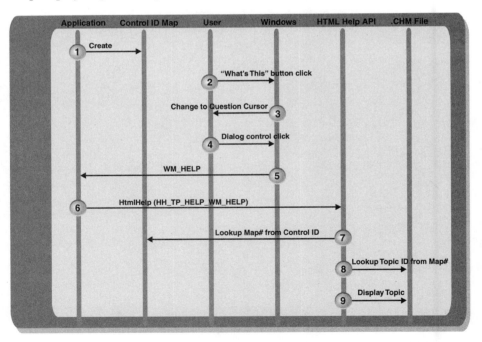

A look under the hood of clicking on a dialog box item with the "What's This" cursor.

The F1 Key

Pressing the F1 function key causes Windows to send the application a WM_HELP message requesting Help for the element of the dialog box which currently has the focus. The application responds to this message in exactly the same way as it does when the user requests Help via the "What's This" button. In fact, the application does not usually distinguish between these two types of Help requests; the differences between them are handled entirely by Windows itself.

Clicking with the Right Mouse Button

If the user clicks an element of a dialog box with the right mouse button, Windows sends a WM_CONTEXTMENU message to the application, indicating which element was right-clicked. At this point the application may decide, depending on the element, to display a context menu. If it does, this menu should include an item labeled "What's This?"

Often, the application will not display a context menu, but instead will immediately call HTML Help. The application supplies the same information in this case as it does for the F1 key and the "What's This" button: namely, which element was clicked, and the control ID map.

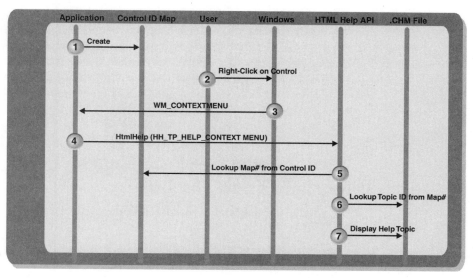

A look under the hood of a request for "What's This" Help from a context menu.

Procedures for Implementing Context-Sensitive Help

The responsibility for assigning map numbers to topics is shared by programmers and Help authors. It's a cooperative effort, and you will have to communicate with each other occasionally.

Typically, a programmer assigns a map number to each area of the application that requires context-sensitive Help. To improve code readability, these numbers are gathered in one or more header (.H) files, which associate a name (also known as a symbolic constant) with each map number.

A Help author uses the HTML Help Workshop to incorporate the header files provided by a programmer into an HTML Help project. The map numbers can then be associated with—or aliased to—specific topic Ids.

The procedures for implementing context-sensitive Help vary widely among different development tools. We'll discuss techniques for Visual C++ and Visual Basic. If you're using some other development tool, you'll probably want to read both sections to get an idea of how context-sensitive Help should be implemented in your environment.

For a full explanation of the HTML Help API calls used in the code fragments below, refer to "HH_HELP_CONTEXT," on page 219, "HH_TP_HELP_WM_HELP," on page 230, and "HH_TP_HELP_CONTEXTMENU," on page 228.

Alternative Implementation Strategies

For clarity, the following procedures outline a specific implementation strategy without discussing alternatives. You may decide that some variation of this strategy is more suitable for your needs. Possible variations include: having the Help author assign map numbers and create header files; using the HH_DISPLAY_TEXT_POPUP command instead of text popup topics; and even using Windows Help for popup topics. The latter possibility might seem peculiar given the migration to HTML Help—but it provides the benefit of supporting rich-text and graphics in popup topics which HTML Help does not.

What a Visual C++ Programmer Needs to Know and Do

Before you start, be sure to read the section titled "Calling HtmlHelp() from Visual C++," on page 206.

You'll be pleased to hear that there is built-in support for automatically generating map numbers in Visual C++. In the dialog editor, the property sheet for each dialog control has a checkbox labeled Help ID. If you check this box, a unique map number for the control will be placed in the file RESOURCE.HM, which is automatically created by Visual C++.

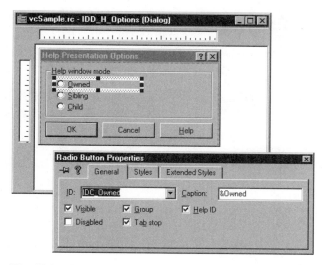

The Help ID checkbox in the property sheet of the Visual C++ dialog editor automatically generates a map number for you.

For example, the RESOURCE.HM file generated for the vcSample application found in the HHKIT\CHAP08\VCSAMPLE folder looks like this:

```
// Developer Studio generated Help ID include file.
// Used by vcSample.rc
//
#define HIDC_Owned              0x808403f3    // IDD_Options
#define HIDC_CallHtmlHelp       0x808303f0    // IDD_File
#define HIDC_Child              0x808403f2    // IDD_Options
#define HIDC_DisplayTopic       0x808303ec    // IDD_File
#define HIDC_HelpContext        0x808303eb    // IDD_File
#define HIDC_Owned              0x808403f3    // IDD_Options
#define HIDC_ReturnValue        0x808303ef    // IDD_File
#define HIDC_Search             0x808303e8    // IDD_File
#define HIDC_Sibling            0x808403f4    // IDD_Options
#define HIDC_WindowType         0x808303ea    // IDD_File
#define HIDC_dwData             0x808303ee    // IDD_File
```

Note: Try to use descriptive names for your control Ids in order to avoid confusion. You're going to have to explain to the Help author what part of the application each map number refers to.

Supplying Map Numbers to HTML Help

The RESOURCE.HM file is almost suitable as is for use by the HTML Help Workshop as input for text popup constants. However, the HTML Help Workshop only accepts files with a ".H" extension for this purpose. So, the file must be renamed before a Help author can use it. One way to take care of this automatically is to add a new post-build step as shown below. Note that this setting should be made for "All Configurations."

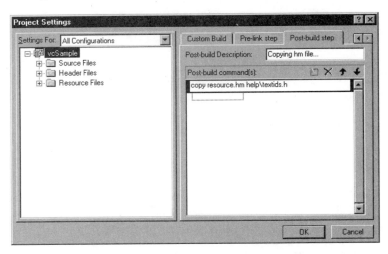

Adding this post-build step to your project settings will automatically update the map numbers every time you build the project.

Standard Button Identifiers

You do not need to create map numbers for certain standard buttons. Buttons with ID values of IDOK, IDCANCEL, and IDHELP have default text popup topics supplied by HTML Help. These default topics can be overridden if you wish. However, there is no default topic for the other standard button ID values IDABORT, IDRETRY, IDIGNORE, IDYES, IDNO, and IDCLOSE.

Note: The IDHELP constant is not recognized by the dialog editor in Visual C++, despite the fact that it appears in the relevant header files. If you create a control with an identifier of IDHELP, you will probably get a compilation error. To work around this problem, explicitly assign the value "9" to the identifier when you create your first Help button, as shown below.

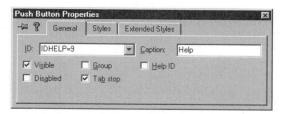

To avoid a compilation error, you must assign the value "9" to IDHELP.

Enabling the "What's This" Help Button

For every dialog box on which you want to support "What's This" Help, you must enable the "What's This" Help button. This is a simple matter of selecting the Context Help option on the Extended Styles tab of the dialog resource property sheet.

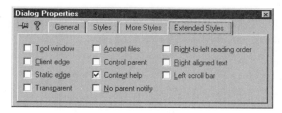

The Context Help checkbox enables the "What's This" Help button.

This checkbox corresponds to the WS_EX_CONTEXTHELP extended style bit during window creation. There is also a Context Help checkbox on the More Styles tab which corresponds to the DS_CONTEXTHELP dialog style. They are functionally equivalent.

As we stated earlier, you cannot have a "What's This" Help button at the same time as a Minimize or Maximize button (or both). The Minimize and Maximize buttons take precedence, and the "What's This" Help button will not appear. This is a limitation of Windows.

Responding to "What's This" Help Requests

Once you have map numbers for all of the text popup topics in the application, you need to write a bit of code to display these topics when appropriate. Each dialog box or other CWnd-derived class that has "What's This" Help will need handlers for the WM_HELP and WM_CONTEXTMENU messages. The WM_HELP message is sent in response to the user pressing F1 or clicking a control in "What's This" Help mode. The WM_CONTEXTMENU message is sent when the user right-clicks a control.

Use ClassWizard to create OnHelpInfo and OnContextMenu member functions for these classes. Note that WM_HELP is incorrectly referred to as WM_HELPINFO in ClassWizard.

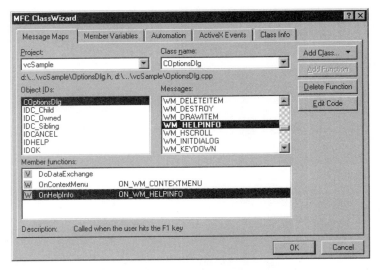

You'll need handlers for WM_HELP (referred to in ClassWizard as
WM_HELPINFO), and WM_CONTEXTMENU.

OnHelpInfo

The code you need in the OnHelpInfo function is fairly straightforward, such as
the following example:

```
BOOL CoptionsDlg::OnHelpInfo(HELPINFO* pHelpInfo)
{
    HtmlHelp((HWND)pHelpInfo->hItemHandle,
      "MyHelp.chm::/MyPopups.txt",
      HH_TP_HELP_WM_HELP, (DWORD)&dwHelpIds);
    return(TRUE);
}
```

Ask the Help author you're working with which file names to use for your project
in place of "MyHelp.chm" and "MyPopups.txt" in the example.

The dwHelpIds argument is the control ID map declared as follows:

```
static const DWORD dwHelpIds[]= {
    IDC_Owned, HIDC_Owned,
    IDC_Sibling, HIDC_Sibling,
    IDC_Child, HIDC_Child,
    0, 0
};
```

The first half of the pair is the control ID, and the second half of the pair is the
corresponding context map number. A pair of zeroes terminates the list.

OnContextMenu

Assuming you don't have custom context menus in your application, the code you need for OnContextMenu is very similar to that for OnHelpInfo:

```
void CoptionsDlg::OnContextMenu(CWnd* pWnd, Cpoint)
{
    HtmlHelp(pWnd->GetSafeHwnd(),
      "MyHelp.chm::/MyPopups.txt",
      HH_TP_HELP_CONTEXTMENU, (DWORD)&dwHelpIds);
}
```

The primary difference between the two functions is the way you get the handle of the control for which Help was requested. Although there are two distinct HTML Help API commands, in the current version they behave identically. The same dwHelpIds control ID map is used for both calls.

Responding to the Help Button

OnHelpInfo and OnContextMenu take care of the text popup topics for all of the dialog controls in the application. What about the conventional Help topics required by the Help button in each dialog box? Unfortunately, Visual C++ doesn't currently support automatically generating map numbers for dialog boxes. However, each dialog box already has a unique number associated with it: its resource ID. You can just use the resource ID of a dialog box as its map number, and supply RESOURCE.H to the Help author for aliasing.

(You will have to let the Help author know which of the ID values in RESOURCE.H require aliasing since there will be many others that do not. One way to approach this problem is to use a consistent naming convention for identifiers that need to be aliased. For example, dialog box templates are typically assigned a symbolic constant which begins with "IDD_".)

To respond to the Help button, use ClassWizard again to create a handler for the BN_CLICKED notification of the IDHELP button. The code for this handler can be as simple as a single line, for example:

```
HtmlHelp(NULL, "MyHelp.chm", HH_HELP_CONTEXT, IDD);
```

Of course, you should check with your Help author for the correct file name to use in place of "MyHelp.chm" in the second argument. What you choose to pass for the first argument depends on your choice of presentation mode for the Help window. You may also want to explicitly specify a window type with the Help file name. These issues are discussed in detail in the section titled "Presentation of the Help Window," on page 201.

In practice you will probably also want to centralize storage of the Help file name. The vcSample application source code demonstrates one possible approach (see "Visual C++ Implementation Notes," on page 248).

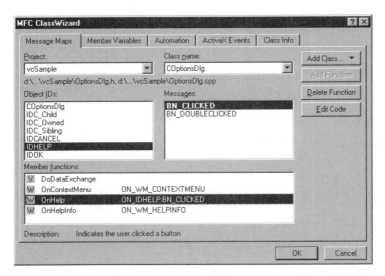

Adding a handler for the Help button of a dialog box is straightforward.

What a Visual Basic Programmer Needs to Know and Do

Before you start, be sure to read the section titled "Calling HtmlHelp() from Visual Basic," on page 209.

The first thing you need to do is use a text editor to create a C-style header file that defines a unique map number for each Help button in your application. You'll probably also want to create one or more separate header files containing map numbers for text popup topics. Each map number definition in the header files should look something like this:

```
#define IDH_Options 2001 // Options dialog
```

Both the IDH_ constant name and its corresponding numeric value are arbitrary, but they must be unique within a given HTML Help project. The C++ comment introducer

```
//
```

and the text following it are optional. The C comment format of

```
/* Options dialog */
```

is also acceptable. The file extension must be ".H"; for example, the file name TEXTIDS.H is acceptable.

At this point you might be wondering why it's necessary to create header files at all since you're not using C or C++. The answer is that you will have to provide these header files to the Help author for inclusion in the Help project. HTML Help Workshop expects C-style header files regardless of what programming language you choose to use. In the absence of a more sophisticated tool, header files are not a bad way to manage map numbers anyway.

Try to use descriptive names in your header files to avoid confusion. You're going to have to explain to the Help author what part of the application each map number refers to.

Assigning Map Numbers to Forms and Controls

Forms and controls in Visual Basic each have a HelpContextID property that is meant to be used for external Help topics—topics that display in their own window when the user clicks Help. Controls also have a WhatsThisHelpID property that is meant to be used for popup Help topics.

When integrating with HTML Help, you must override the default behavior supplied by Visual Basic. As a result, it doesn't really matter how you use the HelpContextID and WhatsThisHelpID properties (or if you use them at all, in fact). However, they are a convenient place to store map numbers and for this discussion we will use them as originally intended.

For every control that has a corresponding text popup topic, assign the map number of the topic to the WhatsThisHelpID property. For every form that has a Help button, assign the map number of the corresponding HTML topic to the HelpContextID property.

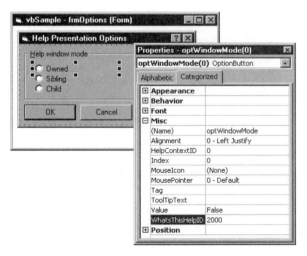

The WhatsThisHelpID and HelpContextID properties must be set manually.

It would be nice if there was some automatic way to handle map number assignment in Visual Basic, but unfortunately you must do it all manually.

Note: HTML Help doesn't support "What's This" Help for windowless controls. As a rule of thumb, if a control has an "hWnd" property at runtime, you can successfully give it a "What's This" Help topic. Otherwise, save yourself the trouble.

Enabling the "What's This" Help Button

For every form on which you want to support "What's This" Help, you must set the WhatsThisHelp and WhatsThisButton properties to True.

The WhatsThisButton and WhatsThisHelp properties must both be set to True.

Also, MinButton and MaxButton must be set to False. If you set either of these properties to True, the "What's This" Help button will not appear. This is a limitation of Windows.

Responding to "What's This" Help Requests

To implement "What's This" Help you must respond to the WM_HELP and WM_CONTEXTMENU messages that Windows sends to your forms. Unfortunately, Visual Basic doesn't fire any events in response to these messages. Visual Basic assumes that you'll want to invoke the WinHelp API function and calls it on your behalf. To override this behavior requires using a technique called subclassing.

Subclassing a form consists of intercepting messages sent to the form before Visual Basic has a chance to see them. After your subclass routine looks at a message, it can decide whether to process the message immediately or pass it on to Visual Basic for default processing.

There are third-party controls available which provide robust subclassing features to Visual Basic applications. If you choose to use one of these third-party controls, you'll have to consult its documentation to find out how to intercept WM_HELP and WM_CONTEXTMENU.

The sample application supplied with this book, which can be found in HHKIT\CHAP08\VBSAMPLE, implements subclassing in pure Visual Basic code by taking advantage of a feature called AddressOf. This feature is new to Visual Basic 5.0, so if you're using Visual Basic 4.0, you'll have to either upgrade to 5.0 or buy a third-party subclassing control.

Warning! Unfortunately, using the AddressOf operator in the Visual Basic debugger tends to be very unstable. It's common for Visual Basic to lock up when you hit errors in the subclassing code, when you try to single step through code, and when you stop at a breakpoint. Though not strictly necessary, using a third-party subclassing control can save you a lot of grief even in Visual Basic 5.0.

Declarations

Every form that supports "What's This" Help requires a single declaration in the General section of the form's code:

```
Private IdPairs() As HH_IDPAIR
```

HH_IDPAIR is a user-defined type declared in HTMLHELP.BAS. It's used to store the control ID map. The control ID map is populated in the Form_Load event.

Form_Load

When a form that supports "What's This" Help is first loaded, it must populate its private IdPairs() control ID map:

```
Call CollectIdPairs(Me, IdPairs)
```

The CollectIdPairs subroutine resides in HTMLHELP.BAS. It's a helper function written in Visual Basic that simply walks through all the controls on the form, looking for ones that have a non-zero WhatsThisHelpID property. It also checks to make sure that the control has a non-zero hWnd property since HTML Help doesn't support windowless controls.

You also need to subclass the form before it's displayed. If you're using a third-party subclassing control, this is probably already taken care of. With the pure Visual Basic implementation of subclassing supplied with the vbSample application, you need to make another subroutine call:

```
Call Subclass(Me)
```

The Subclass subroutine resides in SUBCLASS.BAS. It replaces the window procedure for the form with a function called SubclassWndProc. The SubclassWndProc function assumes that your form has 5 public subroutines for handling HTML Help-specific messages:

```
Public Sub OnContextMenu(hWndControl As Long)
Public Sub OnHelp(hWndControl As Long)
Public Sub OnNavComplete(phhnt As Long)
Public Sub OnTCard(wParam As Long, lParam As Long)
Public Sub OnTrack(phhnn As Long)
```

You only need to implement the first two subroutines to support "What's This" Help. The other subroutines will only be invoked for notification messages and training card messages, but it doesn't hurt to put them in your form even if you don't intend to use them.

OnHelp

Once your program is prepared for "What's This" Help support, responding to WM_HELP is simple:

```
Public Sub OnHelp(hWndControl As Long)

    Call HtmlHelp(hWndControl,_
       "MyHelp.chm::/MyPopups.txt",_
       HH_TP_HELP_WM_HELP, IdPairs(0))

End Sub
```

Ask the Help author you're working with which file names to use for your project in place of "MyHelp.chm" and "MyPopups.txt" in the above example.

If you're using a third-party subclassing control, note that the lParam argument of the WM_HELP message is a pointer to a HELPINFO structure from which you must extract the handle of the control (hItemHandle). Check the code in SubclassWndProc for an example of how to do this.

OnContextMenu

Handling the WM_CONTEXTMENU message is very similar to handling the WM_HELP message:

```
Public Sub OnContextMenu(hWndControl As Long)

    Call HtmlHelp(hWndControl,_
       "MyHelp.chm::/MyPopups.txt",_
       HH_TP_HELP_CONTEXTMENU, IdPairs(0))

End Sub
```

As always, ask the Help author you're working with which file names to use for your project in place of "MyHelp.chm" and "MyPopups.txt" in the above example.

If you're using a third-party subclassing control, note that the wParam argument of the WM_CONTEXTMENU message is the handle of the control.

Responding to the Help Button

Compared with "What's This" Help, supporting a Help button is trivial. You don't need any special declarations, or any code in Form_Load; and there's no need to subclass the form. All you need to do is assign the correct map number to the HelpContextID property of the form, and then add one line of code to the OnClick event of your Help button, for example:

```
Private Sub btnHelp_Click()

    Call HtmlHelp(0, "MyHelp.chm", HH_HELP_CONTEXT,_
      ByVal Me.HelpContextID)

End Sub
```

What you choose to pass for the first argument depends on your choice of presentation mode for the Help window. You may also want to explicitly specify a window type with the Help file name in the second argument. These issues are discussed in detail starting with the section titled "Presentation of the Help Window," on page 201.

In practice you will probably also want to centralize storage of the Help file name. The vbSample application source code, which can be found in HHKIT\CHAP08\VBSAMPLE, demonstrates one possible approach (see "Visual Basic Implementation Notes," on page 245).

What a Help Author Needs to Know and Do

Before you begin, you'll have to sit down with the application programmer and get some information about what you're documenting. The programmer will provide you with one or more header files containing map numbers and associated symbolic constants. You'll be including these header files in your HTML Help project, and using the constants to alias map numbers to specific Help topics.

The programmer will also have to explain which part of the application each map number refers to. This will be a lot easier if the programmer settles on a user-friendly naming convention for the symbolic constants and/or uses descriptive comments in the header files.

Although it's not strictly necessary, you'll probably find it easier to manage your project if there are at least two separate header files: one containing map numbers for "What's This" Help topics, and the other containing map numbers for Help button topics. It's fine to have more than two header files, but try to convince the programmer to keep map numbers for these two types of topics separate.

Help Button Topics

Help button topics are authored in exactly the same manner as any other HTML Help topic, except that they must also be aliased to a context map number. A map number gives the application an efficient way to refer to the topic. The aliasing process entails using the HTML Help Workshop (or your HTML Help authoring tool) to include the appropriate application header file(s), then creating aliases in your HTML Help project file.

Perhaps the easiest way to explain the aliasing process is with an example. The vcSample application found in the HHKIT\CHAP08\VCSAMPLE folder has a HELP subfolder in which the corresponding HTML Help project files are found. The descriptions that follow are taken directly from this project.

Let's take the specific example of the Options dialog box. The application developer indicates that a Help button topic is needed for this dialog, so you create the file OPTIONS.HTM and add it to the HTML Help project.

The next step is to include the header file containing the map numbers for the Help button topics. Open the project in HTML Help Workshop and click the **HTML Help API Information** button, found along the left side of the Workshop window.

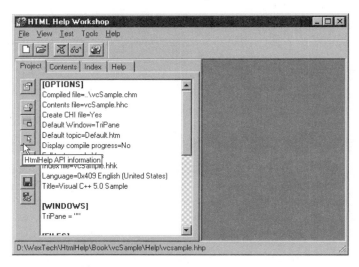

Click this button to display the HTML Help API Information dialog box.

The first tab displayed is titled Map. Click the **Header File...** button to add a header file containing map numbers for Help button topics. If you have more than one such header file, each must be added separately. Don't add header files containing map numbers for "What's This" Help yet. These are taken care of later.

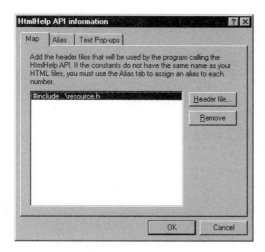

Click the "Header file..." button to add a header file containing map numbers for Help button topics.

Next, click the **Alias** tab. Click the **Add...** button to add a new alias. Type the symbolic name of the map number you want to alias. Finally, choose the name of the corresponding Help topic and click **OK**.

The Alias dialog.

After you have added an alias, you can edit or remove it with the appropriate buttons. The **Include...** button lets you keep aliases in a separate text file if you prefer to manage them yourself.

The Alias tab with a single aliased map number.

The last tab in the HtmlHelp API Information dialog box is titled **Text Pop-ups**. Click it to add "What's This" map numbers and topics to your project. Header files are added, not surprisingly, with the **Header File...** button. Note that header files must have an extension of ".H" or they will not be interpreted correctly by HTML Help. Click the **Text File...** button to add "What's This" Help topics. The format of these files is described in the next section.

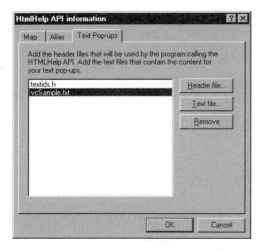

The Text Pop-ups tab, with a header file and topic file added.

"What's This" Help Topics

A text popup file is a plain text file, editable with Notepad, which contains entries that look like this:

```
.topic HIDC_Owned
Sets hWndCaller to the handle of the main window

.topic HIDC_Sibling
Sets hWndCaller to NULL

.topic HIDC_Child
Sets hWndCaller to the handle of the embedded parent
```

The keyword ".topic" introduces a new text popup topic in the file. It is followed by the topic ID, which is either a constant defined in an included header file, or a simple numeric value. On the next line is the text of the topic itself. A blank line is permitted between topics and improves readability.

You can create as many individual text popup files as you want. One possibility is to put every text popup for the entire application into a single text popup file. This may be a fine solution for small applications. At the other extreme, you could create a separate text popup file for each dialog box in the application. Of course you may choose a solution somewhere in between—the only restriction is that all text popups for a single dialog box must appear in the same text popup file.

In any case, you must inform the programmer how you have organized the text popup topics because she needs to provide the text popup file name(s) to the HTML Help API. Making this decision early will help avoid headaches later.

Frequently Asked Questions

Question: *Can I create context-sensitive Help for applications on platforms other than Windows?*

Answer: Yes and no. Of course you can write code to do whatever you want. But the HTML Help API and the context-sensitive Help features of HTML Help are only available on the Windows 95 and NT platforms.

Question: *Can I include graphics in "What's This" Help topics?*

Answer: No, "What's This" Help is implemented with plain text popups.

Question: *I'm not using C or C++. Do I still have to create header files for map numbers?*

Answer: Yes, HTML Help Workshop requires C-style header files in order to alias map numbers to topic Ids.

CHAPTER EIGHT

The HTML Help API

In this chapter we'll explore the programming interface to HTML Help, known as the HTML Help API. This interface is only available to Windows programmers, and is intended to aid the integration of HTML Help projects with Windows applications.

The HTML Help API gives Windows applications much more control over the display of Help than would be possible by simply invoking an external Help viewer—regardless of whether the viewer is an Internet browser or the standalone HTML Help viewer application HH.EXE.

For the programmer: This is where the rubber meets the road. In this chapter, you will find everything you need to know about integrating HTML Help with your Windows application.

For the Help author: You will probably want to skip most of this chapter. However, if your Help project will be integrated with an application, you may want to read some of the introductory material—in particular, the section titled "Presentation of the Help Window," on page 201.

Note: The only programming languages specifically covered by this book are Microsoft Visual C++ 5.0 and Microsoft Visual Basic 5.0. If you use a different development tool, this chapter will still be relevant—but you will probably also need to consult your development tool documentation for tips on how to call API functions declared for C/C++.

What's in this Chapter

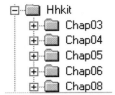

The sample code for this chapter can be found in HHKIT\CHAP08.

Presentation of the Help Window

The first time an application uses the HTML Help API to display a topic using a given window type, HTML Help will create a window for that window type and display it. Subsequent requests to display a topic with the same window type will simply activate the window, since it has already been created—unless it was closed in the meantime, in which case it will be recreated. Generally speaking, there are three different ways this window can be presented to the user: as a sibling, as an owned window, or as a child.

Help Window as a Sibling

In "Sibling" mode, HTML Help behaves in exactly the same manner as WinHelp. A separate top-level overlapped Help window is displayed alongside your application. The user may freely switch between the application and Help windows.

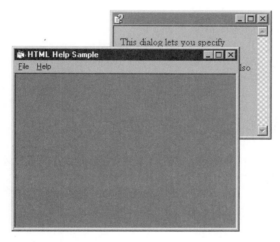

In Sibling mode, the application and Help windows overlap, with the active window on top.

Help Window as an Owned Window

In "Owned" mode, a separate top-level overlapped Help window is displayed alongside your application, as in sibling mode. The difference is that the Help window always remains on top of the application, even when the application window is active. Users may freely switch between the application and HTML Help, but the always-on-top Help window can be a nuisance for the user who wants to concentrate on the application.

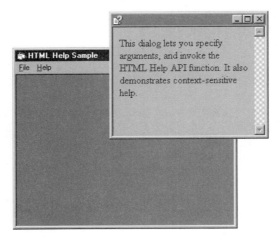

In Owned mode, the application and Help windows overlap, with the Help window always on top—even when the application window is active.

Note: Unlike Windows 95 Help "On Top" windows, an owned window does not stay on top of other applications as well. If you really want a Help window to stay on top of all other windows, you must explicitly set the WS_EX_TOPMOST extended style bit. This is not recommended.

Owned mode is most appropriate for procedural help windows, which describe a step-by-step process for a user to follow in the application. To minimize interference, owned windows should be narrow and positioned along the right-hand edge of the screen.

Help Window as a Child

In "Child" mode, HTML Help can be displayed anywhere within your application. Possibilities include "docked" along one edge of the application frame; an MDI (Multiple Document Interface) child window (as shown in the figure on the opposite page); or a "fly-out" window extension. Simply put, you can display HTML Help wherever you want.

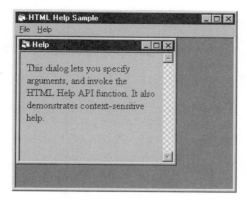

In Child mode, the Help window is completely contained within the application.

If you like the idea of a modeless sibling window, but neither Sibling mode nor Owned mode suits your needs perfectly, you can create a sibling window yourself and then display HTML Help as a child of the sibling. For example, if you want your application to manage the size and position of Help windows according to built-in rules or user preference, this would be one way to approach the implementation.

Overview of the HtmlHelp() Function

All of the HTML Help API commands are accessed through this single entry point. A simplified declaration looks like this:

VC++:   HWND HtmlHelp(HWND hwndCaller, LPCSTR pszFile,
               UINT uCommand, DWORD dwData);

VB: Declare Function HtmlHelp(ByVal hwndCaller As Long,_
               ByVal_pszFile As String, ByVal uCommand As Long,_
               dwData As Any) As Long

Argument	Description
hwndCaller	A handle to an application window, or NULL. This window handle may be used as a parent, an owner, or a message recipient for HTML Help depending on usage (see "Presentation of the Help Window," on page 201). Typically, NULL or the main window of the application would be specified.
pszFile	File to display; optionally also specifies which window type to display it in, delimited with the right angle bracket character ("*filename>window-type*"). For uCommand values that do not require a source file, pszFile may be NULL. Typically, the compiled HTML Help file for the application would be specified.

Argument	Description
uCommand	Specifies the action to perform (see "HTML Help API Commands," on page 213).
dwData	Specifies additional data depending on the uCommand value. For C++, you will typically have to cast this data to DWORD to prevent compiler errors. For Visual Basic, you must pass the correct data type or else you will run the risk of a GPF.

The return value of HtmlHelp() is usually the handle of the HTML Help window displayed/affected by the command, or NULL if the command fails. Unfortunately this means that, at best, you can only determine the success or failure of a given call—you cannot easily determine the *cause* of a failure. Occasionally, you can get a clue by using the HTML Help Messages command on the View menu of the HTML Help Workshop. For this to work, the HTML Help Workshop must be running at the same time as your application.

A Simple Example

The calls below illustrate the code you might want to run in response to the "Help Contents" command in your application:

VC++:
```
HtmlHelp(AfxGetMainWnd()->GetSafeHwnd(), "MyHelp.chm",
    HH_DISPLAY_TOPIC, 0);
```

VB:
```
Call HtmlHelp(Me.hWnd, "MyHelp.chm",_
    HH_DISPLAY_TOPIC, ByVal 0&)
```

In both cases, the handle of the application's main window is provided, and the return value is ignored. The last argument is the topic ID, which can be specified as NULL or an empty string to display the default topic ("/default.htm" unless otherwise specified in the HTML Help project file).

If the file "MyHelp.chm" is contained in the current directory or the Windows\Help directory, the file will be opened immediately; otherwise the user will be prompted to locate the file. Once it has been located, HTML Help remembers the appropriate folder, and the user will not be prompted again unless the file is moved. As a convenience to your users, you may wish to provide a full pathname for the file.

Comparison with the WinHelp() Function

If you've ever used the WinHelp() function, then the HtmlHelp() function will look very familiar. The HtmlHelp API was purposely designed to resemble the WinHelp API in order to make it easier to convert existing applications. Many WinHelp API commands have close equivalents in the HtmlHelp API, although some do not.

For detailed information on the use of each command listed under "HtmlHelp Equivalent," refer to "HTML Help API Commands," on page 213.

WinHelp Command	HtmlHelp Equivalent
HELP_COMMAND	None. You are expected to use scripting, ActiveX controls, and Java applets in place of WinHelp macros.
HELP_CONTENTS	HH_DISPLAY_TOPIC, with NULL specified for the topic ID, will display the default topic.
HELP_CONTEXT	HH_HELP_CONTEXT
HELP_CONTEXTMENU	HH_TP_HELP_CONTEXTMENU is the equivalent command, but it does not behave in exactly the same manner.
HELP_CONTEXTPOPUP	HH_DISPLAY_TEXT_POPUP is the closest equivalent, but it does not currently allow you to display a Help topic—it only supports display of unformatted text supplied by the application.
HELP_FINDER	None. Although there is a command defined called HH_HELP_FINDER, it is the same as HH_DISPLAY_TOPIC. The closest equivalent of the WinHelp Finder dialog is the left pane of an HTML Help tri-pane window.
HELP_FORCEFILE	None.
HELP_HELPONHELP	None.
HELP_INDEX	Same as HELP_CONTENTS.
HELP_KEY	HH_KEYWORD_LOOKUP
HELP_MULTIKEY	HH_ALINK_LOOKUP is similar, but only provides access to a single alternate keyword table.
HELP_PARTIALKEY	None.
HELP_QUIT	HH_CLOSE_ALL
HELP_SETCONTENTS	None.
HELP_SETINDEX	None.
HELP_SETPOPUP_POS	Integrated with HH_DISPLAY_TEXT_POPUP.
HELP_SETWINPOS	No equivalent. However, you could use HH_GET_WIN_HANDLE to obtain a handle to the Help window and reposition it using standard Win32 API functions.

WinHelp Command	HtmlHelp Equivalent
HELP_TCARD	None.
HELP_TCARD_DATA	None.
HELP_TCARD_OTHER_CALLER	None.
HELP_WM_HELP	HH_TP_HELP_WM_HELP

Calling HtmlHelp() from Visual C++

In order to get the declarations for the HTML Help API, you must include the file HTMLHELP.H somewhere in your project. Since this file will (presumably) seldom change, a good place to include it is in the precompiled header for your application—STDAFX.H, by default. You will also need to tell Visual C++ where to find the file. One way to do this is to modify the Include search path via the Directories tab on the Tools | Options dialog box in Developer Studio. HTMLHELP.H is installed with the HTML Help Workshop, by default in the folder C:\PROGRAM FILES\HTML HELP WORKSHOP\INCLUDE.

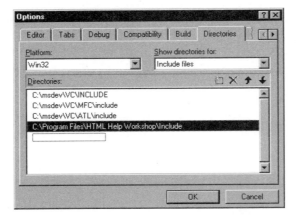

Add the HTML Help Workshop Include directory to the Include files path.

Note: In the unlikely event that you're using a strict ANSI C compiler, you will not be able to include HTMLHELP.H directly because it contains C++ comment delimiters ("//"). Your choices would be to edit HTMLHELP.H, change your compiler options, or switch to C++.

Which Library?

The HTML Help Workshop ships with two different libraries that you can link with. HHCTRL.LIB is an import library for HHCTRL.OCX, which is the DLL containing the HtmlHelp() API. Linking with HHCTRL.LIB will cause HHCTRL.OCX to be loaded when your application starts up. HTMLHELP.LIB is a static library with actual code in it, rather than a simple import library.

Machines that have Internet Explorer 4.01 installed typically load HHCTRL.OCX significantly faster.

So what does this code do? When you call HtmlHelp() for the first time, HHCTRL.OCX will be loaded for you. This defers some processing until the user asks for help, which can reduce the startup time required by your application. On the other hand, it means the user may see a noticeable delay the first time help is requested. This could be annoying, particularly for "What's This" help, which the user expects to pop up immediately.

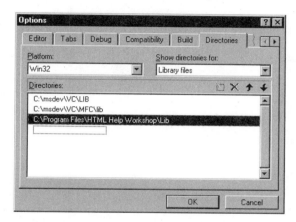

Add the HTML Help Workshop Lib directory to the Library files path.

If you choose to link with either HHCTRL.LIB or HTMLHELP.LIB, you will have to let Visual C++ know where to find these files. The Library search path can be specified in the same manner as the Include search path. The libraries are installed with HTML Help Workshop, by default in the folder C:\PROGRAM FILES\HTML HELP WORKSHOP\LIB. To link directly with one of these libraries, just add HHCTRL.LIB or HTMLHELP.LIB to the "Object/library modules" list on the Link tab of the Project Settings dialog box.

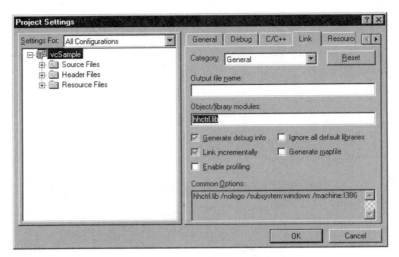

Add either HTMLHELP.LIB or HHCTRL.LIB to the Object/library modules list.

If you're using a
development tool
other than Visual
C++, you probably
won't be able to link
with HTMLHELP.LIB.

If you choose to link with HTMLHELP.LIB, you may find that you get warnings like this:

```
LINK : warning LNK4098: defaultlib "LIBCMT" conflicts with
use of other libs; use /NODEFAULTLIB:library
```

To eliminate this warning, you can do as the message suggests and disable default library search. However, this can be rather inconvenient because you then have to explicitly specify every single library you want to link with. The other options are to ignore the warning, link with HHCTRL.LIB, or load HHCTRL.OCX manually.

Manually Loading HHCTRL.OCX

If you want finer control over when the performance hit occurs for loading HHCTRL.OCX and all of its dependent DLLs, you can use the LoadLibrary() API function to manually load HHCTRL.OCX, and GetProcAddress() to obtain a pointer to the HtmlHelp function.

If you decide to use LoadLibrary() and GetProcAddress(), you will soon find out that there is no function called HtmlHelp() exported from HHCTRL.OCX. In fact there are two flavors of the API function: HtmlHelpA() for ANSI applications, and HtmlHelpW() for Unicode applications. In practice you will probably almost always use HtmlHelpA(). Symbolic constants are provided for the ordinals of both functions in HTMLHELP.H; you can arrange for your application to build successfully as either ANSI or Unicode with a little bit of additional preprocessor code:

```
#ifdef UNICODE
#define ATOM_HTMLHELP_API ATOM_HTMLHELP_API_UNICODE
#else
#define ATOM_HTMLHELP_API ATOM_HTMLHELP_API_ANSI
#endif
```

Loading of the OCX is straightforward:

```
HINSTANCE hInstanceHtmlHelp = NULL;
hInstanceHtmlHelp = LoadLibrary("hhctrl.ocx");
```

To obtain a pointer to the appropriate flavor of the HtmlHelp() function, it's helpful to first declare a type definition for it:

```
typedef HWND (WINAPI *PFNHTMLHELP)(HWND hwndCaller,
  LPCTSTR pszFile, UINT uCommand, DWORD dwData);
```

Actually getting the function pointer is, again, straightforward:

```
PFNHTMLHELP pfnHtmlHelp = NULL;
pfnHtmlHelp =
  (PFNHTMLHELP)GetProcAddress(hInstanceHtmlHelp,
  ATOM_HTMLHELP_API);
```

Calling through the function pointer is almost identical to the call you would use with an implicit link:

```
pfnHtmlHelp(NULL, "MyHelp.chm", HH_DISPLAY_TOPIC, 0);
```

Of course, replace "MyHelp.chm" in this example with the name of your Help file.

And finally, if you want to clean up after you're finished using HTML Help, you can free the library loaded earlier:

```
FreeLibrary(hInstanceHtmlHelp);
```

Be very careful that all HTML Help windows have been destroyed before you call FreeLibrary, or else you are likely to crash your application. You can use the HH_CLOSE_ALL command for this purpose.

These code fragments are for illustration only—in a real application you would naturally include error checking.

Calling HtmlHelp() from Visual Basic

When you install HTML Help, supporting files for Visual C++ are installed along with HTML Help Workshop. There are no equivalent files installed for use with Visual Basic; however, you are free to use the following files that comprise the sample code for this book:

File	Description
HTMLHELP.BAS	A straight translation of the constants, data structures, and function declarations in HTMLHELP.H plus some helper functions.
SUBCLASS.BAS	A pure Visual Basic implementation of subclassing, to enable implementation of context-sensitive Help, notification message handling, and training cards.
SUBCLASS.CLS	A helper class for the functions in SUBCLASS.BAS.
WIN32API.BAS	Declarations of additional Win32 API items used by the sample code.

Some of the declarations in HTMLHELP.BAS and SUBCLASS.BAS depend on declarations in WIN32API.BAS—for example, the HH_POPUP user-defined type declared in HTMLHELP.BAS contains a POINTAPI and a RECT, which are both declared in WIN32API.BAS. If you're already declaring Win32 API functions in your application, you may want to just copy the declarations you need from WIN32API.BAS rather than including it in your project. This will help avoid duplicate declarations.

The "real" declaration of HtmlHelp()—as opposed to the simplified one presented earlier in this chapter—looks like this:

```
Declare Function HtmlHelp Lib "hhctrl.ocx" Alias_
    "HtmlHelpA" (ByVal hwndCaller As Long, ByVal pszFile_
    As String, ByVal uCommand As HH_COMMAND, dwData As_
    Any) As Long
```

As you can see, this refers to the ANSI version of the HtmlHelp() function exported by HHCTRL.OCX ("HtmlHelpA"). If you wanted to call the Unicode version ("HtmlHelpW"), you would have to build a type library, which is well beyond the scope of this book.

One difference you may notice between the simplified and actual declarations is that uCommand is declared as type HH_COMMAND. This is an enumerated type found in HTMLHELP.BAS, which has the advantage of enabling a nifty feature in the Visual Basic code editor to prompt you for possible values, as shown on the next page.

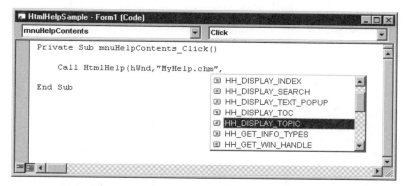

The Visual Basic code editor prompts for uCommand values as you type.

Note: Enumerated types are a new language feature introduced in version 5.0 of Visual Basic. You can theoretically call the HtmlHelp() API from version 4.0 of Visual Basic by editing HTMLHELP.BAS to change the enumerated constants to plain Global Const declarations, and the enumerated type arguments to Long. This has not been tested.

Using HHCTRL.OCX

It's natural to think that you might be able to include HHCTRL.OCX directly in a Visual Basic project and put an instance of the control on a form. Unfortunately, HHCTRL.OCX, while it does contain an ActiveX control, is only designed for use with Internet Explorer.

The first time you call HtmlHelp() from your application, there may be a noticeable delay while the Visual Basic runtime loads HHCTRL.OCX and all of its dependent DLLs. You can use LoadLibrary() to control when this delay occurs if you wish.

Type Safety

The HtmlHelp() function is not really very well suited for use with Visual Basic, mainly because of the polymorphic—and hence, not type-safe—nature of its dwData argument. For starters, you must always pass the correct data type, or else risk crashing your application. It's also easy to forget that for String and Long values, you must explicitly include the ByVal modifier. If you forget to include the ByVal, you may get strange behavior. Furthermore, if you're passing a user-defined type such as HH_POPUP and you include ByVal by mistake, your application will probably crash.

To make matters worse, some parts of the HTML Help API use pointers to pointers—a paradigm not supported by Visual Basic. For example, it's only possible to use the HH_GET_WIN_TYPE command with some fairly ugly kludged code.

Some of the lack of type safety could be partially overcome by creating multiple declarations for the HtmlHelp() function, each typed specifically for certain commands. For example:

```
Declare Function HtmlHelpLong Lib "hhctrl.ocx" Alias_
    "HtmlHelpA" (ByVal hwndCaller As Long, ByVal_
    pszFile As String, ByVal uCommand As HH_COMMAND,_
    ByVal dwData As Long) As Long
```

This declaration would be suitable for use with any command that requires a Long for its dwData argument, for example HH_HELP_CONTEXT. But you still have to match up the right call with each command, so it's not much of an improvement.

A better workaround would be to wrap the entire API in a Visual Basic Class module which has a properly typed method for each HtmlHelp command.

Ideally, HTML Help would ship with a type-safe COM interface to make it friendlier to Visual Basic and other programming languages besides C/C++. In fact this is a planned enhancement for a future version of HTML Help.

Choosing a Presentation Mode

There are three different ways to present a Help window, as discussed in the section titled "Presentation of the Help Window," on page 201. The presentation mode for a given window type is established the first time you display a Help topic using that window type, and can only be changed by destroying and recreating the window.

A Help topic can be directly displayed using either of two HTML Help API commands: HH_DISPLAY_TOPIC or HH_HELP_CONTEXT. These are discussed in detail in the section titled "HTML Help API Commands," on page 213. In both cases, there are two factors that influence the presentation mode: the presence or absence of the WS_CHILD window style in the definition of the window type, and the value of the hwndCaller argument passed to the HtmlHelp() API function.

Sibling Mode

To implement Sibling mode presentation, specify NULL for hwndCaller, and use either the default window type, or any window type that does not include the WS_CHILD window style.

Owned Mode

To implement Owned mode presentation, specify your main application window handle for hwndCaller, and use either the default window type, or any window type that does not include the WS_CHILD window style.

Child Mode

To implement Child mode presentation, specify the parent window for hwndCaller, and use any window type that includes the WS_CHILD window style. But be warned: Defining window types with WS_CHILD through the HTML Help Workshop is not very flexible because you cannot turn off the default styles, which include a title bar and resizable border. You may find that you need to use the HH_SET_WIN_TYPE command to create a window type suitable for use in Child mode (see "HH_SET_WIN_TYPE," on page 222).

HTML Help API Commands

Each of the following sections describes a single HTML Help API command, invoked by calling the HtmlHelp() function with the uCommand argument set to the corresponding constant.

Only the commands implemented in the current version of HTML Help are documented here. There are several additional commands declared in HTMLHELP.H which may be implemented in future versions of HTML Help.

HH_ALINK_LOOKUP

Argument	Description
hwndCaller	Handle of the parent or owner window for the HTML Help window. May be NULL to cause the HTML Help window to be displayed in Sibling mode.
pszFile	Pathname of a compiled HTML Help file. This path may be local or it may be a URL.
dwData	A pointer to an HH_AKLINK.

This command is identical to HH_KEYWORD_LOOKUP except that it searches the alternate keyword index instead of the primary keyword index. Alternate keywords (also known as "ALink Names") are inserted directly into topic files by the Help author using the "Edit-Compiler information" command found in the HTML editor of the HTML Help Workshop.

For more information on invoking HH_ALINK_LOOKUP, refer to "HH_KEYWORD_LOOKUP," on page 220.

HH_CLOSE_ALL

Argument	Description
hwndCaller	Must be NULL for Visual C++, or 0 (zero) for Visual Basic.
pszFile	Must be NULL for Visual C++, or vbNullString for Visual Basic.
dwData	Must be zero.

The HH_CLOSE_ALL command destroys all HTML Help windows associated with the current process. As a byproduct, all currently open compiled HTML Help files are closed.

If you explicitly loaded HHCTRL.OCX with LoadLibrary, you can safely call FreeLibrary after invoking HH_CLOSE_ALL.

Example Code

The following Visual Basic code fragment invokes the HH_CLOSE_ALL command.

```
Call HtmlHelp(0, vbNullString, HH_CLOSE_ALL, 0)
```

HH_DISPLAY_TEXT_POPUP

Argument	Description
hwndCaller	Handle of the top-level parent window over which the popup should appear.
pszFile	Must be NULL for Visual C++, or vbNullString for Visual Basic.
dwData	A pointer to an HH_POPUP.

This command displays a text popup ("What's This" Help). Ironically, it can't be used to display a text popup *topic*. HH_DISPLAY_TEXT_POPUP can be used to display strings supplied by the caller or stored as a Win32 resource; while text popup *topics* stored in a compiled HTML Help file can only be displayed indirectly, via HH_TP_HELP_WM_HELP.

Since this command can't be used to display text popup topics, you might wonder what good it is. There are a couple of possible scenarios in which you may find it useful. One would be if you have text popups for which the content is dynamically determined at runtime, since it's not practical to modify compiled text popup topics. Another possibility is that you have windowless controls or other unique items for which you want to provide "What's This" Help. The HH_TP_HELP_WM_HELP command is limited to providing help for items that have their own child windows.

HH_POPUP

The HH_POPUP data structure is used only by the HH_DISPLAY_TEXT_POPUP command. All of its members are filled in by the caller. HtmlHelp() does not return any data in this structure.

Member	Description
cbStruct	Must be set to the size of the HH_POPUP data structure.
hinst	Instance handle of a module containing string resources, or NULL if a string is supplied in pszText.
idString	ID of a string resource, or zero if a string is supplied in pszText.
pszText	String to display, or NULL if a string resource is specified with hinst and idString.
pt	Top-center position of the popup window, in screen coordinates.
clrForeground	Color of the popup text, or –1 to use the default (black).
clrBackground	Color of the popup background, or –1 to use the default (pale yellow).
rcMargins	Space between popup window border and popup text, or –1 for defaults.
pszFont	A font specification in the format: [facename][,[point size][,[char set][,[BOLD ITALIC UNDERLINE]]]]

You can choose to display a string directly supplied in the HH_POPUP or from a module containing string resources. If you want to specify a string resource, set the hinst member to the instance handle of the module containing the string resources, the idString member to the identifier of the string, and the pszText member to NULL. If you want to display a string directly, set both hinst and idString to zero, and assign the string pointer to pszText.

The pt member determines where the popup should be displayed. This would typically be a position near the item for which "What's This" Help was requested.

The pszFont member allows you to specify the font used in the popup window. To accept the default, Visual C++ users should assign NULL and Visual Basic users should assign vbNullString. To accept defaults for only some parts of the font specification, leave them blank in the string. For example, to select a bold, italicized Arial font with the default size and character set, you would assign "Arial,,,BOLD ITALIC".

The choices for the "char set" portion of the pszFont member may not be obvious. To get an idea of the possibilities, click the Pop-up Attributes command on the Test menu of the HTML Help Workshop, then click the Change button for the Font selection.

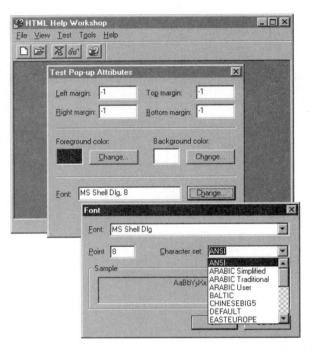

The HTML Help Workshop displays the "char set" options for pszFont.

Example Code

The following Visual Basic code fragment illustrates displaying a text string at the current cursor location, using default colors and margins, with a 10 point MS Sans Serif font.

```
Dim hhp As HH_POPUP
hhp.cbStruct = Len(hhp)
hhp.clrBackground = -1
hhp.clrForeground = -1
hhp.rcMargins.Left = -1
hhp.rcMargins.Top = -1
hhp.rcMargins.Bottom = -1
hhp.rcMargins.Right = -1
Call GetCursorPos(hhp.pt)
hhp.pszText = "A popup text message."
hhp.pszFont = "MS Sans Serif,10"
Call HtmlHelp(0, vbNullString, HH_DISPLAY_TEXT_POPUP, hhp)
```

HH_DISPLAY_TOPIC

Argument	Description
hwndCaller	Handle of the parent or owner window for the HTML Help window. May be NULL to cause the HTML Help window to be displayed in Sibling mode.
pszFile	Pathname of an HTML file or compiled HTML Help file. This path may be local or it may be a URL. To specify a particular window type in which to display the topic, append the window type name with a right angle bracket delimiter ("*filename>window-type*").
dwData	If pszFile refers to a compiled HTML Help file, dwData may point to a filename within it; if dwData is zero, the default topic within the compiled file is assumed. If pszFile refers to a plain HTML file (that is, not a compiled HTML Help file), dwData is ignored and should be set to zero.

The most fundamental HTML Help API command, HH_DISPLAY_TOPIC displays a Help topic using the default window type or a specified window type.

Window Type

If you want to display the topic in a specific window type, you must append the name of the window type to the pathname of the HTML file or compiled HTML Help file in the pszFile argument, using a right angle bracket as a delimiter. For example, if you supply "MyHelp.chm>MyWindow" for the pszFile argument, HTML Help will attempt to display the topic in the "MyWindow" window type. This window type must already have been defined either as part of a compiled help project or with the HH_SET_WIN_TYPE command.

If you do not specify a window type, HTML Help will use the default window type specified in the HTML Help project file. In either case, the window will be created if it does not already exist. It is only when the window is first created that the hwndCaller argument becomes relevant. For subsequent calls after the window has been created, hwndCaller is ignored.

Example Code

The following Visual Basic code fragment illustrates displaying the default topic of the compiled Help file "MyHelp.chm" in Sibling mode, using the window type named "Main."

```
Call HtmlHelp(0, "MyHelp.chm>Main", HH_DISPLAY_TOPIC, ByVal 0&)
```

HH_GET_WIN_HANDLE

Argument	Description
hwndCaller	Must be NULL for Visual C++, or 0 (zero) for Visual Basic.
pszFile	Must be NULL for Visual C++, or vbNullString for Visual Basic.
dwData	The name of the window type.

The return value of HtmlHelp() when using the HH_GET_WIN_HANDLE command is a handle to the window created for the window type named by the dwData argument. If no such window exists, the return value is zero.

Example Code

The following Visual Basic code fragment illustrates obtaining the handle for the window type named "Fred."

```
Dim hWndFred As Long
hWndFred = HtmlHelp(0, vbNullString, HH_GET_WIN_HANDLE, ByVal
"Fred")
```

HH_GET_WIN_TYPE

Argument	Description
hwndCaller	Must be NULL for Visual C++, or 0 (zero) for Visual Basic.
pszFile	The name of the window type for which information is desired, prefixed by the name of the compiled HTML Help file in which the window type is defined, and delimited by a right angle bracket. For example, "MyHelp.chm>MyWindow" selects the window type named "MyWindow" in the compiled Help file MyHelp.chm. You may optionally omit the name of the compiled Help file, e.g. ">MyWindow". The latter syntax will only be successful if you have already displayed a topic from the compiled help file, or if you created the window type at runtime using HH_SET_WIN_TYPE.
dwData	A pointer to *a pointer to* an HH_WINTYPE.

The return value of HtmlHelp() when using the HH_GET_WIN_TYPE command is a handle to the window created for the type named by the pszFile argument. If no such window type has been defined either via HH_SET_WIN_TYPE or within an open compiled HTML Help file, the return value is –1. If the window type has been defined, but doesn't currently have a window created for it, the return value is zero.

This command is unlike most Win32 API functions that return information. Rather than filling in a data structure owned by the application, it returns a pointer to a data structure owned by HTML Help. You must not modify any members of this data structure; if you want to change the properties of a window type, use the HH_SET_WIN_TYPE command instead.

For a detailed description of the HH_WINTYPE data structure, refer to the section titled "HH_WINTYPE," on page 222.

Note: Because of the fact that this command deals directly with pointers, it's highly unsuitable for use with Visual Basic. If you're really adventurous, you can supply a Long variable by reference for the dwData argument. The HH_WINTYPE pointer value will be stored in the Long variable, which you can then use to copy the contents of the data structure into a locally declared user-defined type. There is a helper function called GetWinTypeFromPointer supplied in HTMLHELP.BAS for this purpose.

Example Code

The following Visual C++ code fragment illustrates obtaining information for the window type named "Wilma."

```
HH_WINTYPE *phhwtWilma = NULL;
HWND hWndWilma = HtmlHelp(NULL, "MyHelp.chm>Wilma",
HH_GET_WIN_TYPE, (DWORD)&phhwtWilma);
```

HH_HELP_CONTEXT

Argument	Description
hwndCaller	Handle of the parent or owner window for the HTML Help window. May be NULL to cause the HTML Help window to be displayed in sibling mode.
pszFile	Pathname of a compiled HTML Help file. This may be a local pathname or a URL. To specify a particular window type in which to display the topic, append the window type name with a right angle bracket delimiter (*"filename>window-type"*).
dwData	A context map number. This number must be aliased in the compiled help file.

The HH_HELP_CONTEXT command is very similar to the HH_DISPLAY_TOPIC command; but instead of referring to the topic by its name, you use a context map number.

For more information, read the description of the HH_DISPLAY_TOPIC command, in particular the section titled "Window Type," on page 217. For a complete discussion of context-sensitive Help, refer to "Understanding and Creating Context-Sensitive HTML Help," on page 175.

Warning! The current version of HTML Help doesn't pay any attention to the window type you append to pszFile. Topics displayed via HH_HELP_CONTEXT are always displayed in the default window. This will be fixed in a future release.

Example Code

The following Visual C++ code fragment illustrates displaying the topic mapped to the number represented by the symbolic constant IDH_MyTopic in MyHelp.chm, using sibling mode, in the window type named "Main."

```
HtmlHelp(NULL, "MyHelp.chm>Main", HH_HELP_CONTEXT,
    IDH_MyTopic);
```

HH_KEYWORD_LOOKUP

Argument	Description
hwndCaller	Handle of the parent or owner window for the HTML Help window. May be NULL to cause the HTML Help window to be displayed in Sibling mode.
pszFile	Pathname of a compiled HTML Help file. This path may be local or it may be a URL.
dwData	A pointer to an HH_AKLINK.

The HH_KEYWORD_LOOKUP command searches the keyword index of the compiled HTML Help file specified via the pszFile argument. The keywords to search for, and the action to take in the event that no match is found, are specified via the HH_AKLINK data structure passed via the dwData argument.

HH_AKLINK

The HH_AKLINK data structure is used only by the HH_ALINK_LOOKUP and HH_KEYWORD_LOOKUP commands. All of its members are filled in by the caller. HtmlHelp() does not return any data in this structure.

Member	Description
cbStruct	Must be set to the size of the HH_AKLINK data structure.
fReserved	Must be set to zero.
pszKeywords	One or more keywords, delimited by semicolons.
pszUrl	If fIndexOnFail is FALSE, indicates the URL of a topic to display in the event of failure to find a matching keyword. Unlike most URLs passed to HtmlHelp, you cannot append the window type with an angle bracket delimiter; you must use the pszWindow member instead.
pszMsgText	If fIndexOnFail is FALSE, and pszUrl is NULL, specifies the text

Member	Description
	of a message box to display in the event of failure to find a matching topic. Used in conjunction with pszMsgTitle.
pszMsgTitle	If fIndexOnFail is FALSE, and pszUrl is NULL, specifies the title of a message box to display in the event of failure to find a matching topic. Used in conjunction with pszMsgText.
pszWindow	Specifies the window in which to display the topic found as a result of the keyword search, the non-found topic specified with pszUrl, or the Index tab if fIndexOnFail is TRUE.
fIndexOnFail	If TRUE, the Index tab of pszWindow is displayed when the keyword search fails to find any matching topics.

If the keyword search is successful, the matching topic is displayed in the window type specified via the pszWindow member of the HH_AKLINK structure.

If the keyword search does not find any matching topics, the action taken depends on the values of the other members of the HH_AKLINK structure:

- First, if fIndexOnFail is TRUE, then the Index tab is displayed in the left pane of the window type specified with pszWindow. You must ensure that this window type is a tri-pane window.

- If fIndexOnFail is FALSE, HtmlHelp next checks the pszUrl member. If it is not NULL (vbNullString in Visual Basic), its value is interpreted as the URL of a topic to display, again using pszWindow as the window type. You can use this technique to author your own topic indicating the failure of the keyword search.

- If fIndexOnFail is FALSE, and pszUrl is NULL, HtmlHelp finally attempts to display a simple message box using the pszMsgTitle member for the caption, and the pszMsgText member for the actual message.

Note: In the current version of HTML Help, keyword searches are case-sensitive. For example, if you have a keyword "Options" in the Help file, it won't be found by a search for "options." One possible workaround for this is to convert all keywords to lowercase in the Help file, then convert all keyword searches to lowercase. Case-sensitivity may be removed in a future release of HTML Help.

Example Code

The following Visual Basic code fragment illustrates searching the compiled file RHYMES.CHM for either of the keywords "Jack" or "Jill."

```
Dim hhak as HH_AKLINK
hhak.cbStruct = Len(hhak)
hhak.pszKeywords = "Jack;Jill"
hhak.fIndexOnFail = True
hhak.pszWindow = "TriPane"
Call HtmlHelp(frmMain.hWnd, "rhymes.chm", HH_KEYWORD_LOOKUP,
hhak)
```

HH_SET_WIN_TYPE

Argument	Description
hwndCaller	Must be NULL for Visual C++, or 0 (zero) for Visual Basic.
pszFile	Must be NULL for Visual C++, or vbNullString for Visual Basic.
dwData	A pointer to an HH_WINTYPE.

This command allows you to create or modify window types at runtime. This means you are not restricted to using window types defined by the Help author in a compiled HTML Help file. In fact you can use window types to display plain HTML files—no compilation is required if you choose to create the window types at runtime.

When modifying existing window types, be warned that some changes will not take effect unless the window is destroyed and recreated. In fact, some attributes cannot be changed at all. If you can't get the effect you want by modifying an existing window type, consider creating a similarly defined type with a different name.

Note: The namespace for window types consists of the union of the names of all window types created by the current process, and the names of all window types defined in compiled HTML Help files opened by the current process. In the event of a name collision, the first window type referenced will be used. For example, if you open "MyFile1.chm" with window type "Deluxe", then open "MyFile2.chm" which also has a window type named "Deluxe," the one from MyFile1.chm will be used.

Each process has its own window type namespace. In no event will window types from another process be visible in the namespace of the current process. In other words, you do not need to worry about disturbing other applications when you manipulate window types.

HH_WINTYPE

The HH_WINTYPE data structure is used by both the HH_GET_WIN_TYPE and HH_SET_WIN_TYPE commands. It is somewhat intimidating because of the large number of members, but in practice you probably will only have to deal with a small subset of its potential complexity. One approach to avoiding such headaches is to let the Help author define window types at compile time using the HTML Help Workshop whenever possible.

In the following member descriptions, IN means that the member may be used by HH_SET_WIN_TYPE, OUT means that the member may be used by HH_GET_WIN_TYPE, and IN/OUT means that the member may be used by both commands.

Member	Description
`cbStruct`	IN. Must be set to the size of the HH_WINTYPE data structure.
`fUniCodeStrings`	IN. If you set this member to TRUE, all string members of the HH_WINTYPE will be treated as Unicode; otherwise they will be treated as ANSI. This behavior is independent of whether you are calling the Unicode or ANSI version of the HtmlHelp() API function (HtmlHelpW and HtmlHelpA respectively). Strings returned via HH_GET_WIN_TYPE are always ANSI.
`pszType`	IN/OUT. Name of the window type.
`fsValidMembers`	IN. A set of bit-flags describing which of the other members of the HH_WINTYPE should be changed. See the HHWIN_PARAM table, on page 226, for possible values.
`fsWinProperties`	IN/OUT. A set of bit-flags describing the properties of the window type. See the HHWIN_PROP table, on page 226, for possible values.
`pszCaption`	IN/OUT. Specifies the caption to display in the title bar of the window type. If the HHWIN_PROP_CHANGE_TITLE property is set, this member is ignored.
`dwStyles`	IN/OUT. A set of bit-flags specifying the styles to use when creating the window. These bits are documented with CreateWindow in the Win32 API. Unless the HHWIN_PROP_NODEF_STYLES property is set, these style bits are combined with the default style bits of WS_VISIBLE, WS_CLIPSIBLINGS, WS_BORDER, WS_DLGFRAME, WS_SYSMENU, WS_THICKFRAME, WS_MINIMIZEBOX, and WS_MAXIMIZEBOX.
`dwExStyles`	IN/OUT. A set of bit-flags specifying the extended styles to use when creating the window. These bits are documented with CreateWindowEx in the Win32 API. Unless the HHWIN_PROP_NODEF_EXSTYLES property is set, these style bits are combined with the default style bits of WS_EX_WINDOWEDGE and WS_EX_APPWINDOW.

Member	Description
rcWindowPos	IN/OUT. Specifies the size and position of the window. When setting, individual members of the rcWindowPos RECT structure may be set to –1 in order to leave those members unchanged. For example, setting left and top to zero while setting right and bottom to –1 would cause the window to be moved to the upper-left corner of its parent but keep the same size.
nShowState	IN. Specifies the initial show state of the window. Possible values are documented with ShowWindow in the Win32 API.
hwndHelp	OUT. Handle of the help window. This is the same as the return value of the HtmlHelp() function for any command that displays a topic in the window.
hwndCaller	OUT. Handle of the caller. This is the same as the hwndCaller argument passed to HtmlHelp() when the window is first created as a result of displaying a topic.
paInfoTypes	IN. This member is not used in HTML Help version 1.1, and should be set to NULL.

The remaining members of the HH_WINTYPE structure are only valid for tri-pane windows. A tri-pane window is specified by setting the HHWIN_PROP_TRI_PANE bit in the fsWinProperties member.

Member	Description
hwndToolBar	OUT. Handle of the window containing the toolbar buttons.
hwndNavigation	OUT. Handle of the navigation window (containing the table of contents, index, etc.).
hwndHTML	OUT. Handle of the HTML window pane which acts as a host for SHDOCVW.DLL.
iNavWidth	IN/OUT. Specifies the width of the navigation pane when the tri-pane window is expanded.
rcHTML	OUT. Size and position of the window referenced by the hwndHTML member.
pszToc	IN. Specifies the file or URL to use for the table of contents.
pszIndex	IN. Specifies the file or URL to use for the index.
pszFile	IN. Specifies the file or URL to display in the HTML pane.
pszHome	IN/OUT. Specifies the file or URL to display in the HTML pane when the Home button is clicked.
fsToolBarFlags	IN. A set of bit-flags which specify the buttons to be displayed in the toolbar. See the HHWIN_BUTTON table below for possible values.

Member	Description
fNotExpanded	IN/OUT. Specifies whether or not the navigation pane should be expanded.
curNavType	This member is ignored.
tabpos	IN/OUT. Specifies where the tabs should be placed in the navigation pane. See the HHWIN_NAVTAB table below for possible values.
idNotify	IN. Specifies the ID to pass as the wParam argument for WM_NOTIFY messages. You must also set the HHWIN_PARAM_PROPERTIES bit in the fsValidMembers member, and the HHWIN_PROP_TRACKING bit in the fsWinProperties member. See the section "Notification Messages," on page 230, for details.
tabOrder	This member is ignored.
cHistory	This member is ignored.
pszJump1	IN. Specifies the text to display on the Jump1 button. To display the Jump1 button, you must include the HHWIN_PARAM_TB_FLAGS bit in the fsValidMembers member, and the HHWIN_BUTTON_JUMP1 bit in the fsToolBarFlags member. In addition, you must also set the pszUrlJump1 member.
pszJump2	IN. Specifies the text to display on the Jump2 button. To display the Jump2 button, you must include the HHWIN_PARAM_TB_FLAGS bit in the fsValidMembers member, and the HHWIN_BUTTON_JUMP2 bit in the fsToolBarFlags member. In addition, you must also set the pszUrlJump2 member.
pszUrlJump1	IN. Specifies the URL of the topic to display when the Jump1 button is clicked. You must also set the pszJump1 member.
pszUrlJump2	IN. Specifies the URL of the topic to display when the Jump2 button is clicked. You must also set the pszJump2 member.
rcMinSize	This member is ignored.
cbInfoTypes	This member is not used in HTML Help version 1.1, and should be set to zero.

Bits that may be set in the fsValidMembers member are shown in the following table. Each bit corresponds to a single member of the HH_WINTYPE structure that will be examined by HtmlHelp when invoking the HH_SET_WIN_TYPE command. Members which do not have a corresponding bit in fsValidMembers are examined on every call to HH_SET_WIN_TYPE. These include idNotify, hwndCaller, and pszCaption. You may find it helpful to call HH_GET_WIN_TYPE before calling HH_SET_WIN_TYPE in order to obtain appropriate defaults for such members.

HHWIN_PARAM bit value	Corresponding member
HHWIN_PARAM_PROPERTIES	fsWinProperties
HHWIN_PARAM_STYLES	dwStyles
HHWIN_PARAM_EXSTYLES	dwExStyles
HHWIN_PARAM_RECT	rcWindowPos
HHWIN_PARAM_NAV_WIDTH	iNavWidth
HHWIN_PARAM_SHOWSTATE	nShowState
HHWIN_PARAM_INFOTYPES	painfoTypes (ignored)
HHWIN_PARAM_TB_FLAGS	fsToolBarFlags
HHWIN_PARAM_EXPANSION	fNotExpanded
HHWIN_PARAM_TABPOS	tabpos
HHWIN_PARAM_TABORDER	tabOrder
HHWIN_PARAM_HISTORY_COUNT	cHistory
HHWIN_PARAM_CUR_TAB	curNavType

Bits that may be set in the fsWinProperties member are shown in the following table. These bits are only honored for an HH_SET_WIN_TYPE command when the HHWIN_PARAM_PROPERTIES bit is set in the fsValidMembers member.

HHWIN_PROP bit value	Description
HHWIN_PROP_ONTOP	Topmost window (ignored).
HHWIN_PROP_NOTITLEBAR	Turns off the default WS_CAPTION window style.
HHWIN_PROP_NODEF_STYLES	Turns off all default style bits. Use the dwStyles member to explicitly specify all desired window styles.
HHWIN_PROP_NODEF_EXSTYLES	Turns off all default extended style bits. Use the dwExStyles member to explicitly specify all desired extended window styles.
HHWIN_PROP_TRI_PANE	Makes the window type a tri-pane, with toolbar on top, navigation pane on the left, and HTML pane on the right. Note that the navigation pane will only be displayed if you also set the pszToc member.
HHWIN_PROP_NOTB_TEXT	Turns off the display of text on the toolbar buttons of a tri-pane window.

HHWIN_PROP bit value	Description
HHWIN_PROP_POST_QUIT	Causes a WM_QUIT message to be posted to the window referenced by the hwndCaller member when the HTML Help window is closed.
HHWIN_PROP_AUTO_SYNC	Causes the table of contents in the navigation pane to be automatically synchronized with the topic in the HTML pane.
HHWIN_PROP_TRACKING	Causes notification messages to be sent. You must also set the idNotify member. See the section "Notification Messages," on page 230, for details.
HHWIN_PROP_TAB_SEARCH	Causes a Search tab to be included in the navigation pane of a tri-pane window.
HHWIN_PROP_TAB_HISTORY	Causes a History tab to be included in the navigation pane of a tri-pane window.
HHWIN_PROP_TAB_FAVORITES	Causes a Favorites tab to be included in the navigation pane of a tri-pane window.
HHWIN_PROP_CHANGE_TITLE	Causes the title bar of the HTML Help window to be automatically updated with the title of the current topic in the HTML pane.
HHWIN_PROP_NAV_ONLY_WIN	Causes the toolbar and HTML pane of a tri-pane window to be hidden.
HHWIN_PROP_NO_TOOLBAR	Causes the toolbar of a tri-pane window to be hidden.

Bits that may be set in the fsToolBarFlags member are shown in the following table. These bits are only honored for an HH_SET_WIN_TYPE command when the HHWIN_PARAM_TBFLAGS bit is set in the fsValidMembers member.

HHWIN_BUTTON bit value	Button to be displayed
HHWIN_BUTTON_EXPAND	Show/Hide
HHWIN_BUTTON_BACK	Back
HHWIN_BUTTON_FORWARD	Forward
HHWIN_BUTTON_STOP	Stop
HHWIN_BUTTON_REFRESH	Refresh
HHWIN_BUTTON_HOME	Home
HHWIN_BUTTON_BROWSE_FWD	(Ignored)

HHWIN_BUTTON bit value	Button to be displayed
HHWIN_BUTTON_BROWSE_BCK	(Ignored)
HHWIN_BUTTON_NOTES	Notes (not implemented)
HHWIN_BUTTON_CONTENTS	Contents (not implemented)
HHWIN_BUTTON_SYNC	Locate
HHWIN_BUTTON_OPTIONS	Options
HHWIN_BUTTON_PRINT	Print
HHWIN_BUTTON_INDEX	Index (not implemented)
HHWIN_BUTTON_SEARCH	Search (not implemented)
HHWIN_BUTTON_HISTORY	History (not implemented)
HHWIN_BUTTON_FAVORITES	Favorites (not implemented)
HHWIN_BUTTON_JUMP1	Jump1
HHWIN_BUTTON_JUMP2	Jump2
HHWIN_BUTTON_ZOOM	Font
HHWIN_BUTTON_TOC_NEXT	(Ignored)
HHWIN_BUTTON_TOC_PREV	(Ignored)

You may use any one of the following values to set the tabpos member of the HH_WINTYPE structure. They are not bit flags and may not be combined.

HHWIN_NAVTAB value	Tab position
HHWIN_NAVTAB_TOP	At the top of the navigation pane.
HHWIN_NAVTAB_LEFT	At the left of the navigation pane.
HHWIN_NAVTAB_BOTTOM	At the bottom of the navigation pane.

HH_TP_HELP_CONTEXTMENU

Argument	Description
hwndCaller	Handle of the window which the user right-clicked.
pszFile	Pathname of a text popup topic within a compiled HTML Help file. This should be a local pathname rather than a URL, in order to provide immediate feedback to the user.
dwData	A pointer to an array of DWORD pairs, described below.

This command is meant to be invoked when the application receives a WM_CONTEXTMENU message. The WM_CONTEXTMENU message is sent in response to a user right-clicking any application window. If the application doesn't have a custom context menu for the window, it can simply pass on the request to HTML Help. HTML Help will display the appropriate context-sensitive popup help topic. For hwndCaller, use the handle supplied as wParam with the WM_CONTEXTMENU message.

There are some cases where, even if you do not implement custom context menus, you will probably want to allow the default processing for the WM_CONTEXTMENU message rather than pass on the request to HTML Help. In particular, a right-click on the title bar of any window is supposed to display the system menu; and a right-click of a Windows EDIT control (known in Visual Basic as a TextBox) is supposed to display a context menu with items such as Cut, Copy, and Paste.

Control ID Map

The dwData argument for this command must point to a control ID map, in the form of an array of DWORD pairs. The first half of the pair is a window identifier (control ID), and the second half is a popup topic ID. The last pair in the array must have both values set to zero in order to terminate the list.

HTML Help will compare the ID of the hwndCaller window with each ID in the array of pairs. If a match is found, the corresponding popup topic will be displayed. Otherwise, a message will be displayed which says "No help topic is associated with this item."

You may find that the readability of your application code is improved if you use a data structure rather than a straight DWORD array to store the ID pairs. For example, in Visual Basic you could declare:

```
Type HH_IDPAIR
    dwControlId As Long
    dwTopicId As Long
End Type
```

In fact, you will find this declaration in the HTMLHELP.BAS module in the sample code accompanying this book, in the HHKIT\CHAP08\VBSAMPLE folder. Instead of passing a DWORD array, you would pass an HH_IDPAIR array, with one element for each control on a form, plus one extra element with ID values of zero to terminate the list.

Similarly, for C++ you could declare:

```
typedef struct tagHH_IDPAIR {
    DWORD dwControlId;
    DWORD dwTopicId;
} HH_IDPAIR;
```

The Visual Basic sample code also contains a helper function called "CollectIdPairs" which will walk through all of the controls on a form and build an HH_IDPAIR array using the control IDs and the topic IDs stored in the WhatsThisHelpID property of each control. A similar function could be written for a C++ application by making use of the GetWindowContextHelpId function in the Win32 API.

HH_TP_HELP_WM_HELP

Argument	Description
hwndCaller	Handle of the window which the user right-clicked.
pszFile	Pathname of a text popup topic within a compiled HTML Help file. This should be a local pathname rather than a URL, in order to provide immediate feedback to the user.
dwData	A pointer to an array of DWORD pairs, as for HH_TP_HELP_CONTEXTMENU.

This command is meant to be invoked when the application receives a WM_HELP message. The WM_HELP message is sent in response to two different user actions: pressing F1 or clicking a control after clicking the "What's This" Help button. For hwndCaller, use the hItemHandle member of the HELPINFO structure passed with the WM_HELP message.

The behavior and use of this command is identical to the HH_TP_HELP_CONTEXTMENU command.

Notification Messages

HtmlHelp can optionally send notification messages to an application window so that the application can track and/or respond to user activity in the Help system. There are two types of notification message: HHN_NAVCOMPLETE is sent whenever a new topic is displayed, and HHN_TRACK is sent whenever one of the toolbar buttons in a tri-pane window is clicked. In many cases, clicking one of these buttons will also result in a new topic being displayed, in which case both notification messages will be sent.

One possible use for notification messages would be to support synchronization of a table of contents in one window with the displayed topic in another window. HTML Help only supports synchronization natively for a table of contents and topic pane displayed in the same tri-pane window.

If your application requires even tighter integration with its Help system, it's possible to explicitly send messages in response to user action or from HTML script code. This capability is described in the section titled "Training Cards," on page 235.

Enabling Notification Messages

HTML Help will only send notification messages for HTML Help window types with appropriate property settings. Specifically, the hwndCaller and idNotify members of the HH_WINTYPE structure must be non-zero. You must also set the HHWIN_PARAM_PROPERTIES bit in the fsValidMembers member, and the HHWIN_PROP_TRACKING bit in the fsWinProperties member. By default, idNotify is zero, and the hwndCaller member is set to the value of its namesake in the HtmlHelp argument list when the window is first created.

It's possible to set the HHWIN_PROP_TRACKING bit by manually editing the HTML Help project file, but the idNotify and hwndCaller values can only be set via the HTML Help API. The hwndCaller member is set implicitly the first time a topic is displayed in a particular window type. It may be overridden via HH_SET_WIN_TYPE; note that this does not change the presentation mode.

If a user closes a topic window, it will be recreated automatically the next time you display a topic using that window type. However, the idNotify and hwndCaller values will be reset, and you must call HH_SET_WIN_TYPE again to re-enable notification messages.

Visual Basic

The following code fragment illustrates enabling notification messages for the HTML Help window type "Main."

```
Dim hWndHelp As Long
Dim phhwt As Long
hWndHelp = HtmlHelp(0, "Main", HH_GET_WIN_TYPE, phhwt)
If (phhwt <> 0) Then
    ' Copy the structure
    Dim hhwt As HH_WINTYPE
    Call GetWinTypeFromPointer(hhwt, phhwt)

    ' Reset members to enable notification messages
    hhwt.cbStruct = Len(hhwt)
    hhwt.fsValidMembers = HHWIN_PARAM_PROPERTIES
    hhwt.fsWinProperties = hhwt.fsWinProperties Or_
        HHWIN_PROP_TRACKING
    hhwt.idNotify = 9999
    hhwt.hwndCaller = Me.hWnd

    ' Set it
    hWndHelp = HtmlHelp(0, vbNullString,_
        HH_SET_WIN_TYPE, hhwt)
End If
```

The value 9999 assigned to hhwt.idNotify is arbitrary. It only becomes important if the window assigned to hhwt.hwndCaller will be receiving notification messages from multiple sources. Since you do not have any control over the ID values assigned to controls automatically by Visual Basic, the safest bet is to use a form for hhwt.hwndCaller which doesn't have any controls on it.

The handle you assign to hhwt.hwndCaller must belong to a subclassed window which is prepared to receive WM_NOTIFY messages. Refer to "Receiving Notification Messages," on page 233, for details.

Visual C++

The following code fragment illustrates enabling notification messages for the HTML Help window type "Main."

```
// Get the specified window type
HH_WINTYPE *phhwt = NULL;
HWND hWndHelp = HtmlHelp(NULL, "Main", HH_GET_WIN_TYPE,
   (DWORD)&phhwt);

if (phhwt) {
    // Copy the returned structure
    // NOTE: DO NOT MODIFY THE RETURNED STRUCTURE!!
    HH_WINTYPE hhwt;
    memcpy(&hhwt, phhwt, min(sizeof(hhwt), phhwt->cbStruct));

    // Reset members to enable notification messages
    hhwt.cbStruct = sizeof(hhwt);
    hhwt.fsValidMembers = HHWIN_PARAM_PROPERTIES;
    hhwt.fsWinProperties |= HHWIN_PROP_TRACKING;
    hhwt.idNotify = 9999;
    hhwt.hwndCaller = AfxGetMainWnd()->GetSafeHwnd();

    // Set it
    hWndHelp = HtmlHelp(NULL, NULL, HH_SET_WIN_TYPE,
       (DWORD)&hhwt);
}
```

The pointer you get back from the HH_GET_WIN_TYPE command refers to an HH_WINTYPE structure owned by HTML Help which should be considered read-only. For this reason, the structure is copied into a local variable before being modified and passed back with HH_SET_WIN_TYPE.

The value 9999 assigned to hhwt.idNotify is arbitrary, just like control IDs. Just make sure you don't have a control on the window represented by hhwt.hwndCaller with the same ID value as you assign to hhwt.idNotify.

The handle you assign to hhwt.hwndCaller must belong to a window which is prepared to receive specific WM_NOTIFY messages. Refer to the next section, "Receiving Notification Messages," for details.

Receiving Notification Messages

HTML Help notification messages are sent via the standard Windows message WM_NOTIFY. By examining the control ID value supplied with the WM_NOTIFY message, an application can determine the source of the message. The control ID is supplied both as the wParam argument and the idFrom member of the NMHDR structure passed as the lParam argument. The idFrom member is preferred.

Once an application has determined that a particular WM_NOTIFY message is from an HTML Help window, it must examine the "code" member of the NMHDR structure. The code value will be either HHN_NAVCOMPLETE to indicate that a new topic has been displayed, or HHN_TRACK to indicate that a toolbar button has been clicked on a tri-pane window.

For the HHN_NAVCOMPLETE notification, the NMHDR structure should be recast to HHN_NOTIFY. After that, an application can obtain the URL of the new topic via the pszUrl member of the HHN_NOTIFY structure.

For the HHN_TRACK notification, the NMHDR structure should be recast to HHNTRACK. After that, an application can obtain the URL of the current topic via the pszCurUrl member, the ID of the toolbar button which was clicked via the idAction member, and the window type information via the phhWinType member.

In the event that a toolbar button click results in a new topic being displayed, an HHN_TRACK notification is sent first, followed by an HHN_NAVCOMPLETE notification.

Visual Basic

Assuming you're using the subclass implementation supplied with the sample code, you need to call the Subclass function before you can receive notification messages. Typically this would be done in the Form_Load event. The hWnd property of this form should be assigned to the hwndCaller of the window type for which notification messages are desired.

You also need an OnNavComplete handler function and an OnTrack handler function implemented in the subclassed form. For example:

```
Public Sub OnNavComplete(phhnn As Long)

    ' Display notification info in debug window
    Dim hhnn As HHN_NOTIFY
    Call GetHHN_NOTIFYFromPointer(hhnn, phhnn)
    Debug.Print "OnNavComplete: '" &_
      hhnn.pszUrl & "'"

End Sub

Public Sub OnTrack(phhnt As Long)

    ' Display notification info in debug window
    Dim hhnt As HHNTRACK
    Call GetHHNTRACKFromPointer(hhnt, phhnt)
    Debug.Print "OnTrack: idAction " &_
      Format(hhnt.idAction) & " '" &_
      hhnt.pszCurUrl & "'"

End Sub
```

In both cases, the lParam argument of the WM_NOTIFY message is passed to the handler function as a Long value, and you need to convert it to something useful. The GetHHN_NOTIFYFromPointer and GetHHNTRACKFromPointer helper functions serve this purpose. Once you have a populated HHN_NOTIFY or HHNTRACK structure, it's up to you what to do with it. The sample code simply dumps some of the structure members to the debug window.

Note that the subclass implementation for these notification messages is not 100% bulletproof because it doesn't check the ID value of the sender. It's theoretically possible for a control to use the same notification codes as HTML Help (HHN_NAVCOMPLETE and HHN_TRACK). Again, the safest bet is to use a form for hhwt.hwndCaller that doesn't have any controls on it.

Visual C++

Normally when you want to receive a notification message in an MFC CWnd-derived class, you add some ON_NOTIFY macros to the message map. This lets you have a separate handler function for each notification source and each notification code.

Unfortunately, the way that HTML Help sends notification messages isn't compatible with the way that MFC dispatches them. So, you will have to override the OnNotify virtual function and manually pick out the notifications of interest. At least you can use ClassWizard to override OnNotify.

In the following sample code, the window class receiving the notification messages (CMainFrame) is derived from CMDIFrameWnd. If your notification target window is derived from some other base class, just replace the occurrence of CMDIFrameWnd below with the appropriate base class name.

```
BOOL CMainFrame::OnNotify(WPARAM wParam, LPARAM lParam,
  LRESULT* pResult)
{
    NMHDR *pNMHDR = (NMHDR *)lParam;
    if (pNMHDR->idFrom == 9999) {
        switch (pNMHDR->code) {
            case HHN_NAVCOMPLETE: {
                HHN_NOTIFY *phhnn = (HHN_NOTIFY *)pNMHDR;
                TRACE("OnNavComplete: '%s'\r\n",phhnn->pszUrl);
                break;
            }
            case HHN_TRACK: {
                HHNTRACK *phhnt = (HHNTRACK *)pNMHDR;
                TRACE("OnTrack: idAction %d "
                  "pszCurUrl '%s'\r\n",
                  phhnt->idAction,phhnt->pszCurUrl);
                break;
            }
        }
        return(TRUE);
    }
    return CMDIFrameWnd::OnNotify(wParam, lParam, pResult);
}
```

For notification messages which were not sent from an HTML Help window, make sure you call the base class OnNotify function to perform default processing, as shown above. This will properly dispatch any normal notifications you may have in your message map.

This sample code does nothing more than output some of the members of the notification structures to the debugger. It's up to you what to do with these notifications in your own applications.

Training Cards

The "training card" feature of HTML Help offers the most control over the interaction between HTML Help and an application. Don't be fooled by the name—you can use this feature to implement whatever you want: It doesn't have to be anything like the original WinHelp concept of training cards.

The training card mechanism is very simple. The HTML Help ActiveX control supports a TCard method which can be called from script in an HTML topic. The arguments of this method are packaged up into the wParam and lParam arguments of the WM_TCARD message which is sent to the hwndCaller of the current HTML Help window type. When the application receives the WM_TCARD message, it can do whatever it wants with it. Possibilities include demonstrating to a user how to perform some action, changing the displayed help topic, and so on.

You can use any scripting language you like to invoke the TCard macro. In the specific case of Internet Explorer, both VBScript and JScript are supported. The TCard method has two numeric arguments which are passed unchanged via the WM_TCARD message.

In addition to the TCard macro, there is also a TCard command parameter available with the HTML Help ActiveX control. When using the TCard command parameter, no script code is required. When the user clicks a visible representation of the control, the WM_TCARD message is sent automatically.

Unlike the TCard method, the TCard command parameter permits sending a string for the second argument. In this case, the recipient of the WM_TCARD message must be prepared to deal with lParam as a string pointer. This is explained in more detail with the sample source code below.

Inserting the HTML Help ActiveX Control

The easiest way to get an instance of the HTML Help ActiveX Control into an HTML topic is to use the wizard included in the HTML Help Workshop. While editing an HTML topic, click the Tags menu and select the HTML Help Control menu item. There is also a corresponding toolbar button if you prefer.

There are two possible ways you might want the control inserted for use with TCard. Choose "Training Card," and then click the Next button.

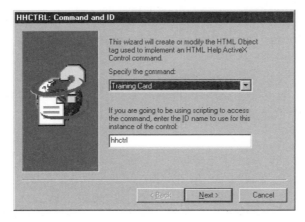

Choose "Training Card."

The next step of the wizard gives you a choice between displaying the control as a button, or not displaying it at all. If you want to invoke TCard directly in response to a user clicking the control, choose Button. Otherwise, choose Hidden.

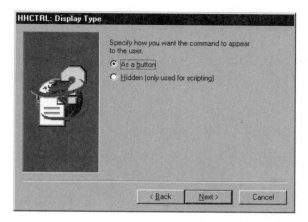

Choose As A Button for a visible instance, or Hidden if you just want to call the TCard macro from script code.

The last wizard step lets you choose values to pass for wParam and lParam.

Note: When you insert a "hidden" instance of the HTML Help ActiveX control, it may still register as a tiny area on the HTML page which causes the mouse pointer to change to a hand as though it were an <A> tag or other hyperlink. This is a visual anomaly only: Nothing happens when the control is clicked.

Calling the TCard method from script code

The TCard method of the HTML Help ActiveX control is a simple method with two numeric arguments (both required), and no return value. This method can be called just as easily using either VBScript or JScript in Internet Explorer.

Note: Unlike with the TCard command described above, it is not possible to pass a string for the second argument. However, there is a Click method that invokes the TCard command attached to an instance of the control. You could theoretically use Dynamic HTML in Internet Explorer 4.01 to modify the TCard command and then invoke it with the HHClick method. We leave this as an exercise for someone needing the ability to pass arbitrary strings from script code.

The examples below all assume that you have inserted an instance of the HTML Help ActiveX control on your page with the default ID name of "hhctrl." It doesn't matter whether the control is hidden or visible.

Invoking TCard from a Hyperlink

If you'd like to call the TCard method in response to a user click of an <A> tag, there are two possibilities. Either the click calls the TCard method and then jumps to another page, or it just calls the TCard method. The tag syntax for these two cases is somewhat different.

To simply call the TCard method without jumping to another page, you need to use the javascript custom URL type:

```
<A HREF="javascript:hhctrl.TCard(123,456)">
   Call TCard
</A>
```

To invoke TCard and jump to another page, you need a tag that looks something like this:

```
<A HREF="Options.htm" onClick="hhctrl.TCard(123,456)">
   Call TCard, then jump to Options
</A>
```

If you would like to call TCard from a button, use this tag:

```
<INPUT TYPE="BUTTON" VALUE="Call TCard"
   onClick="hhctrl.TCard(123,456)">
```

This is usually preferable to displaying the HTML Help ActiveX control itself as a button with the TCard command parameter. The control's button appearance doesn't integrate as well with the browser, and the TCard invocation isn't as flexible.

In all cases, you can invoke a script function to do other processing if you wish, for example:

```
<SCRIPT language="VBScript">
   Sub MySub()
         ' Do some other stuff here
         Call hhctrl.TCard(123,456)
   End Sub
</SCRIPT>
<A HREF="Options.htm" onClick="MySub()">
   Call TCard, then jump to Options
</A>
```

Handling the WM_TCARD message

The only real trick to handling the WM_TCARD message concerns the fact that the lParam argument may either be a straight numeric value or a string pointer. The best way to deal with this ambiguity is to follow a convention in which a certain value or range of values in wParam mean that lParam should be interpreted as a string. This assumes you have complete control over the Help project used with your application.

The generalized solution presented in the code fragments below uses the IsBadStringPtr API function to determine whether the lParam value could possibly refer to a string. This solution is not bulletproof however, because it is theoretically possible for a numeric value to coincide with a valid string pointer value.

Visual C++

Use ClassWizard to create a handler for the WM_TCARD message on the window class which will be used as the hwndCaller for your Help window(s).

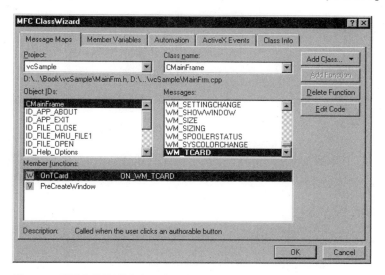

Create a WM_TCARD handler function with ClassWizard.

What you do in response to the WM_TCARD message is of course entirely up to you. The vcSample application simply displays the argument values in the output window of the debugger:

```
void CMainFrame::OnTCard(UINT idAction, DWORD dwActionData)
{
    if (IsBadStringPtr((LPCSTR)dwActionData,256)) {
        TRACE("CMainFrame::OnTCard: %ld, %ld\r\n",
            idAction,dwActionData);
    } else {
        TRACE("CMainFrame::OnTCard: %ld, '%s'\r\n",
            idAction,dwActionData);
    }
}
```

The use of IsBadStringPtr to check the dwActionData argument is a bit of a kludge, as is the arbitrary length check of 256. In a real application, it would be better to treat dwActionData as a string only if idAction has a certain value or range of values.

Visual Basic

Handling the WM_TCARD message in a Visual Basic application presents a similar problem to other Help-related messages such as WM_CONTEXTMENU and WM_HELP. Visual Basic does not provide an event for these messages, so it is necessary to subclass a form in order to be able to detect when these messages have been received. The vbSample application in HHKIT\CHAP08\VBSAMPLE uses a native Visual Basic 5.0 implementation of subclassing which is not particularly robust. Again, you are strongly encouraged to find a third-party subclassing control instead.

Using the sample subclass implementation, handling the WM_TCARD message is just a matter of implementing an OnTCard subroutine as follows:

```
Public Sub OnTCard(wParam As Long, lParam As Long)

    If (IsBadStringPtrp(lParam, 256)) Then
        Debug.Print "OnTCard:" & Str(wParam) & Str(lParam)
    Else
        Dim strlParam As String
        strlParam = GetStringFromPointer(lParam)
        Debug.Print "OnTCard:" & Str(wParam) & " '" &
           strlParam & "'"
    End If

End Sub
```

What you do in response to the WM_TCARD message is of course entirely up to you. The vbSample application simply displays the argument values in the output window of the debugger.

As before, the use of IsBadStringPtr to check the lParam argument is a bit of a kludge, as is the arbitrary length check of 256. In a real application, it would be better to treat lParam as a string only if wParam has a certain value or range of values. Note that the GetStringFromPointer function is a helper found in HTMLHELP.BAS.

Sample Applications

The HHKIT\CHAP08 folder contains two subfolders, VBSAMPLE and VCSAMPLE, containing source code for sample applications written in Visual Basic 5.0 and Visual C++ 5.0 (with MFC). The applications are functionally almost identical, to demonstrate the same concepts using both development tools. First we'll look at the features of the application, independent of which version is being run; then we'll look at the implementation details specific to each programming language.

Don't consider the sample application to be a model of a perfectly integrated help system. Its purpose is merely to demonstrate several of the features you may want to use in your own applications.

Application Overview

The sample application is a simple HTML Help tester, similar to the "Test HtmlHelp API" and "Test Keyword lookup" commands in HTML Help Workshop, but with more features. It uses MDI to allow you to open multiple HTML Help files simultaneously. You can display Help topics by topic ID or context map number, using your choice of the three presentation modes. You can also perform API-level keyword search, and view notification and training card messages in the output window of the debugger. The sample application provides context-sensitive Help in the form of "What's This" popup topics and Help buttons on some dialogs.

User's Guide

On the **File** menu, click the **Open** command. You will be presented with a standard File Open dialog box. Select any compiled HTML Help file. An MDI child window will be created for the file as shown below:

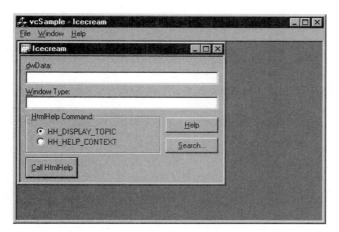

A compiled HTML Help file opened in the sample application provides an interface similar to the "Test HtmlHelp API" command in the HTML Help Workshop.

From the File window, you can specify arguments for the HTML Help API commands HH_DISPLAY_TOPIC or HH_HELP_CONTEXT. For HH_DISPLAY_TOPIC, the dwData field specifies a topic ID—typically the name of an HTML file contained within the compiled HTML Help file. You may leave this field empty to select the default topic. For HH_HELP_CONTEXT, the dwData field specifies a context map number. For both commands, the Window Type field specifies the name of a window type in which to display the topic.

The File window also supports context-sensitive help, both with its Help button and via "What's This" Help. There is no "What's This" Help button because Windows doesn't support displaying such a button at the same time as minimize and maximize buttons. However, you can click with the right mouse button or press F1 to display the "What's This" popup topic for a given field.

Clicking the Help button, or selecting the Help Topics command from the Help menu, will display Help in an external tri-pane window (in sibling mode).

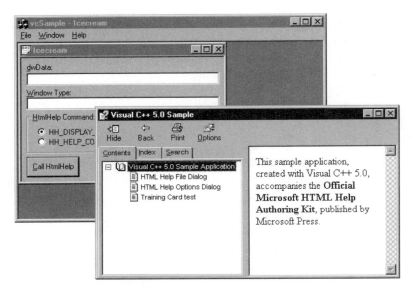

The Help Topics command displays a tri-pane window in sibling mode.

If you click the **Search** button on the **File** window, a dialog box will be displayed that lets you specify arguments for the HH_KEYWORD_LOOKUP and HH_ALINK_LOOKUP commands of the HTML Help API.

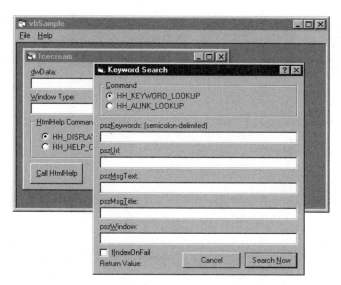

The Keyword Search dialog box is displayed when you click the Search button on the File window.

At the top of the dialog box is a pair of option buttons that allow you to choose between the HH_KEYWORD_LOOKUP and HH_ALINK_LOOKUP commands. The remaining fields in the dialog box represent members of the HH_AKLINK data structure (see "HH_AKLINK," on page 220). When you click the Search Now button, the field values are gathered into an HH_AKLINK and passed to the HTML Help API as the dwData argument of the chosen command. The return value is displayed in the label at the bottom of the dialog box.

You can select the presentation mode of the Help window via the Options command on the Help menu. The presentation mode option is used only for external topics displayed via the Call HtmlHelp button on the File window, and the Search Now button of the HH_KEYWORD_LOOKUP dialog box. It is not used for internal Help topics displayed by clicking the Help button or invoking the Help Topics command from the Help menu.

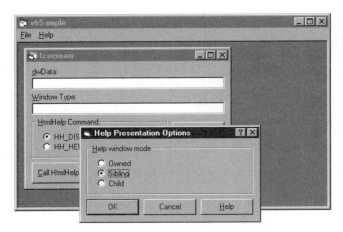

Choosing the Options command on the Help menu displays this dialog box, allowing you to select the Help presentation mode.

Because of the difficulty in defining well-behaved child window types via the HTML Help Workshop, the sample application always uses a window type called "Embedded" when you select Child mode. In this mode, the Window Type field of the File window is ignored. The Embedded window type is created at runtime by the sample application using the HH_SET_WIN_TYPE command of the HTML Help API.

Finally, you can enable notification messages using the **Notification Messages** command on the **File** menu.

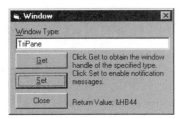

This dialog box lets you enable notification messages.

Once enabled, notification messages are simply reported in the debugger of the application. Training card messages are included. If you want to see an example of training card messages, click Contents on the Help menu, then enable notification messages for the TriPane window as shown above. Select the topic titled "Training Card test" from the table of contents, and click any of the tests. The WM_TCARD messages received by the application are reported in the debugger.

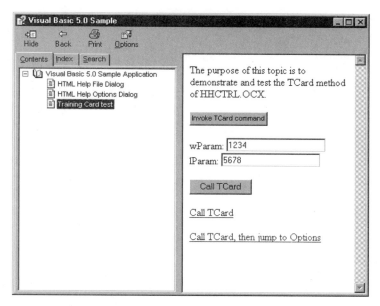

The Training Card test topic.

If you look at the HTML source of this topic, you'll see a variety of different ways of invoking the TCard command and method. The topic is designed to let you change the wParam and lParam values passed via the TCard method. However, a bug in the current version of HTML Help prevents you from changing the values in the edit fields.

Visual Basic Implementation Notes

Using HTML Help from a Visual Basic application presents several challenges. The HTML Help API is not friendly to Visual Basic because of its non-typesafe interface and its use of pointers within structures. Visual Basic also doesn't provide events for certain useful window messages, for example: WM_HELP and WM_CONTEXTMENU for context-sensitive Help, WM_NOTIFY for notification messages, and WM_TCARD for training cards.

These problems have been discussed individually in other parts of this book. The purpose of this section is to provide an overview of the architecture of the vbSample application, with particular emphasis on those parts of the code intended to be reusable in other applications.

HTMLHELP.BAS

The key part of the vbSample application for interfacing with HTML Help is the file HTMLHELP.BAS. The first part of this file contains a straight translation of the constants, data structures (user-defined types), and the HtmlHelp() API function declaration from the C++ header file HTMLHELP.H which is provided with the HTML Help Workshop.

The second part of HTMLHELP.BAS is a set of additional declarations and helper functions designed to make the HTML Help API more usable. These items are summarized in the following table.

Declaration	Description
HH_WINTYPE_KLUGE	A private user-defined type used by the GetWinTypeFromPointer function.
HHN_NOTIFY_KLUGE	A private user-defined type used by the GetHHN_NOTIFYFromPointer function.
HHNTRACK_KLUGE	A private user-defined type used by the GetHHNTRACKFromPointer function.
HH_IDPAIR	A public user-defined type used by the CollectIdPairs function.
CollectIdPairs	This subroutine walks through the Controls collection of a form and populates a dynamic array of HH_IDPAIR with control ID and WhatsThisHelpID values for use with the HH_TP_HELP_WM_HELP and HH_TP_HELP_CONTEXTMENU commands.
GetStringFromPointer	A function which takes a Long pointer value and converts it to a Visual Basic string. You can use it to convert the lParam argument of the WM_TCARD message in an OnTCard handler. It's also used extensively by the other Get…FromPointer functions to convert structure members.
GetWinTypeFromPointer	This function takes a Long pointer value to an HH_WINTYPE and populates another HH_WINTYPE with its contents. It's the only way to make the HH_GET_WIN_TYPE return value useful.
GetHHN_NOTIFYFromPointer	A function which populates an HHN_NOTIFY, given a pointer. It is meant to be used to convert the lParam argument of the HHN_NAVCOMPLETE notification message.
GetHHNTRACKFromPointer	Similar to GetHHN_NOTIFYFromPointer, this function populates an HHNTRACK, and is meant to be used to convert the lParam argument of the HHN_TRACK notification message.

SUBCLASS.BAS and SUBCLASS.CLS

The Public Subclass function in SUBCLASS.BAS is a pure Visual Basic implementation of subclassing that allows you to catch Windows messages for which no Visual Basic events are provided.

Warning! The implementation of Subclass uses the Visual Basic AddressOf feature to change the window procedure of a form. As stated in the Visual Basic documentation, using AddressOf can destabilize the Visual Basic debugger. You are strongly encouraged to find a third-party subclassing control, or at the very least, disable subclassing while debugging.

To subclass a form, all you need to do is call the Subclass function anywhere within the form code; typically, this would be in the Form_Load event.

```
Call Subclass(Me)
```

In addition, the form must provide public handler functions for each of the messages that the subclass implementation might receive:

Public Sub	Purpose
OnContextMenu	Called in response to WM_CONTEXTMENU
OnHelp	Called in response to WM_HELP
OnNavComplete	Called when WM_NOTIFY is received and the code value is HHN_NAVCOMPLETE
OnTCard	Called in response to WM_TCARD
OnTrack	Called when WM_NOTIFY is received and the code value is HHN_TRACK

Although it is not strictly necessary to implement all five handler functions for every subclassed form, it is still recommended. If you get an unexpected message for which you do not have a handler, it can be difficult to debug.

WIN32API.BAS

This module contains declarations for Win32 API functions used by SUBCLASS.BAS and HTMLHELP.BAS. You might want to merge these with the Win32 API declarations you're already using in your application.

Form Files

There are several form files in vbSample which aren't really intended to be reused in other applications. However, you might find it helpful to look at the code in these forms. A brief description of each form follows.

Form	Description
frmAbout	Standard About box.
frmFile	An MDI child form representing an open HTML Help file. This form implements context-sensitive Help and allows the user to invoke HH_DISPLAY_TOPIC and HH_HELP_CONTEXT.
frmHelp	An MDI child form for hosting HTML Help in child mode. Also demonstrates receiving notification messages.

Form	Description
frmMain	The main MDI container form for the application. Demonstrates creating the Embedded window type for use in child mode.
frmOptions	A standard dialog box for selecting the presentation mode, this form also demonstrates context-sensitive Help.
frmSearch	As well as permitting the user to invoke HH_KEYWORD_LOOKUP and HH_ALINK_LOOKUP, this form demonstrates an alternative implementation of "What's This" Help using HH_DISPLAY_TEXT_POPUP.
frmWindow	Illustrates calling HH_GET_WIN_TYPE and HH_SET_WIN_TYPE, specifically for the purpose of enabling notification messages.

Visual C++ Implementation Notes

This section describes the parts of the sample application which are unique to the vcSample implementation created using Visual C++ 5.0.

The vcSample project was created using the MFC AppWizard. It is a fairly standard MDI application using the MFC doc/view architecture. The only document type defined is the compiled HTML Help file, and it has only one view—a CFormView-derived class referred to as the File window in the User's Guide above. The commands added by the Wizard for creating and editing the document were removed because the document in this application is read-only.

A brief description of each of the custom application classes can be found in the following table.

Class	Description
CChildFrame	A custom MDI child frame used to contain CFileView. Its purpose is only to change the default frame styles and make the view be fixed-size.
CFileView	The CFormView-derived class displayed for each HTML Help file opened by the user. As well as allowing the user to invoke the HH_DISPLAY_TOPIC and HH_HELP_CONTEXT commands, it also supports context-sensitive Help.
CHelpWnd	A trivial class derived from CMDIChildWnd in order to host HTML Help in child mode. It does little more than resize the HTML Help child window to fit.
CMainFrame	Standard CMDIFrameWnd-derived class generated by AppWizard. It is also the recipient of notification messages, demonstrated in the OnTCard and OnNotify member functions.
COptionsDlg	A straightforward CDialog-derived class for selecting the presentation mode, this class also implements context-sensitive Help.
CSearchDlg	Another straightforward CDialog-derived class, allowing the user to invoke HH_KEYWORD_LOOKUP and HH_ALINK_LOOKUP. This class offers

Class	Description
	an alternative implementation of "What's This" Help using HH_DISPLAY_TEXT_POPUP.
CWindowDlg	A CDialog-derived class that permits the user to enable notification messages.

Frequently Asked Questions

Question: *On which platforms is the HTML Help API available?*

Answer: The HTML Help API is only available on the Windows 95 and Windows NT platforms. For Windows NT, only the x86 version is currently supported—the HTML Help API is not available on RISC-based versions of NT.

Question: *Is there a COM interface to HTML Help?*

Answer: There is no COM interface to HTML Help in version 1.1. A COM interface is planned for a future version of HTML Help.

Question: *Can I call the HTML Help API from HTML script code?*

Answer: No, that requires a COM interface. The only features you can use from script are the commands and methods of the HTML Help ActiveX control.

Question: *Can I call the HTML Help API from Java?*

Answer: In order to call HtmlHelp() from Java, you must use J/Direct or create a wrapper to provide a native Java interface.

C H A P T E R   N I N E

HTML Help on Other Platforms

Although many parts of HTML Help are specific to the Windows platform, a useful subset of HTML Help features is available for any Java-capable Internet browser via the HTML Help Java applet.

For the Help author: We'll explore the features that are available on each platform, and explain how you should compose your topics differently when targeting a web site rather than a compiled HTML Help file.

For the programmer: You may be called upon to assist with writing script code, but generally this chapter probably isn't relevant to you.

For the web author: We'll explain how to use the HTML Help Java applet to enhance a web site, and how you can construct an HTML Help site to be friendly to all browsers.

What's in this Chapter

The sample code for this chapter can be found in HHKIT\CHAP09.

How HTML Help Works on Other Platforms

The topics in an HTML Help system are of course written in HTML; they can be displayed in a web browser. But an HTML Help system is more than just a collection of web pages.

The HTML Help table of contents and keyword index files (.HHC and .HHK, respectively) use a standard file format known as a Sitemap. The Sitemap format is understood by the HTML Help compiler, the HTML Help ActiveX control, and most importantly for this chapter, the HTML Help Java applet.

The HTML Help Java applet is a portable implementation of some of the most important features of the HTML Help ActiveX control. These features include the table of contents, index, and related topics. A complete list can be found in the next section.

Which Features of HTML Help Are Available?

Although HTML Help is targeted at the Windows platform, its most important features are directly supported on other platforms via the HTML Help Java applet. Alternatives exist for many of the unsupported features. The following table summarizes the availability of each major feature.

HTML Help Feature	Cross-Platform Availability
Table of Contents	Supported by Java applet.
Explicit keyword index	Supported by Java applet.
Implicit keyword index	Not available.
Related topics	Supported by Java applet (except for display as popup menu).
Popup topics	Not available (but various alternatives exist).
Tripane window	Not available (but you can emulate it with framesets; refer to "Sample Site: IceCream," on page 266 for an example).
Window types	Not available (but you can use frames and the window.open script method to do similar things).
Information types	Not available.
ALink index	Not available.
Full-text search	Not available (but there are other solutions available).
HTML Help API	Not available.

Each of these features is discussed in more detail below.

Table of Contents

The HTML Help Java applet directly supports displaying a table of contents file (default extension .HHC). However, it doesn't load the table of contents file as quickly as can be done from a compiled HTML Help file. This is particularly true when downloading the file over the Internet using a dial-up connection. The difference becomes more noticeable with larger files.

You can decrease the load time by breaking up your table of contents into multiple files; the applet will load each as necessary. Refer to "Improving Performance with Merge," on page 256, for more information.

Synchronizing the table of contents with the currently displayed topic is not supported automatically. You can write some script code to take care of this (see "Sample Site: IceCream," on page 266, for an example), but it only works for those parts of the table of contents which have already been loaded. If you break up the table of contents into multiple files using Merge, synchronization won't always work.

The applet ignores any specified target window type since window types are not supported. It also ignores information types.

Explicit Keyword Index

The HTML Help Java applet directly supports displaying a keyword Index file (default extension .HHK). As with the table of contents, it will not load as quickly as it would in a compiled HTML Help file. Unlike the table of contents, the keyword index cannot be broken up into multiple files.

Information types in the keyword index file are ignored by the applet.

Implicit Keyword Index

With a compiled HTML Help file, you can insert Compiler Information OBJECT tags into your HTML topic files. These tags are extracted at compile time, which permits the index to be built automatically. Since there is no compilation step when using the Java applet, these tags don't do anything.

Furthermore, such object tags display poorly in a browser. As a result, you will probably want to avoid including Compiler Information OBJECT tags in HTML topic files that are intended to be viewed outside the context of a compiled HTML Help file.

Related Topics

The HTML Help Java applet directly supports displaying a Related Topics dialog box. It does not support displaying related topics on a popup menu; a dialog box will always be displayed regardless of whether you set the popup menu option.

Popup Topics

Popup Help topics are not supported by the applet as they are with the ActiveX control, but there are various things you can do instead which may be satisfactory.

The window.alert method can be called from script to display a dialog box with any arbitrary text message. However, it's fairly ugly, supports only text (not HTML), and forces the user to click the OK button to dismiss it. Windows Help users are accustomed to a popup topic behavior where they can click anywhere to dismiss the popup.

You could write a trivial Java applet to display a nicer looking dialog box, but it would otherwise suffer from most of the same drawbacks as window.alert.

A separate browser window can be displayed using window.open, and the popup topic can be loaded into that window. This allows HTML source for the topic, but the user still has to take explicit action to close the window.

You could have a small frame as part of your frameset displayed perhaps at the bottom of your topic frame. Clicking a "popup" link could load a new HTML page (the popup topic) into this frame, with an appearance something like a footnote. The user of course would not have to take any action to dismiss the topic, because it's an integral part of the frameset. However, it takes up valuable screen real estate even when it's not being used.

Some browsers support the display of tooltips containing the value of the TITLE attribute of an <A> tag. You could use this feature, perhaps in combination with one of the other alternatives already mentioned, to support text-only popups which do not need to be dismissed by the user. This is probably as close as you can get to the Windows Help popup topic model without using a custom ActiveX control, but not all browsers support it.

Tripane Window

An important part of the HTML Help feature set is the ability to display an integrated tripane window containing a toolbar button pane at the top, a navigation control pane on the left (for table of contents, index, and so forth), and a topic pane on the right. Because this tripane window is implemented by the HTML Help ActiveX control, it's not supported on other platforms.

However, a browser frameset can be made to look quite a lot like a tripane window, and support most of the same user interface features. For a sample implementation, take a look at "Sample Site: IceCream," on page 266.

Window Types

Window types are not supported by the HTML Help Java applet. However, you can use browser frames to accomplish almost all of the same things. This includes specifying a target frame for topics displayed from the table of contents, index, and related topics dialog box.

Information Types

Information types are not supported, and there is no simple alternative.

ALink Index

There is no equivalent to the ALink index, and even if there were, there is no equivalent to the HTML Help API that would let you search it.

Full-Text Search

Full-text search isn't supported directly, but there are many third-party solutions available for web sites that should work fine in conjunction with your HTML Help site. If you're hosting a web site on NT Server, one possibility is Microsoft Index Server.

HTML Help API

The HTML Help API is only supported by Windows 95 and $x86$ versions of Windows NT.

Creating Portable HTML Help Projects

The fantasy is that HTML and Java are "write once, run anywhere" languages. The reality is far more sobering, as you're probably well aware if you have done any web site development.

The HTML Help Java applet has been tested on a wide variety of platforms including Macintosh and various flavors of Unix. However, portability to all platforms is not guaranteed. Your best bet is to research the platforms required by your user base, and test with those platforms before deploying your site.

If you're working on an HTML Help system that you intend to deliver in compiled form as well as a portable web site, you may find that it is not practical to single-source the Help system. For example, if you put script code in each topic to synchronize with the table of contents, the code will fail when the topic is displayed in a compiled HTML Help window instead of a browser. If you use Compiler Information tags to insert keywords directly into a topic file, these are likely to be visible to the end user in a browser as unresolved objects.

As a result, you will probably find that you need to target one format or the other initially. After the primary target is complete, you can convert the project to a suitable format for the other target.

If you write client-side script code, be sure to use JavaScript rather than VBScript for maximum portability. If you really want to take advantage of a feature peculiar to one browser, test for the browser version in script code beforehand. For example, the IceCream sample uses Dynamic HTML in Internet Explorer 4.01 only to resize the applet to fit its parent frame.

It's possible to substitute the HTML Help ActiveX control for the Java applet when a user has an ActiveX-capable browser (which at the moment means Internet Explorer 3.0 or later). If your web server runs Active Server Pages, you can use server-side script code to detect whether the browser is ActiveX-capable, for example:

```
<% Set bc = Server.CreateObject("MSWC.BrowserType") %>
<% If (bc.ActiveXControls = TRUE) Then   %>
Your browser supports ActiveX controls.
<%  Else  %>
Your browser doesn't support ActiveX controls.
<%  End If  %>
```

This HTML fragment is taken from the sample page ACTIVEX.ASP, which can be found in the HHKIT\CHAP09 folder.

However, if you're satisfied with the behavior of your web site using the Java applet, there is probably not much incentive to substitute the ActiveX control for a subset of your users.

Improving Performance with Merge

The HTML Help Java applet supports merging multiple table of contents (.HHC) files at runtime. To a user, these appear as a single large table of contents. The advantage to breaking up such a large file is performance—the applet won't load included files until the user expands a branch of the table of contents that exposes a Merge parameter. Using Merge, you can arrange for an arbitrarily large table of contents to initially load much more quickly.

Unfortunately, the current version of the HTML Help Workshop doesn't support the Merge parameter. If you use the HTML Help Workshop to build your table of contents files, you will have to hand-edit these files after you're finished to add the Merge parameter.

Each table of contents entry in the .HHC file looks something like this:

```
<LI><OBJECT type="text/sitemap">
    <param name="Name" value="Ice Cream Creation Simulator">
    <param name="Local" value="html/icec3v76.htm">
</OBJECT>
```

There are other parameters such as Type and ImageNumber which can be applied to a table of contents entry, but Name and Local are the most important. The Name parameter specifies the string to be displayed to the user in the table of contents tree-view. The Local parameter specifies the document to load when the user selects this item in the tree-view.

A Merge entry looks very similar to a regular entry, for example:

```
<LI><OBJECT type="text/sitemap">
    <param name="Name" value="Loading...">
    <param name="Merge" value="Express.hhc">
</OBJECT>
```

When the HTML Help Java applet encounters a Merge entry, it will display the Name string in the tree-view until the file named by the Merge parameter has been fully loaded. After that, the contents of the Merge file are seamlessly integrated.

Note that Merge entries found at the top level of the table of contents hierarchy will actually degrade performance because they have to be separately loaded at the same time as the original table of contents file.

For an example of Merge in action, see "Sample Site: IceCream," on page 266.

Working with the HTML Help Java Applet

Just as the HTML Help ActiveX control can be inserted with an OBJECT tag, the applet can be inserted with an APPLET tag. For supported commands (table of contents, index, and related topics), the parameters for these two are mostly compatible. So, you could use the HTML Help Workshop to insert an OBJECT tag for the ActiveX control with all the appropriate parameter values, and then change the OBJECT tag to an APPLET tag while leaving the parameter values alone. This would let you use the wizard interface instead of hand-editing parameter values.

However, if you prefer to hand-edit the APPLET tag or use some other tool, the following sections contain all the information you need.

Note: All pathnames supplied to the applet must be relative to the path of the document containing the applet tag. The security model of most Java Virtual Machines will not allow the applet to read files which are located above its containing document in the hierarchy.

Applet Tag Format

The following example, taken from the IceCream project, is fairly typical of what an APPLET tag for the HTML Help Java applet looks like:

```
<applet code="HHCtrl.class" align="baseline" width="300"
height="300" name="HHCtrl" archive="HHCtrl.zip">
        <param name="command" value="contents">
        <param name="item1" value="icecream.hhc">
        <param name="background" value="ffffff">
        <param name="cabbase" value="HHCtrl.cab">
        <param name="flags" value="0x200,0x7">
</applet>
```

The applet tag and the attribute values contained within the angle brackets are handled by the browser. The code attribute tells the browser the name of the applet you want to run, and must be set to "HHCtrl.class." The archive attribute is a Netscape Navigator extension which allows Java applet class files to be collected into a single uncompressed zip file.

The align, width, and height attributes determine the size and position of the applet on the page. The name attribute is required if you want to use script code to refer to the applet—for example, to call the syncURL method.

Most of the parameter values contained between the <applet> and </applet> tags are handled by the applet itself. An exception is the cabbase parameter, a Microsoft Internet Explorer extension which allows Java applet class files to be collected into a single cab file, similar to the zip files used for Navigator.

The most important parameter for the applet is "Command." This determines which of the three available navigational interfaces will be presented: Table of Contents, Keyword Index, or Related Topics button. You can think of these as being three distinct applets.

Parameter Reference

All of the applet-specific parameter values are summarized in the table below. Each parameter is described in detail in its own section following the table.

Parameter name	Applies To	Description
Background	Contents, Index	Specifies the background color.
Background-Image	Contents, Index	Specifies a background image.
Button	Related Topics	Specifies the button caption.
Command	All	Specifies the navigational interface to use: Contents, Index, or Related Topics.
Flags	Contents	Specifies display attributes.
Font	Contents	Specifies the font attributes.
Frame	All	Specifies the frame in which to load topics.
Item1, Item2, Item3...	All	Provides additional information, dependent on the Command value.

Background

The Background parameter lets you set the background color for the Contents and Index commands. Syntax for the Background parameter is:

```
<param name="background" value="RRGGBB">
```

The *RRGGBB* value is a six-digit hexadecimal number, with 2 digits for each of the primary colors red, green, and blue. For example, "ffffff" is white, "000000" is black, "c0c0c0" is light gray, and "ff0000" is red.

Notes: For the Index command, only a thin stripe above and below the keyword list is affected by the Background parameter. The background color of the list itself is always white. For best results, set the value of the Background parameter to match the value of the bgcolor parameter of the body tag.

The Sitemap format allows for a Background parameter also, but the current version of the applet ignores it.

Background Image

This parameter lets you specify a background image for Contents and Index views. Syntax for the Background Image parameter is:

```
<param name="background image" value="filename">
```

The *filename* value is the path, relative to the document containing the applet, of the GIF or JPEG file to use as the background image.

Notes: For the Index command, only a thin stripe above and below the keyword list is affected by the BackgroundImage parameter. The background of the list itself is always plain white.

The Sitemap format allows for a Background Image parameter also, but the current version of the applet ignores it.

Button

The Button parameter sets the caption of the Related Topics button. Syntax for the Button parameter is:

```
<param name="button" value="caption">
```

The *caption* value is displayed on the face of the Related Topics button. If the button isn't large enough to fit the caption text, the text will be truncated. Generally speaking, you can probably get better results by setting the width and height attributes to 0, and scripting the Related Topics command by using the HHClick method of the applet. Then you are free to use an <A> tag, form button, image, or whatever you like to activate the Related Topics command.

This parameter is ignored with the Contents or Index commands.

Command

The Command parameter determines the type of navigational interface that the applet is to provide. Syntax for the Command parameter is:

```
<param name="Command" value="command-string">
```

The *command-string* value can be one of "Contents," "Index," or "Related Topics." The Contents command displays a table of contents in a tree-view style. The Index command displays a keyword index in a combo-box style. The Related Topics command displays a button which, when clicked, presents a dialog box with a list of related topics for the user to choose from.

Each command uses one or more Item values as well. Refer to the Item parameter for further details.

Flags

The Flags parameter lets you control certain visual attributes of the Contents tree-view. Syntax for the Flags parameter is:

```
<param name="Flags" value="ExWinStyle,WinStyle">
```

The ExWinStyle and WinStyle values are hexadecimal numbers in the format $0xn$. These values are composed of bit values, one for each attribute. The following table describes how each style bit affects the display. To combine styles, simply add their values.

Bit value	Symbolic name	Description
ExWinStyle 0x200	WS_EX_CLIENTEDGE	Sunken edge
WinStyle 0x1	TVS_HASBUTTONS	Plus/minus squares
WinStyle 0x2	TVS_HASLINES	Draw lines between items
WinStyle 0x4	TVS_LINESTATROOT	Start lines at root

The easiest way to assign the Flags parameter value is to use the HTML Help ActiveX control wizard in the HTML Help Workshop. The Java applet supports a subset of the flags available to the ActiveX control, and ignores any other flag values.

To specify multiple styles, use a logical OR of the styles. Here are a few examples:

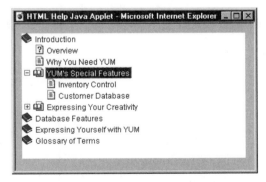

<param name="Flags" value="0x0,0x1">
(Contents tree-view with plus/minus squares.)

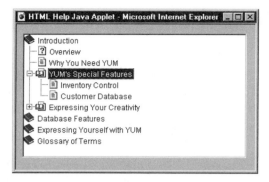

<param name="Flags" value="0x200,0x3">
(Contents tree-view with sunken edge, plus/minus squares, and lines drawn between items.)

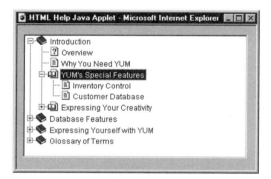

<param name="Flags" value="0x200,0x7">
(Contents tree-view with sunken edge, plus/minus squares, and lines drawn between items, starting at the root.)

Note: The Sitemap format allows for a "Window Styles" parameter and an "ExWindowStyles" parameter that are equivalent to the WinStyle and ExWinStyle components of the Flags parameter. However, the current version of the applet ignores these Sitemap parameters.

Font

The Font parameter specifies the font attributes for the Contents tree-view. Syntax for the Font parameter is:

```
<param name="Font" value="font-specification">
```

The syntax of the font-specification value is:

```
[facename][,[point size][,[charset][,[color][,[BOLD ITALIC
UNDERLINE]]]]]
```

The default value is: "Helvetica,12,,000000". The charset item is ignored by the applet; it is only used by the HTML Help ActiveX control. The color item is a hexadecimal number in the format *RRGGBB*, just like the Background parameter.

You can omit values to accept their defaults. For example, a value of ",10" specifies a 10-point font using the default typeface and color.

To specify a plain font, omit the last item. You can specify more than one of the modifiers in the last item, for example, ",,,,BOLD ITALIC" specifies a font which is both bold and italicized.

Notes: Because Java runs on many different platforms, the available font faces will vary. The Java Virtual Machine will attempt to provide the font that most closely matches the specified face.

The font may also be specified in the Sitemap file (.HHC or .HHK) rather than in the APPLET tag. However, in the current version, the Sitemap font specification is ignored by the applet.

Frame

The Frame parameter specifies the target frame for loading documents. Syntax for the Frame parameter is:

```
<param name="Frame" value="frame-name">
```

The target frame may also be specified via the FrameName parameter in the Sitemap file (.HHC or .HHK) for Contents or Index. In this case, the Sitemap FrameName parameter overrides the applet Frame parameter.

Item1, Item2, Item3...

The Item parameters are interpreted differently depending on the value of the Command parameter.

Command	Item Parameter Description
Contents	Item1 specifies the path, relative to the HTML page containing the applet, of the .HHC Sitemap file.
Index	Item1 specifies the path, relative to the HTML page containing the applet, of the .HHK Sitemap file.
Related Topics	There can be any number of Item parameters, starting with Item1. Each specifies an entry in the Related Topics list in the format

Command	Item Parameter Description
	"*title;path*". The title is displayed to the user in the Related Topics dialog box. The path specifies an HTML page to load when the user selects the corresponding entry. Again, this path is relative to the HTML page containing the applet.

Method Reference

All of the applet methods are summarized in the table below. Each method is described in detail in its own section following the table.

Method name	Applies To	Description
HHClick	Related Topics	Equivalent to a user click of the Related Topics button.
getAppletInfo	All	Returns a version information string.
syncURL	Contents	Selects the table of contents entry which matches the caller-supplied URL.

In order to invoke an applet method from script code, you must set the Name attribute in the APPLET tag.

HHClick

The HHClick method can be used to display the Related Topics dialog box from an applet instance with the Related Topics command parameter. This is useful if you want to provide an alternative user interface to the button displayed by the applet. You can set the width and height attributes of the APPLET tag to 0 so that the applet has no visible representation.

The following HTML fragments are taken from the file html/icec3rcn.htm which is part of the IceCream sample project. Here is an example of a Related Topics APPLET tag which doesn't show a button:

```
<APPLET code="HHCtrl.class" width="0" height="0"
name="HHCtrl" archive="../HHCtrl.zip">
    <PARAM name="Command" value="Related Topics">
    <PARAM name="Item1" value="YUM's Special
Features;icec9uib.htm">
    <PARAM name="Item2" value="Inventory
Control;icec112k.htm">
    <PARAM name="Frame" value="frmTopic">
    <PARAM name="cabbase" value="../HHCtrl.cab">
</APPLET>
```

This <A> tag invokes the Related Topics dialog box from a text hyperlink:

```
<A HREF=javascript:document.HHCtrl.HHClick()>Related
Topics</A>
```

This INPUT tag invokes the Related Topics dialog box from a button:

```
<INPUT type="button" onClick=document.HHCtrl.HHClick()
value="Related Topics"
</INPUT>
```

getAppletInfo

The getAppletInfo method is provided for diagnostic purposes only. It returns version information for the applet in human-readable form. The following script fragment displays the version information in a message box:

```
alert(document.HHCtrl.getAppletInfo())
```

The file JavaVersion.htm, supplied in the HHKIT\CHAP09 folder, displays the applet version information.

syncURL

The syncURL method allows you to select the table of contents entry corresponding to a particular URL from an instance of the applet using the Contents command. It does not display the document; it only selects it in the contents tree-view.

This method has one argument, which is the URL to synchronize. It must be in exactly the same format as the URLs found in the Sitemap (.HHC) file loaded by the applet. For example, you cannot pass a fully qualified URL and expect it to work with relative URLs specified in the .HHC file. Backslashes and forward slashes are not equivalent. The only exception is case—a URL which matches in all other respects doesn't need to have the same upper and lower case characters.

The IceCream sample demonstrates normalizing URLs in script code to implement a Sync button and an AutoSync feature. Refer to "Sample Site: IceCream," on page 266, for more information.

Another problem with syncURL is that it only works with those parts of the .HHC file which have been loaded by the applet. If you use Merge to break up your table of contents for improved performance, syncURL will quietly fail for any URL which hasn't been loaded yet.

Deploying the Java Applet

The most efficient way to deliver the HTML Help Java applet with your site is to supply a cab file for Internet Explorer users and an uncompressed zip file for Netscape Navigator users. These require the cabbase parameter and the archive attribute of the APPLET tag to be set accordingly. The applet files must reside on the same site as their containing document(s) and the Sitemap files.

There are some limitations on relative paths imposed by the Java security model. These limitations can vary from one platform to another. For example, when an

HTML page containing the applet is viewed in Netscape Navigator using the `file://` protocol, relative paths cannot walk up the directory structure. This means that you can't specify a path to a Sitemap file like "../../mycontents.hhc". When viewed using the `http://` protocol, this relative path is valid.

If you simply put the applet files, containing document, and Sitemap files into the same folder, your site should work regardless of the client platform.

Sample Site: IceCream

At the beginning of this book, we used a sample compiled HTML Help file called IceCream to explain and illustrate some of the features of HTML Help. A modified version of the IceCream project was also used as the basis for a sample site using the HTML Help Java applet. The IceCream site can be found in the HHKIT\CHAP09 folder. Display default.htm in your browser to see it in action.

Although the IceCream site documents an application, we don't recommend that you use the HTML Help Java applet for this purpose. The only way to achieve a reasonable level of application integration is with the HTML Help API and a compiled HTML Help file. Refer to "The HTML Help API," on page 199, for more information.

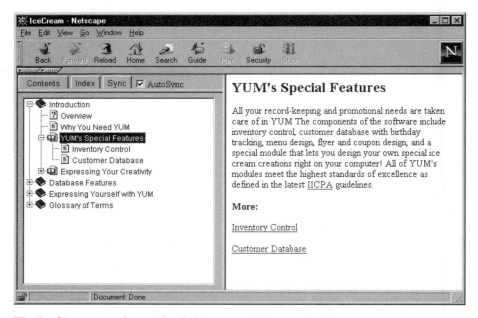

The IceCream sample running in Netscape Navigator 4.04.

The IceCream sample site requires a browser capable of rendering frames, executing JavaScript code, and hosting Java applets. The site has been tested with Netscape Navigator 3.0 and 4.04, and Microsoft Internet Explorer 3.02 and 4.0.

Note: The HTML Help Java applet will run properly in Microsoft Internet Explorer 3.0 only if you have upgraded to 3.02 *and* you have updated the Java VM (WINDOWS\SYSTEM\MSJAVA.DLL or WINNT\SYSTEM32\MSJAVA.DLL) to at least version 4.79.1518. You can update your Java VM by visiting **www.microsoft.com/java**.

Site Features

The IceCream site demonstrates most of the features of the HTML Help Java applet, and uses script code to implement a synchronization capability across the entire site. You can borrow freely from this sample to create your own sites.

Tripane look

The IceCream site uses a group of HTML framesets to emulate the appearance of the HTML Help tripane window. In the diagram below, the hierarchy of HTML files in the IceCream frameset is shown with the frame names in parentheses.

```
Default.htm

  JavaControl.htm (frmControl)          html/intro.htm (frmTopic)

    JavaTab.htm (frmTab)

    JavaContents.htm (frmApplet)
```

The IceCream frameset.

The file JavaTab.htm contains a form with three buttons—Contents, Index, and Sync—and an AutoSync checkbox. Clicking the Contents button loads JavaContents.htm into the frmApplet frame; this is the initial state of the frameset when first loaded. Clicking the Index button loads JavaIndex.htm into the frmApplet frame. Topic files displayed from the table of contents or index are loaded in the frmTopic frame.

Sync button

The Sync button invokes the OnSync function in JavaTab.htm:

```
function OnSync()
{
    // Extract base location from current document
    var strBase = NormalizeURL(document.location.toString());
    strBase = strBase.substring(0,
```

```
                    strBase.lastIndexOf("javatab.htm"));

          // Get location of current topic
          var strTopic = NormalizeURL(
            parent.parent.frmTopic.document.location.toString());

          if (strTopic.indexOf(strBase) == 0) {
                  // Current topic is relative to base
                  // Strip base from left hand side
                  strTopic = strTopic.substring(strBase.length);
          }


          // Sync it in the table of contents
          parent.frmApplet.document.HHCtrl.syncURL(strTopic);
    }
```

This function assumes that the .HHC file is located in the same folder as
JavaTab.htm itself and that the document files are either in the same folder or a
subfolder. OnSync gets the current document name from the frmTopic frame,
normalizes it, makes it relative to the current folder (if possible), and calls the
syncURL method of the applet.

Normalization is required because the browser may return URLs with different use
of slash and backslash characters. The syncURL method only works with URLs
that are identical (except for case) to the original (relative) URLs found in the
.HHC file. The NormalizeURL function looks like this:

```
    function NormalizeURL(strURL)
    {
        // Start by converting to lower case
        var str = strURL.toLowerCase();
        strURL = "";
        var cLast = '';
        for (var i = 0; i < str.length; i++) {
            var c = str.charAt(i);
            if (c == '\\') {
                // Convert backslash to forward slash
                c = '/';
            }
            if (c == '/') {
                if (cLast == '/') {
                    // Collapse multiple slashes to single slash
                    continue;
                }
            }
            strURL = strURL + c;
            cLast = c;
        }
        return(strURL);
    }
```

NormalizeURL steps through each character of its argument, converting backslash ('\') to slash ('/'), and collapsing multiple slash characters to a single slash. This compensates for different browser behaviors.

AutoSync feature

All of the topic files in the IceCream site (except for html/intro.htm—more on this later) contain a call from the onLoad event of the BODY tag back into JavaTab.htm like this:

```
<BODY onLoad=parent.frmControl.frmTab.OnNewTopic()>
```

The OnNewTopic function looks at the state of the AutoSync button, and if checked, calls the OnSync function:

```
function OnNewTopic()
{
    if (document.formTab.chkAutoSync.checked) {
        OnSync();
    }
}
```

This all works fine as long as parent.frmControl.frmTab is available at the time the topic file is loaded. But the very first topic file, html/intro.htm, usually loads before JavaControl.htm because of the way the frameset is structured. So, auto-synchronization doesn't work for this introductory topic file.

Also, synchronization doesn't work at all for entries that haven't yet been loaded into the table of contents via Merge. Which leads us to our next topic . . . .

Merged Table of Contents

It's not really necessary for such a small project, but IceCream has a Merge entry in its table of contents to illustrate the Merge feature. The topmost entries in the table of contents hierarchy are all found in the file ICECREAM.HHC. One of these entries is titled "Expressing Yourself with YUM." When the user expands this entry to see topics beneath it in the hierarchy, the HTML Help Java applet loads EXPRESS.HHC and merges it with the currently displayed items.

Mostly the Merge feature is transparent to a user. For a large file or a slow network connection, the user may briefly see a "Loading..." message appear in the table of contents until the merged items replace it. And as mentioned before, the synchronization feature only works with table of contents entries that have actually been loaded. If a user navigates to a topic via a link in another topic, it's possible that synchronization may quietly fail.

Related Topics

The Overview topic (html/icec3rcn.htm) found immediately beneath the Introduction in the table of contents contains three examples of how you can use the Related Topics feature of the HTML Help Java applet. The first is simply a button displayed by the applet; the second, an <A> tag which invokes the HHClick method of the applet; and the third, a form button which invokes the HHClick method. In practice, if you were using either of the second two methods, you would set the width and height attributes of the applet to 0 (zero) so that it doesn't show.

Popup topics

Popup topics aren't supported in the way that Windows Help users are accustomed. The IceCream sample uses the admittedly ugly workaround of calling the alert method to display a message box. It also sets the TITLE attribute of the <A> tag so that in browsers that support it, a tooltip will be displayed when the user moves the mouse over the popup hyperlink.

Frequently Asked Questions

Question: *Which platforms are supported by the HTML Help Java applet?*

Answer: The applet is designed to run in any Java-capable Internet browser. However, there are no guarantees that it will work on any particular platform. You must test with your target platforms to be sure.

Question: *Why does the applet take so long to load my table of contents file?*

Answer: If you have a large table of contents file, the load time will increase accordingly, and it will be particularly noticeable for a slow network connection. You can improve the load time by using the Merge feature to break up your table of contents.

Question: *Why do some browsers report a security violation when attempting to display my site?*

Answer: The security model may be implemented slightly differently in the Java Virtual Machine of each platform. For best results, put the applet class files in the same folder as your .HHC and .HHK files.

Appendix

Even though this is the Appendix, this chapter contains information that will be very important to your being able to create and distribute HTML Help systems.

For the Help author and web author: We'll discuss what components need to be installed so that a user can run a compiled HTML Help system, and what tools are available for distributing these components. We'll also look at the image editing and conversion tools that come with the HTML Help workshop, and at other HTML Help features that you may want to incorporate into your Help systems.

For the programmer: We'll discuss what components need to be installed so that a user can run a compiled HTML Help system, and how you can display a WinHelp popup or topic from an HTML Help system.

What's in the Appendix

Distributing Compiled HTML Help Systems

If you will be creating compiled HTML Help systems (as opposed to systems that run inside a browser) you must make sure that the following components are properly installed on your users' machines:

- Microsoft Internet Explorer or Internet Explorer runtime engine

- Microsoft HTML Help runtime components

The Microsoft Internet Explorer runtime engine contains the core elements needed to interpret and display an HTML Help window (SHDOCVW.DLL, MSHTML.DLL, and so forth). It is not a fully functional browser.

The HTML Help runtime components contain the modules needed to correctly interpret and display HTML Help-specific constructs, including the table of contents, index, full text search, and so on.

Free Setup Programs

Internet Explorer Runtime Setup

At the time of this writing, a freely-distributable setup program that installs the Internet Explorer runtime engine was in development and should be available by the time you are reading this.

You will only need to distribute this setup program if you are not sure if your users will have Internet Explorer installed.

For more information, please visit the Microsoft HTML Help web page at
http://www.microsoft.com/workshop/author/htmlhelp/

Or, visit the Official Microsoft HTML Help Authoring Kit update page at
http://mspress.microsoft.com/mspress/products/1408

HTML Help Runtime Components Setup

The HTML Help Workshop does contain a free-distributable setup program (HHUPD.EXE) that will install and register the HTML Help runtime components, listed here.

Component name	Description
HHCTRL.OCX	HTML Help ActiveX control
ITSS.DLL	Dynamic link library that handles compiled HTML
ITIRCL.DLL	Full-text search DLL
HH.EXE	HTML Help viewer

You will find this setup program in the REDIST folder underneath the folder where HTML Help Workshop has been installed. This setup program can be called from other setup programs, and can be made to run in "quiet" mode so that it does not interfere with the setup program you may have already created. For a complete list of command line options, run HHUPD.EXE /?.

Important Note: You should always include the latest HTML Help runtime components when distributing your compiled HTML Help systems. While your users may have the necessary components already installed, they may not have as recent a version of those that your Help system requires. HHUPD.EXE makes it painless to make sure your users have the correct version of the components they need.

Other HTML Help Workshop Tools

Microsoft's HTML Help Workshop comes with two additional programs that you may find useful. The Microsoft HTML Help Image Editor allows you to take screen shots, convert graphics, edit images, and maintain catalogues of graphic images. The RTF to HTML converter allows you to convert WinHelp projects to HTML Help.

Microsoft HTML Help Image Editor

A discussion of all the features of the Image Editor is beyond the scope of this book. We will, however, explore the features that allow you to take screen shots, change color depth, and save graphics in different file formats.

To Run the HTML Help Image Editor

You can also run the Image Editor by clicking the Tools menu in the HTML Help Workshop.

1   Click the **Start** button.

2   Click **Programs**.

3   Click the **HTML Help Workshop** program group.

4   Click **HTML Help Image Editor**.

The Image Editor will load, as shown below.

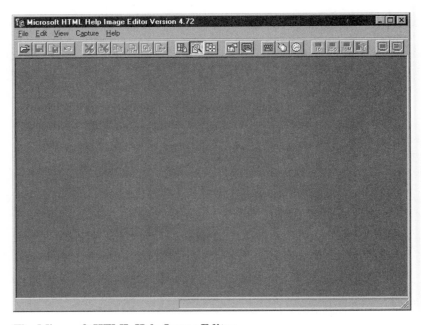

The Microsoft HTML Help Image Editor.

Taking Screen Shots

The HTML Help Image Editor is particularly good at taking screen shots. In fact, most of the screen shots for this book were created and edited using the Image Editor.

You will find most of the commands you need for taking screen shots under the Capture menu. Before plunging in, make sure you set your preferences because one of the most useful features found in the Preferences dialog box is the ability to automatically reduce screen capture to 16 colors when an image is captured. This saves you the step of having to reduce the images to 16 colors later.

Note: You don't have to reduce your images to 16 colors if you don't want to, but most dialog boxes and toolbars only contain 16 colors, so reducing the color depth of these images greatly reduces file size without compromising image quality.

Saving in Different File Formats

While HTML Help can deal with graphics in virtually any format, including .BMP and .WMF files, many browsers cannot, so you will need to make sure your graphics have been saved in either a .JPG or .GIF format. You can use the Image Editor's Save As command to save an image in either of these (as well as other) formats.

The Image Editor also has a batch facility that allows you to convert many graphics at the same time. This is useful if you already have many graphics in one format that need to be converted to another format. You will find this batch feature by clicking **File** and choosing **Multiple File Conversion**.

Changing Color Depth

Detailed information about the type of graphics you should include in your HTML Help projects and how many colors these graphics should contain is beyond the scope of this book (but is covered in virtually every book on generic HTML authoring, including the two books cited on page 5). There are however, some simple guidelines that will help you in creating and editing images.

- Most screen shots can be saved as 16-color images with no loss in clarity. Your system is almost certainly set to display 256 to 16.7 million colors, so if you take screen shots you will need to reduce the number of colors if you want to reduce the image file size.

- GIF files can contain no more than 256 colors. If you have an image that contains more than 256 colors, such as a photographic scan, you will need to reduce the image to 256 colors if you want to save it in a .GIF format.

- You can use the Image Editor's batch facility to change the color depth of more than one image at a time.

RTF to HTML Help Converter

If you have a WinHelp project, The HTML Help Workshop includes a conversion utility that will help jump start your migration to HTML Help. While not perfect, the HTML Help Workshop's conversion tool will do a lot of the grunt work in taking a WinHelp project and converting it to an HTML Help project.

Converting a WinHelp project to HTML Help is a two-step process. The first step converts the source RTF file(s) to HTML equivalents. The second step involves making sure the Workshop converts the WinHelp table of contents file (.CNT file) to its HTML Help equivalent when you compile your HTML Help System.

To Convert a WinHelp Project to HTML Help

1   If it's not already running, start the HTML Help Workshop.

2   From the **File** menu, choose **New**.

3   When the New dialog box appears, click **Project**.

4   When the New Project wizard appears, make sure **Convert WinHelp Project** is selected, as shown below.

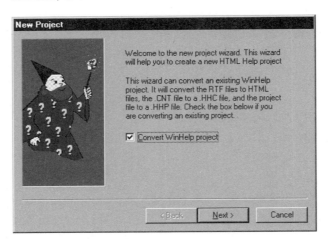

5   Click **Next**.

6   Specify the source of the WinHelp Project and the destination of the HTML Help project, as shown on the opposite page.

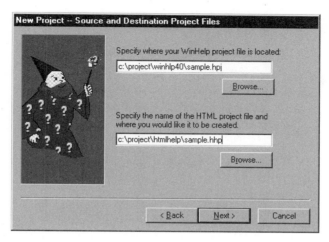

7 Click the **Finish** button.

To Have the HTML Help Workshop
Convert the WinHelp .CNT File into an .HHC File

1 Click the **Change Project Options** button.

2 Click the **Files** tab.

3 Enter a name for the contents file (.HHC file).

4 Make sure **Automatically Create Contents File When Compiling** is selected.

The dialog box should look like the one shown on the next page.

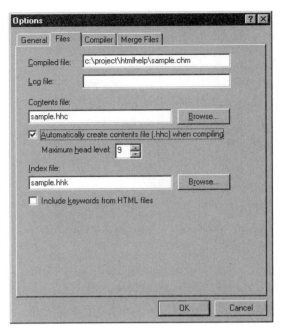

5 Click **OK**.

6 Click the **Save Project And Compile** Button.

Very Important: If you will be editing the .HHC file, make sure you turn off the auto generation of the contents file option, because the HTML Help Workshop will overwrite any changes you make if this option is turned on.

Other HTML Help Commands and Workshop Features

Related Topics

We saw in Chapter Six how you can create links to other topics that contain information related to the current topic using ALinks and Keyword search links. Using this feature you could create a button, or virtually any type of hotspot, that when clicked displays a list of targets to which the user can jump.

HTML Help determines the list of targets at runtime and displays them either in a popup menu or in a dialog box.

A lot of authors like this mechanism for displaying target topics and choose to employ a dialog box or popup menu of target topics even when the author is hard-coding the topics to which the user can jump. Consider the example shown below.

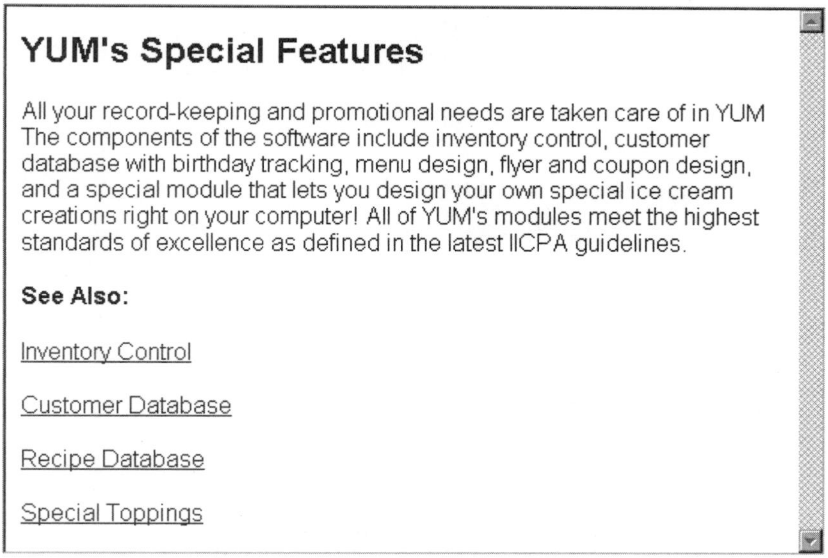

YUM's Special Features

All your record-keeping and promotional needs are taken care of in YUM The components of the software include inventory control, customer database with birthday tracking, menu design, flyer and coupon design, and a special module that lets you design your own special ice cream creations right on your computer! All of YUM's modules meet the highest standards of excellence as defined in the latest IICPA guidelines.

See Also:

Inventory Control

Customer Database

Recipe Database

Special Toppings

An HTML Help topic with hard-coded links to other topics.

Here the Help author has hard coded four links at the end of the topic. Using the Related Topics command, the author can consolidate these four links into one button that, when clicked, displays a popup menu, as shown below.

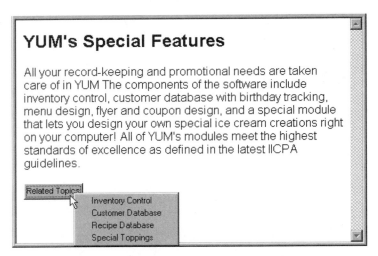

Using the Related Topics button to group hard-coded links.

Notes on the Related Topics Command

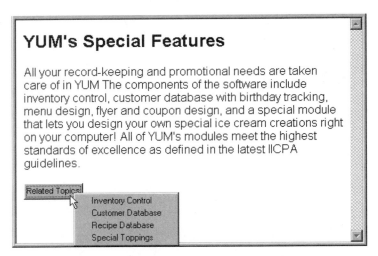 Insert HTML Help ActiveX Control button.

You insert a Related Topics button by positioning your insertion pointer where you want the button to appear, clicking the Insert HTML Help ActiveX Control button, and selecting Related Topics from the drop down list. The HTML Help ActiveX Wizard will guide you through the rest.

The Related Topics button does not have to be a big pushbutton. It can appear as practically anything that you want, including static text with a chiclet button.

The list of target topics can appear in either a popup menu or in a dialog box.

WinHelp Popups and Jumps

If you absolutely must have popups with rich text and graphics, and you know your HTML Help system will only be used on the Microsoft Windows platform, you can create a link that displays a WinHelp popup or displays a WinHelp topic in a WinHelp window.

You create a WinHelp popup or jump by placing your insertion pointer where you want the popup or jump to appear, clicking the Insert HTML Help ActiveX control, and selecting WinHelp Topic from the drop-down list. The HTML Help ActiveX Wizard will guide you through the rest.

Splash Screens

Using another feature of the HTML Help ActiveX control, HHCTRL.OCX, you can display an author-specified graphic whenever a particular topic is displayed. This capability is most often used to display a splash screen when the HTML Help system is first loaded.

Consider the example shown below:

HTML Help system with splash screen.

Here we are giving our Help system a little more pizzazz by displaying a logo when the system is first loaded. You specify that you want a splash screen using the Insert HTML Help ActiveX Command wizard. This means that the command to display a splash screen is embedded into a particular HTML Help topic page, as opposed to being part of the project file

Some Notes on Using Splash Screens

Since the command to display the splash screen is embedded into a topic, be careful to design your Help system so that topic is displayed only once, when the HTML Help system is first loaded. Otherwise, the user will see the splash screen whenever she accesses the topic. (Note: You can specify which topic to display when a .CHM file is first loaded from the Options dialog box.)

The image can be virtually any type of graphic that the HTML Help display engine can render, including .BMP, .WMF, .GIF, and .JPG.

You can specify how long you want the image to display before it disappears.

You will need to distribute the splash screen image with your HTML Help system, because it does not get compiled into the .CHM file.

Glossary of Terms

ActiveX
An ever-growing group of software building blocks adhering to a set of rules and specifications for interoperability.

ALink
A hypertext link between topics in a Help file, generated at runtime based on hidden keywords shared by the topics.

Child mode
A Help window presentation mode in which the Help window is displayed anywhere within your application as a child window.

Container
A software component that can host one or more ActiveX controls.

Context-sensitive Help
Help which displays the topic corresponding to the application feature in use when Help was requested.

Control
A reusable chunk of pre-built software that can be used to build or enhance an application.

Control ID Map
A NULL-terminated array of DWORD pairs in which the first half of the pair is a control ID and the second half of the pair is a context map number. A Control ID Map is passed to the HtmlHelp API function as an argument to the HH_TP_HELP_WM_HELP and HH_TP_HELP_CONTEXTMENU commands.

Data structure
A C++ term; equivalent to a User-Defined Type in Visual Basic.

Help button
A standard feature of Windows dialog boxes that displays a Help topic describing how to use the dialog box.

Help topic
Information in a Help file pertaining to a particular subject. A Help topic is generally introduced by a heading, contains descriptive text, graphics, or both, and may also offer hypertext or hotspot links to related Help topics.

Map number
A numeric value associated with a topic ID, commonly used by applications to specify a topic when calling context-sensitive Help.

Owned mode
A Help window presentation mode in which a separate top-level overlapped Help window is displayed alongside your application, as in sibling mode; but the Help window always remains on top of the application, even when the application window is active.

RTF file
Acronym for Rich Text Format. RTF uses a system of tags to encode document formatting information—such as fonts, alignment, styles, fields, graphics, and so forth—into a text file. The Windows Help Compiler used coded RTF files for its source files.

Sibling mode
A Help window presentation mode in which a separate top-level overlapped Help window is displayed alongside your application.

Sitemap
A file in XML format that describes a table of contents or keyword index. These files typically have a file extension of .HHC or .HHK, respectively.

Structure
See data structure.

Subclassing
A Visual Basic term that means intercepting messages for alternative processing before Visual Basic sees them.

Text popups
HTML Help popups, consisting only of plain text without any graphics or HTML features.

Topic ID
A name used by HTML Help to uniquely identify a Help topic within a given project.

User-defined type
A Visual Basic term; equivalent to a data structure in C++.

What's This Help
Popup Help topics that briefly describe the use of a single control or group of controls in a dialog box.

Index

To **challenge** the World Wide Web's most **innovative** sites with **ultra**-cool ones of your own, **read this.**

U.S.A. **$29.95**
U.K. £27.99 [V.A.T. included]
Canada $39.95
ISBN 1-55615-948-X

To build the smartest, most visually compelling Web sites you've ever seen, just take the techniques in HTML IN ACTION to the limits of your imagination. Bruce Morris, publisher of *NCT Web Magazine, The Web Developer's Journal,* and *Wacky HTML,* offers a powerhouse collection of the techniques and tricks you need to get the most from HTML. You'll review HTML basics; examine the use of graphics, multimedia, and animation; explore Java and HotJava; and deploy vanguard technologies such as CGI scripts and ActiveX™ tools. In short, HTML IN ACTION pushes the limits of what can be done with HTML—so you can push them even further.

The HTML IN ACTION companion CD includes:
- TrueType® fonts
- Microsoft® Internet Explorer
- Internet Control Pack
- Starter set of ActiveX controls

Microsoft Press

IMPORTANT—READ CAREFULLY BEFORE OPENING SOFTWARE PACKET(S). By opening the sealed packet(s) containing the software, you indicate your acceptance of the following Microsoft License Agreement.

MICROSOFT LICENSE AGREEMENT

(Book Companion CD)

This is a legal agreement between you (either an individual or an entity) and Microsoft Corporation. By opening the sealed software packet(s) you are agreeing to be bound by the terms of this agreement. If you do not agree to the terms of this agreement, promptly return the unopened software packet(s) and any accompanying written materials to the place you obtained them for a full refund.

MICROSOFT SOFTWARE LICENSE

1. GRANT OF LICENSE. Microsoft grants to you the right to use one copy of the Microsoft software program included with this book (the "SOFTWARE") on a single terminal connected to a single computer. The SOFTWARE is in "use" on a computer when it is loaded into the temporary memory (i.e., RAM) or installed into the permanent memory (e.g., hard disk, CD-ROM, or other storage device) of that computer. You may not network the SOFTWARE or otherwise use it on more than one computer or computer terminal at the same time.

2. COPYRIGHT. The SOFTWARE is owned by Microsoft or its suppliers and is protected by United States copyright laws and international treaty provisions. Therefore, you must treat the SOFTWARE like any other copyrighted material (e.g., a book or musical recording) except that you may either (a) make one copy of the SOFTWARE solely for backup or archival purposes, or (b) transfer the SOFTWARE to a single hard disk provided you keep the original solely for backup or archival purposes. You may not copy the written materials accompanying the SOFTWARE.

3. OTHER RESTRICTIONS. You may not rent or lease the SOFTWARE, but you may transfer the SOFTWARE and accompanying written materials on a permanent basis provided you retain no copies and the recipient agrees to the terms of this Agreement. You may not reverse engineer, decompile, or disassemble the SOFTWARE. If the SOFTWARE is an update or has been updated, any transfer must include the most recent update and all prior versions.

4. DUAL MEDIA SOFTWARE. If the SOFTWARE package contains more than one kind of disk (3.5", 5.25", and CD-ROM), then you may use only the disks appropriate for your single-user computer. You may not use the other disks on another computer or loan, rent, lease, or transfer them to another user except as part of the permanent transfer (as provided above) of all SOFTWARE and written materials.

5. SAMPLE CODE. If the SOFTWARE includes Sample Code, then Microsoft grants you a royalty-free right to reproduce and distribute the sample code of the SOFTWARE provided that you: (a) distribute the sample code only in conjunction with and as a part of your software product; (b) do not use Microsoft's or its authors' names, logos, or trademarks to market your software product; (c) include the copyright notice that appears on the SOFTWARE on your product label and as a part of the sign-on message for your software product; and (d) agree to indemnify, hold harmless, and defend Microsoft and its authors from and against any claims or lawsuits, including attorneys' fees, that arise or result from the use or distribution of your software product.

DISCLAIMER OF WARRANTY

The SOFTWARE (including instructions for its use) is provided "AS IS" WITHOUT WARRANTY OF ANY KIND. MICROSOFT FURTHER DISCLAIMS ALL IMPLIED WARRANTIES INCLUDING WITHOUT LIMITATION ANY IMPLIED WARRANTIES OF MERCHANTABILITY OR OF FITNESS FOR A PARTICULAR PURPOSE. THE ENTIRE RISK ARISING OUT OF THE USE OR PERFORMANCE OF THE SOFTWARE AND DOCUMENTATION REMAINS WITH YOU.

IN NO EVENT SHALL MICROSOFT, ITS AUTHORS, OR ANYONE ELSE INVOLVED IN THE CREATION, PRODUCTION, OR DELIVERY OF THE SOFTWARE BE LIABLE FOR ANY DAMAGES WHATSOEVER (INCLUDING, WITHOUT LIMITATION, DAMAGES FOR LOSS OF BUSINESS PROFITS, BUSINESS INTERRUPTION, LOSS OF BUSINESS INFORMATION, OR OTHER PECUNIARY LOSS) ARISING OUT OF THE USE OF OR INABILITY TO USE THE SOFTWARE OR DOCUMENTATION, EVEN IF MICROSOFT HAS BEEN ADVISED OF THE POSSIBILITY OF SUCH DAMAGES. BECAUSE SOME STATES/COUNTRIES DO NOT ALLOW THE EXCLUSION OR LIMITATION OF LIABILITY FOR CONSEQUENTIAL OR INCIDENTAL DAMAGES, THE ABOVE LIMITATION MAY NOT APPLY TO YOU.

U.S. GOVERNMENT RESTRICTED RIGHTS

The SOFTWARE and documentation are provided with RESTRICTED RIGHTS. Use, duplication, or disclosure by the Government is subject to restrictions as set forth in subparagraph (c)(1)(ii) of The Rights in Technical Data and Computer Software clause at DFARS 252.227-7013 or subparagraphs (c)(1) and (2) of the Commercial Computer Software — Restricted Rights 48 CFR 52.227-19, as applicable. Manufacturer is Microsoft Corporation, One Microsoft Way, Redmond, WA 98052-6399.

If you acquired this product in the United States, this Agreement is governed by the laws of the State of Washington.

Should you have any questions concerning this Agreement, or if you desire to contact Microsoft Press for any reason, please write: Microsoft Press, One Microsoft Way, Redmond, WA 98052-6399.

Register Today!

Return this
Official Microsoft® HTML Help Authoring Kit
registration card for
a Microsoft Press® catalog

U.S. and Canada addresses only. Fill in information below and mail postage-free. Please mail only the bottom half of this page.

1-57231-603-9   ***OFFICIAL MICROSOFT®***   *Owner Registration Card*
HTML HELP AUTHORING KIT

_____

NAME

_____

INSTITUTION OR COMPANY NAME

_____

ADDRESS

_____

_____

CITY   STATE   ZIP

Microsoft ® *Press*
Quality Computer Books

**For a free catalog of
Microsoft Press® products, call**
1-800-MSPRESS

NO POSTAGE
NECESSARY
IF MAILED
IN THE
UNITED STATES

BUSINESS REPLY MAIL
FIRST-CLASS MAIL   PERMIT NO. 53   BOTHELL, WA

POSTAGE WILL BE PAID BY ADDRESSEE

MICROSOFT PRESS REGISTRATION
OFFICIAL MICROSOFT®
HTML HELP AUTHORING KIT
PO BOX 3019
BOTHELL WA   98041-9946

Il.l.l.l.l.ll...l.l...llll.l.l.l..l.l.ll.ll..l